To Roger H. Nye, Colonel, U.S. Army, 1924–96
Teacher, Mentor, Colleague, Friend

This is an aspect of military science which needs to be studied above all others in the Armed Forces: the capacity to adapt oneself to the utterly unpredictable, the entirely unknown. —Michael Howard, Chesney Memorial Gold Medal Lecture, 3 October 1973

CONTENTS

INTRODUCTION

On Military Change

Harold R. Winton

All human institutions must inevitably deal with the tension between continuity and change, between preserving that which has met the needs of the past and adapting to the challenge of change in a confusing present and uncertain future. This is true in politics, law, economics, and the arts; but this tension is particularly evident in military institutions in which tradition and the need for disciplined acceptance of authority in the chaos of battle vie with the equally strong pressures to meet the demands of new realities of social transformation and, especially in the twentieth century, new means of waging war. The present work examines how five different military institutions dealt with this tension during the time between the two world wars. It also attempts to synthesize from these examinations valid historical generalizations and insights that may have contemporary relevance in the era of significant political, social, and technological changes that confront the armed forces of all major powers in the post–Cold War era. Three of the included studies, those examining the British, French, and German armies, grew out of papers that were presented at the April 1994 conference of the Society for Military History held in Washington DC; the other two, those depicting the American and Soviet armies, were added at the invitation of the editors to provide a wider base of evidence from which to draw meaningful generalizations about the dynamics of the change process. Dennis Showalter graciously agreed to provide a synthesis of all five essays.

The process of military change, or reform, is extremely complex.[1] Although there is no magic formula for success, there are certain steps that it seems to follow. The first is to determine a generally accurate picture of the nature of future war. To paraphrase Clausewitz, such a determination is the most significant and comprehensive question the erstwhile reformer must address. Even if he gets everything else right, if he mis-appreciates the essential dynamics of the next major conflict, he may well find his army perfectly prepared for the wrong type of war. He must next determine the operational concepts that will most likely bring victory in this anticipated environment. These operational concepts then have to be translated into a doctrine that will provide sufficient guidance for the force to use in its war preparation without being so specific that it binds too tightly the hands of the future commanders who will have to use it. The process to this point demands ruthless intellectual honesty and critical self-examination and is usually accompanied by a significant amount of internal debate. Sooner or later, however, debate must end, or at least become mitigated on the major points. This is because doctrine is not an end in itself. It is, rather, the conceptual core around which decisions must be made concerning how the force should be organized, trained, and equipped to win the next war.

Although the process is to some extent iterative, these decisions begin to signify a transition from the analysis to the implementation phase of the change effort. Once they are made, experimental organizations, frequently working with prototype equipment and troops that are only imperfectly trained in the new methods, must be fielded and tested at progressively higher levels to assess the efficacy of the emerging doctrine. These tests are then evaluated and more precise decisions made as to the specifics of the doctrine, the form and equipment of the new organizations, and the extent to and pace at which the new model can begin to supersede the old. If the estimates upon which the foregoing decisions have been made are generally accurate and if there is a logical coherence between these estimates and the consequent formulations of doctrine, organization, equipment, training, and force structure, the military institution has a reasonable chance of beginning the next war adequately configured to make the always necessary adjustments. If, however, either of these conditions does not obtain and the force in question finds itself fighting an enemy force for which they do, the consequences can be devastating.

The complexity of military change is influenced by three fundamental factors: the endemic uncertainty of the environment, the external forces imposed by the political and social structure within which the army exists, and the characteristics and values of the institution itself.

There are many uncertainties associated with the reform process, but two of the most significant are those associated with strategic require-ments and technology. Ascertaining where the armed force is likely to fight, against whom, under what circumstances, and for what purposes is critical. At some times, such as during the height of the Cold War, the answers to these questions appeared to NATO nations to be relatively straightforward. When one peered beneath the surface, however, a number of imponderables still emerged: Would the war be nuclear or non-nuclear? Would chemical weapons be employed? How much warning would the alliance have and how would political leaders react to ambiguous indicators that most likely would be covered by strategic deception? How would the flow of refugees affect deployment plans? If one finds oneself in a situation where the identity of the potential adversary is *unclear* (such as the American armed forces have in the post–Cold War era), or where there is significant political debate over the role of the service in an anticipated war (as there was concerning the British army in the mid- to late 1930s), the strategic imponderables escalate significantly.

Technological uncertainty is equally perverse. The technical capabilities of emerging weapons systems can be determined with some degree of precision in laboratories and on ranges. However, the tactical and operational capabilities of these systems employed against similar enemy systems or countersystems while operating under wartime conditions can only be approximated. The implications of these capabilities can only be assessed through an informed and imaginative military judgment.

A number of external factors influence military adaptation. They include cultural norms, geography, historical experience, political institutions, and resource availability. The American militia tradition and the French theory of the nation in arms—two distinct manifestations of the values held by democratic societies—have placed significant restraints on military reform efforts in the United States and France. Britain's geographic situation of being isolated from yet close to the Continent, while for several centuries acting as the epicenter of a worldwide empire, created a tension for the British army that persists to this day. Prussia's historical experience of being invaded by the Russians, the Swedes, the Austrians, and the French created a mentality that placed a high premium on the maintenance of an effective army. The influence of the communist party on the Soviet army is but one of many striking examples of how political institutions profoundly affect the course of military reform. And one of the most significant issues resulting from an amalgam of all these factors is the resource question: What portion of the nation's, goods, services, and manpower will be put at the disposal of the armed forces during times of peace to prepare for war? The answer to this question significantly affects a service's policy for adapting to an uncertain future.

But the internal characteristics and activities of military institutions also shape reform. Here one must include factors such as "service culture"; the various branches that constitute the service; organizations and processes for doctrinal development; the existence of professional forums in which issues can be debated; personalities of key leaders and reformers; the military education system; simulations, war games, and exercises; and the analysis of contemporary wars. A service's "culture" is a complex aggregate of its attitudes toward a variety of issues including its role in war, its promotion system, its relation to other services, and its place in the society it serves. The most critical variable for reform, however, may be its ability to tolerate dissent and balance such dissent with the ever-present requirement for discipline and obedience, which is the sine qua non of effective combat performance.[2] Every military service is composed of a number of subspecialties, each of which has a particular combat role and each of which has a stake in preserving that role. These specialized entities play a significant role in military adaptation. During the interwar period, organizations and processes for doctrinal development were in their infancy; since World War II, however, many military institutions of the major powers have recognized the need for doctrines and have been much more aggressive in developing them.

Although a formal organization and process for doctrinal development does not guarantee success, it at least provides a recognized forum in which doctrinal issues can be formally assessed.[3] Informal forums such as military periodicals and institutes in which doctrinal issues can be debated must, however, supplement these other more formal structures. During the interwar period, such forums were often the most obvious places for the debates to take place. The personalities of key leaders at or near the top of an organization and those of the reformers themselves exert a key and at times decisive influence on the course of military reform. Hans von Seeckt, Henri Pétain, George Milne, Douglas MacArthur, and M. V. Frunze, as well as Heinz Guderian, Charles de Gaulle, J. F. C. Fuller, Billy Mitchell, and Mikhail Tukhachevsky influenced the course of events in their respective services not only by their *ideas* but also by the *temperamental style* with which their ideas were put forth.

If successful reform is dependent on a harmonious balance between creative ideas and critical inquiry, the structure and values of a service's military education system themselves will profoundly influence its course. Again, a formal military education system will not guarantee success, for it can become simply another mechanism for inculcating orthodoxy. If, however, it is inspired by a genuine search for creative answers to the enduring questions of military art and science, and if it demands that the proposed answers meet the tests of logic and evidence, it can be one of the most important ingredients in a successful reform effort. New ideas must sooner or later be tested to determine their utility. These tests can take the form of simulations, which in our present age include the use of computer models; war games carried out strictly as maneuvers on maps; or the use of actual exercises employing prototypical forces. (This typology is listed in a generally ascending order of cost and fidelity, but all three are important and useful.) Finally, an adaptable armed force must carefully assess the contemporaneous developments of actual wars in which it is either uninvolved or involved only by proxy. While such wars simply cannot be ignored, the utility of such analyses is largely a function of the professional acumen of the observers and the perspicacity and intellectual honesty of the service leaders who must make decisions based on the implications of their observations.[4]

Military reform, then, is driven by a curious trinity of its own. The poles of this trinity are endemic strategic and technological uncertainty, the dictates of the political and social values of the state, and the defining characteristics of the military service itself. Furthermore, just as the danger, chance, uncertainty, and privation of combat demand a genius for war, so also the ambiguities and complexities of peacetime military change demand a genius for adaptation. Such genius is defined in both intellectual and psychological terms.

Intellectually the reformer requires a solid grounding in military art that is developed through a combination of real and vicarious experience. The actual experience will be largely the product of historical accident—the wars and peacetime activities to which military service has exposed the reformer. There is little that can be done about this except to seek out the most challenging assignments that fortune has made available. There is, however, a great deal that can be done about the latter. Here the lifetime habit of study and reflection pays its greatest dividends: teaching the reformer to ask good questions and providing an internalized set of criteria with which to assess a wide range of possible answers. These skills are then translated into a peacetime equivalent of *coup d'oeil*, the ability to see, almost at a glance, which methods of future warfare have the best chance of working well in the context of only dimly foreseen circumstances and, perhaps even more important, which methods do not.

But intellect is not enough. The peacetime leader requires "the courage to follow this faint light wherever it may lead"; he must also possess a temperament that identifies itself with his institution and, equally important, allows the institution to identify itself with *him*.[5] In other words, although he has the authority and responsibility to act by fiat if he must to maintain the effectiveness of the institution for the discharge of its wartime responsibilities, he also has the obligation to *persuade* others that he is taking reform in the right direction. If the advocate of change has not yet captured the reins of power (which is frequently the case), his temperament and his persuasive skills become particularly significant.[6] It should come as no surprise that men who possess these intellectual and psychological qualities in precisely the right blend suitable for their particular time and circumstances are very rare indeed—one reason that the record of military adaptation in peacetime is more often a tale of sorrow than of joy.

Ample evidence to support the above proposition is found in the five studies that constitute the core of this work. Each of these essays also offers historical analysis of the underlying factors influencing the attempts to adapt to new realities, and thus each contributes to the ongoing debate about not only what happened between the wars in the military institutions under consideration but also why it happened as it did. Eugenia Kiesling argues that if one looks at the interwar French army from the point of view of the substantial infrastructural impediments to reform with which it constantly contended, rather than at the disastrous campaign of May–June 1940 in which it was decisively defeated, its failure to adopt the far-reaching doctrinal and organizational changes that would have been required for it to have fought more effectively against the Wehrmacht become much more comprehensible. James Corum has a much different task. His brief explains why the German army of the interwar years was able to produce an operational-level doctrine that was so strikingly successful in the opening campaigns of World War II. His explanation focuses on institutional excellence rather than on individual brilliance, particularly the cultural norm of a general staff mentality. This frame of mind produced a comprehensive approach to reform that ruthlessly assessed the military past, honestly evaluated the pros and cons of various approaches to improving that past, and systematically implemented the conclusions flowing from this evaluation. Corum's essay also confronts the vexing question of why German tactical and operational expertise was not matched by similar strategic acumen. Similar to Kiesling's examination of the French military experience, my study of the British army between the wars seeks to explain why an effective doctrine of armored warfare was not adopted. Such an explanation seems particularly necessary because the British developed the tank during World War I and, in the persons of J. F. C. Fuller and B. H. Liddell Hart, possessed two of the world's most prominent theoreticians of armored warfare. This essay focuses on one variable in the change process—the ability of external actors to influence army doctrine and organization—and argues that such ability was limited and highly dependent on favorable circumstances.

Jacob Kipp's analysis of the interwar Soviet army is of necessity concerned with the political regime that spawned it; but here, unlike the British case, external political influence was decisive. Kipp rejects, however, the Communist Party's interpretation that victory in the Great Patriotic War was prima facie evidence of successful reform, as well as the argument that the Red Army's adaptation to new technology was merely the continuation of a long historical process of modernization begun under Peter the Great. Instead, Kipp discovers in the interwar Soviet army not only the seeds of the initial disasters of June 1941 and the eventual triumph over fascism in 1945, but also the moral bankruptcy evident in Stalin's reign of terror that led eventually to the ossification of the Soviet state.

One of the recurring major themes of American military history has been the unpreparedness of the armed forces at the outbreak of war. David Johnson's study of the interwar American army, which includes very considerable attention to the Army Air Corps, is a continuation of this tradition. Johnson argues that in addition to the adverse effects of an isolationist-minded electorate and a parsimonious Congress, the War Department was hampered in its efforts at meaningful military change by the intellectual and institutional defects that significantly exacerbated its resource restraints. In sum, the five studies here presented chronicle a rich mixture of failure and success at the business of managing change in military institutions, with decidedly more of the former than the latter. They also demonstrate a number of widely cast nets as the various analysts have attempted to grapple effectively with prickly issues of historical interpretation.

A brief word is required on the rationale for selection of the five studies included in this work. Each of the military institutions under consideration developed or attempted to develop both the material capacity and the institutional concepts for the conduct of modern, industrialized warfare on a continental scale. Each also participated in one or more campaigns in World War II on a scale that provided evidence against which to validate the utility of the forces and concepts developed. The editors considered including analyses of the Japanese and Italian interwar military experiences. However, neither of these armies met the criteria referred to above. Therefore, while recognizing that the lack of a more catholic approach might disappoint some readers, the editors ultimately concluded that in this instance the study of the dynamics of military adaptation would be most usefully served by maintaining a relatively discriminating focus.

This brings us to the two-fold relevance of the present work. First, it is explicitly a collection of historical analyses that the authors and editors hope will provide useful insights into the dynamics of the military reform processes of the French, German, British, Soviet, and American armies during the interwar era and, by extrapolation, into their combat effectiveness in World War II. For the historian, the informed understanding of the past is its own reward. However, each of the authors and editors is or has been involved in his or her particular way with the education of military professionals. Thus we are mindful of our responsibility to challenge and shape the intellects of our nation's future military leaders. We fervently hope that this collection, if imaginatively and critically studied, may have a significance that transcends its purely historical utility. The military leaders of the interwar years faced a daunting future influenced to greater or lesser degrees by strategic and technological uncertainty; external constraints and stimuli; and the challenges of directing the energies of large, complex institutions. Perhaps by considering the extent to which these challenges were or were not effectively met and the underlying causes for subsequent success or failure, the military leaders of today and tomorrow, academics who educate them, defense analysts who advise them, and concerned citizens who have a vested interest in the skill with which they prepare themselves and their institutions for a similarly uncertain future, can all find a measure of profit.

In guiding this work the editors have sought to establish a general framework for analysis, but they have not attempted to influence significantly the individual author's interpretation of the events and ideas under discussion. Furthermore, the views expressed herein do not reflect the official positions of any of the Department of Defense organizations with which the contributors are associated. As a final note, the editors wish to acknowledge their deep appreciation for the positive, formative influence on their personal and professional intellectual development by Col. Roger H. Nye, to whom this work is dedicated.

Notes

1. Although there is a semantic difference between the word "change," which is generic, and the word "reform," which implies a process of change less sweeping and more gradual than revolution yet more comprehensive and rapid than incrementalism, the two terms are used interchangeably here. For a taxonomy of attitudes regarding the pace and scope of change in the British army between the wars, which may have more general applicability, see Harold R. Winton, *To Change an Army: General Sir John Burnett-Stuart and British Armored Doctrine, 1927–1938* (Lawrence: The University Press of Kansas, 1988), 27–30.

2. Michael Howard opined that such a balance "lies at the root of military education and of military training at every level." See Michael Howard, "Military Science in an Age of Peace," *Journal of the Royal United Services Institute for Defence Studies* 119 (March 1974): 6. This balance also lies at the root of military adaptation at every level.

3. An articulate analysis of the importance of the doctrinal development process can be found in the essay of I. B. Holley Jr., "An Enduring Challenge: The Problem of Air Force Doctrine," in *The Harmon Memorial Lectures in Military History*, ed. Harry R. Borowski (Washington: Office of Air Force History, 1988), 425–39.

4. For the interwar period the most obvious example was the Spanish Civil War.

5. "The courage to follow this faint light wherever it may lead" is borrowed from Clausewitz's description of military genius. See Carl von Clausewitz, *On War*, ed. and trans. Michael Howard and Peter Paret (Princeton: Princeton University Press, 1978), 102.

6. Adm. William Moffett, who artfully moved the U.S. Navy toward defining the aircraft carrier as the central capital ship rather than as a fleet auxiliary, was a man who exemplifies the temperament and persuasive skills required of a successful reformer. See Stephen Peter Rosen, *Winning the Next War: Innovation and the Modern Military* (Ithaca NY: Cornell University Press, 1991), 76–80. Rosen also points out that Moffett was a man of great bureaucratic savvy, perhaps another essential attribute of the modern reformer.

THE CHALLENGE OF CHANGE

1. RESTING UNCOMFORTABLY ON ITS LAURELS

The Army of Interwar France

Eugenia C. Kiesling

Military reform has two distinct meanings. It can be an effort to rectify apparent deficiencies within an army, often advertised as a return to the institutions of an uncorrupted past, or it can denote change to meet new conditions. The period between the two world wars ought in principle to have been a fruitful one for reform in the latter sense—new technology offered a means for fundamental change and the horrors of four years of trench warfare offered a motive. That the army of interwar France, in fact, undertook few reforms during the interwar period is well known and usually ascribed to lack of vision. According to this argument, if French soldiers had only understood the requirements of modern technology they would have seen the imperative to adapt to new conditions. This essay will take a different approach. Rather than looking backward from the disaster of May–June 1940 to explain why the French took the wrong path, it explores the tensions faced by an army pulled in various directions, by confidence in the doctrines that had won the Great War, by awareness of changing technological and political conditions, and by adherence to the principle that both its missions and its resources could be determined only in the political arena.

Background

The basic structure of the army with which France would fight the Second World War dated to 1872, three years before the official constitution of the Third Republic. The army created after the humiliating Treaty of Frankfurt was manned by conscripts, trained by professional cadres, organized by a general staff educated at the new École Supérieure de Guerre, led by a Conseil Supérieur de la Guerre, and equipped with modern weapons. Committed to an offensive doctrine it understood, however, that troops would have to attack in dispersed formations to survive against the defensive firepower of breechloading repeating rifles.[1] Military service, which was initially popular as a manifestation of republican patriotism and postwar revanchism, lost its appeal to young Frenchman as the century waned. At the same time, the high-handed behavior of the largely monarchist and Catholic officer corps in the Dreyfus Affair raised questions about the army's commitment to republican institutions.[2] While fin de siécle republicans disdained the army's values, professional soldiers resented the rapid diminution in the rewards—tangible and psychological—of military service.

The Third Republic's first experience of military reform arose directly from the tension between republican politicians and conservative army officials. Appointed minister of war by the new Radical Socialist government in 1901, Gen. Louis André set out deliberately to republicanize the army and to strengthen the War Ministry's authority over the general staff through selective promotion of officers.[3] The reforms culminated in 1905 with the reduction of citizens' obligatory military service from three years to two in a calculated effort to reduce their exposure to life under right-wing officers. André's program of promoting and retiring officers on the basis of their political and religious sentiments insulted and angered the army, whose initiation to military reform took the form of an attack on its fundamental convictions by a military regime that many soldiers rejected as unrepresentative of their France.[4] This would not be the last time that military "reform" in France was aimed less at the army's efficiency than at its ideology.

A second prewar period of military reform was inaugurated by Ministers of War Adolphe Messimy and Alexandre Millerand, who, though affiliated with the Radical Socialist and Independent Socialist parties, respectively, felt France was threatened more by Germany than by her own officer corps.[5] The reforms of this period of "nationalist revival" included restoration of the powers of the general staff vis-à-vis the War Ministry,[6] the attenuation of promotion on the basis of political affiliation, the unification of posts of chief of staff and wartime commander in chief designate,[7] and the restoration of three-year service.[8] Though aimed at French preparedness for war, the Messimy-Millerand reforms were received ungratefully by the army, which objected both to certain specific components of the reforms and to political intervention in principle.[9]

That military reform before World War I tended to be something done to the army rather than done by it, did nothing to endear the concept to members of the French high command, and the consequences of a prewar doctrinal reform movement within the army itself reinforced their suspicions. Although the infantry regulations promulgated in 1875, 1904, and 1914 encouraged attacking soldiers to disperse so as to lessen their exposure to enemy fire, a contrary school of thought, briefly triumphant in the 1894 regulations, argued that only closely packed formations could retain the cohesion necessary to triumph over an enemy's greater weight of lead.[10] The regulations in force from 1904 on called for attacks to be carried out in skirmishing order, but official caution lost out to the intoxicating heresies spread in lectures at the École Supérieure de Guerre by Colonels Ferdinand Foch and Louis de Grandmaison.[11] Their "cult of the offensive," the notion that élan and cold steel would defeat firepower, never became official doctrine but found enthusiastic adherents among French (and foreign) officers up to and including Gen. Joseph Joffre himself.

During the war the cost of this spontaneous diversion from infantry instructions was measured in hundreds of thousands of dead. The "cult of the offensive" gave the French high command a second perspective on the nature of military reform. If not forced upon them by politicians it could sneak up through unauthorized channels.[12] French military leaders would not forget the price paid for tolerating the enthusiasms of reformers whose ideas had not been thoroughly vetted throughout the chain of command.[13]

The Great War

In spite of the French army's consistent failure in the Great War to achieve successes commensurate with its appalling casualty lists, the butcher's bill incurred by the disciples of the "cult of the offensive" did not spark any concerted effort at doctrinal reform. The acquisition of huge numbers of machine guns and artillery pieces; the adoption of new heavy artillery, tanks, and airplanes; and the innovative use of automotive transport all occurred without any systematic rethinking of French military organization, strategy, or doctrine. The range of possible reforms was limited by the imperative to expel the Germans from French territory quickly. Moreover, calls for reform hinted at past errors and military leaders would neither admit to having squandered French lives nor tolerate such charges from civilians.[14] Operationally, the French rejected innovation and instead opted for improvements upon traditional methods. For example, they continued throughout the war to mount large offensive operations but learned to coordinate infantry advances with support from massive artillery guns—and later tanks—and to employ the "creeping barrage" demonstrated by Gen. Robert Nivelle at Verdun in the fall of 1916.[15] By the end of the war the French army had integrated its lessons into a comprehensive offensive doctrine called the methodical battle (*la bataille conduite*) whose defining feature was the tightly controlled and integrated advance of infantry, artillery fire, and tanks for which the rate of movement was determined by that of the massive artillery formations.[16]

Reactions to the Great War

The prewar and wartime experiences of the French army combined to militate against postwar reform: partly because previous reforms had all too often been imposed upon the army by hostile politicians, partly because a call for change implied criticism of France's military leaders, but most of all because the French army emerged from the Great War with a strategy and body of doctrine in which it felt confident. Reform typically aims to correct perceived defects or deficiencies and the victorious French army saw itself as neither defective nor deficient. The largest and best-equipped army in the world in 1919, it maintained that self-image through the interwar period. This is not to say that the army remained unchanged from 1919 to 1939 but, rather, that the new materials, formations, and ideas evolved gradually and without any sense of "diversion" from the established path.

The French military situation at the end of the Great War was conducive to satisfaction, not change. The events of 1914–18 had demonstrated that modern war was a struggle not of armies but of mobilized nations. At the level of grand strategy, the key to victory was the efficient mobilization not only of military manpower but also of industrial and agricultural production, transportation, finance, science, public opinion, and every other national asset. Great War experience seemed to indicate that when the huge armies created and fed by national mobilization met in battle, defensive firepower would shatter offensive spirit. To attack successfully required an enemy weakened by his own fruitless offensive efforts, a massive concentration of supporting firepower, and a skillfully employed offensive doctrine. The twin premises that war was "total" at the level of grand strategy and that the defender had the advantage at the operational level led France to conclude that any German attempt to revise the Treaty of Versailles by force of arms would produce a conflict of a sort that France could win.

Although Germany's larger population, greater industrial output, and propensity for surprise attack offered an advantage if used in a short war, French leaders believed their country would hold the advantage in a long contest. Claiming a unique ability to exploit the principles of the nation *armée* and a special understanding of defensive firepower, France also counted on the material support provided by its allies. These considerations led France to adopt a "long war" strategy that was designed to bring victory over Germany only after several years of struggle. During that time the French army planned to use its large cadre of reservists to maintain an impenetrable defense. Forced to attack at great cost, the Germans would only hasten the day when the balance of resources would permit an allied coalition to go over to the offensive. That offensive would overcome German defenses because the doctrine of the methodical battle would magnify Allied material superiority. To make the long war strategy economical in French blood and French treasure, France would eschew premature offensives and would attempt to fight the long defensive struggle on foreign soil. Therein lay the strategic logic behind the construction of the Maginot Line: the fortification of the eastern and northeastern frontiers would force the Germans to choose between fruitless assaults against a well-defended frontier or a circuitous approach through Belgium. The latter contingency was the more likely, and French war plans called for the use of most of the available mobile forces to meet any German move into Belgium.[17]

France entered the 1920s with a strategy for national defense; an army of six hundred thousand officers and men; an arsenal of state-of-the-art artillery, tanks, and airplanes; and a doctrine with which it felt comfortable.[18] The new material developed during the Great War only supplemented the traditional arms. Further developments would render infantry, artillery, and cavalry more mobile and more powerful, but their essential roles and responsibilities remained unchallenged: "artillery conquers, infantry occupies." The cavalry, whose wartime contributions had been meager, had high expectations for the future. Reinforced with mobile artillery, machine guns, and armored cars, it promised to serve as a tool for exploration, screening, surprise attack, and exploitation.[19] Not even the development of the tank stimulated any official demand for doctrinal change because the recent war had already presented the answers. French doctrine called for two kinds of tanks—light tanks to accompany the infantry and heavy tanks to break through fortified positions—but this was not a matter of reform.[20] Thirty-five hundred

Renault FT light tanks existed in French arsenals, and the heavy tank, the Char C, was under development.

If the French army saw no pressing need for reform in the aftermath of the Great War, it was equally true that the sorts of changes likely to be approved by the elected representatives of a war-weary people were not in the army's best interest. French citizens expected their years of agony to be rewarded by the reduction of military service from the three years established in 1913 to one, a proposal that would shrink the army by two-thirds. Although the army hoped to compromise on the issue by obtaining two-year service, the Conseil Supérieur de la Guerre acknowledged on 21 October 1920 the political imperative of reducing the period of conscript service to eighteen months—as soon as German disarmament allowed it.[21] By establishing eighteen-month service the recruitment law of 1 April 1923 shrank the active army to thirty-two infantry divisions, five artillery groups, five cavalry divisions, and two aerial divisions; but the high command did not expect to retain even those numbers.[22] The new law directed the government to reassess the manpower situation in 1925 with an eye to further reducing the required length of military service.[23]

In the face of inexorable pressure for shorter military service, the army could only suggest that France's smaller forces could be made more effective by the peacetime preparation of wartime resources. The primary lesson of the recent war had been that modern wars were not won by standing armies and stockpiled materiel but by a nation's ability to harness its productive energies during wartime. As Col. Jean Fabry told the Senate's army committee, "it is no longer an army that must be put into action, but the entire nation; it is no longer a matter of arming a front, but all of the national resources have to be applied to the war effort."[24] Using this analysis, the size of the nation's army was less important than the efficiency of the industrial machine behind it. Army Chief of Staff Gen. Edmond Buat suggested as early as 1920 that the Conseil Supérieur de Défense Nationale (CSDN) should draft legislation to establish the legal framework for wartime mobilization of France's national resources. By the spring of 1922 members of the chamber of deputies were urging the CSDN to produce a draft of the measure for consideration in conjunction with the eighteen-month service law.[25]

Calls for simultaneous action on the separate matters of length of conscript service and national organization for war came from representatives of two opposing points of view. For men such as Colonel Fabry, a comprehensive national mobilization scheme was a necessary instrument in an age of total war and was rendered more imperative by the reduction of the active army. For legislators more sensitive than Fabry to the electorate's distaste for military service, national mobilization proposals were of rhetorical interest—to be used to justify a lightened military burden and then to be forgotten.[26] The latter attitude prevailed and interest in the proposed "Loi sur l'organisation de la nation pour le temps de guerre" waned with the agreement on eighteen months of service.

Had the measure been passed in its original form, which included provisions both for the wartime conscription of French women and the requisition of private property, it would have constituted a major reform not only of the French army but also of the French state. That, of course, was the politicians' objection. The deputy who called this law "the most militaristic that a country has ever known" had a point.[27] This was certainly not the sort of law likely appeal to voters who had just suffered through one bloody conflict and who rebelled at the prospect of another. In particular, the Senate refused to accept provisions for governmental requisition of private property.[28] The law would not be passed until 11 July 1938, and then in a version much milder than the original.[29] The failure of the effort begun by Buat in 1920 meant that although France chose to wager that her superior ability to mobilize for total war gave her an advantage over nations endowed with superior resources, she failed throughout the interwar period to ensure the effectiveness of her national mobilization. French leaders had acknowledged after the Great War that a haphazard, inefficient, and inequitable mobilization had cost French dearly during that conflict; similar improvisation could easily contribute to defeat in 1940.

The evisceration of General Buat's strong national organization law aroused no regret within the army. Too socialistic for military tastes, it smacked, moreover, of the unhealthy notion that a militia backed by an efficient industrial mobilization could replace the regular army. Worse, the emphasis on projects focused on national mobilization impeded the army's eventually fruitless struggle to retain the eighteen-month service established in 1923.

The Army Laws of 1927–1928

Military reform was a central issue for the deputies of the left-wing majority elected to the Chamber in May 1924; once again "reform" reduced itself essentially to the issue of conscript service. The one-year service demanded by the voters proved to be impossible, however, without an accompanying larger set of changes. In the first place the reduced manpower available under twelve-month service meant that France could no longer field even the twenty active divisions required by the country's regional military organization. Moreover, the proposed sixteen divisions would be not be ready for war. None of them would be at full strength and their soldiers would not be adequately trained.[30] To avoid ever having an army manned solely by untrained recruits, induction had to be staggered so that half of each new conscript class reported every six months. Biennial induction meant that half of any division would be at best only half-trained at any given time, while the other half would not have finished basic training and the bifurcated unit as a whole would be unready for combat. In order to go to war an active-service regiment had to replace its seven hundred to one thousand first-semester recruits with two thousand reservists from the *disponibilité* (the ready reserve), composed of the three youngest reserve classes.[31] As one French general succinctly described the situation, the active duty conscripts provided a "peacetime army" while the reservists were "wartime army."[32]

For these reasons the one-year service proposal stimulated the high command to demand reforms of the reserve organization to compensate for the weakening of the active army.[33] A reduced army would no longer have enough active units to handle reserve training and mobilization, the professional soldiers would be occupied with recruit training, and no trained, second-year conscripts would be available to take up the slack. The solution proposed by the army was to create a separate system of mobilization bureaus to organize, equip, and train the reservists. To compensate for manpower reduction, the army proposed to increase the number of professional cadres to 106,000 and to hire fifteen thousand civilian *agents militaires* to assume responsibility for the mobilization bureaus and other extraneous duties.[34] The army also suggested that the problems created by twelve-month service could be mitigated by a program of premilitary education to prepare young Frenchmen for military service.

Save for the generally unpopular idea of premilitary training, all of these measures were included in the reform legislation. Nevertheless, the army remained justifiably uneasy about the reserve organization. If reservists were wholly separated from the active army after a single year of active duty, who could guarantee that they would be combat-ready when called up for war? As no reserve training had occurred between the Great War's end and 1927, French military leaders had reason to worry that men released to the authority of the mobilization centers would cease to be soldiers. To ensure that one-year service did not leave France with a purely nominal reserve army, the high command insisted upon three further reforms: reservists would be organized into permanent formations based on their active-service units, they would train regularly, and the training would take place within complete units.[35] From the beginning of recruit training until their final retirement from the reserves, groups of men were to serve together continuously in units that drew their cohesion from long acquaintance both in the barracks and in civilian life. As the general staff explained, "Men who will fight together in wartime must already have had the opportunity to get to know one another in time of peace. They must already know their leaders and their leaders must know them."[36] Reservists would be liable for a three-week reserve training exercise sometime during their three years in the *disponibilité*, two such exercises during their sixteen years in the active reserve, and a one-week call-up during their eight years in the second reserve. Because reserve training would be organized by unit rather than by class, it would increase the bonds within the unit and provide a more realistic preparation for war.

The package of laws passed in 1927 and 1928 both reduced conscript service to twelve months as of 1930 and imposed the compensatory reforms on the reserve army—at least in principle.[37] In practice, however, the permanent units and the unit reserve call-ups mandated by Parliament proved impractical. Most French soldiers did not serve in reserve units formed of comrades from active duty years, and reservists were normally called up for training by class rather than by unit. Because the reserve mobilization centers lacked the facilities to train reservists, they sent the soldiers for training to the overburdened active units, which had to combine reservists with recruits or improvise ad hoc formations. Thus the reform legislation failed in its objective of creating two separate and self-sufficient armies of active-duty conscripts and reservists. The reduced active army could train—as long as its obligations to the reservists did not interfere—but was not suited for war. The reservists were expected to fight but could train only haphazardly and at great inconvenience to the active army.[38]

Postwar Doctrine

The structure imposed upon the army by the reform legislation of 1927–28 exerted enormous influence on French military doctrine. The army it created was better suited to defend rather than attack, and the French government gave that defensive orientation concrete support by fortifying the nation's eastern and northeastern frontiers.[39] Moreover, doctrine had to be simple enough to be taught to conscripts in six months and to be executed by units most of whose commissioned and noncommissioned leaders were reservists themselves.[40] Because reserve exercises were held too infrequently to keep citizen soldiers abreast of doctrinal changes, doctrine also had to be stable; active units could not learn new methods without creating confusion when the reservists joined them in time of war. Behind every doctrinal decision was the premise that France had an army of interchangeable parts in which reservists trained as visitors in one unit and fought as members of another, and newly trained conscripts had to join with older men whose basic military training had occurred years in the past. Thus doctrine had to be suitable for soldiers who rarely refreshed their military skills and changes could be introduced only at the cost of creating rifts between formations and individuals trained in the old and new methods of fighting.

The arguments for a simple and stable doctrine were, of course, the very same arguments used against doctrinal reform. If French methods were, in Gen. Robert Touchon's words, "rigid and constrained, especially in comparison to the rapid German attacks," they nevertheless were what was wanted for "an army composed primarily of reservists, very impressionable."[41] The energies of the French army went not into reforming a doctrine believed to be sound but into advertising the deficient doctrine's merits. The need to maintain confidence and the practical impediments to communicating new doctrine acted together to discourage novel ideas. Far from seeking to innovate, the high command reiterated the validity of regulations bearing the imprimatur of the general staff.

The military journals and the École Supérieure de Guerre worked to prove the validity of existing doctrine through carefully managed historical analysis.[42] In 1919 the college created a new history course "whose essential mission was to present the lessons of the last war," lessons that reinforced the currently held doctrine.[43] When the French general staff established a new journal, the *Revue Militaire Générale* in 1937, authors were instructed to "limit themselves to exploiting history . . . without detailed recital of events."[44] The army's controlled approach to the study of history is exemplified by the favorite interwar staff college text, Marius Daille's account of the battle of Montdidier.[45] Daille's account was not a historical study but an exegesis of lessons for the present. His conclusions—the importance of centralized command and the superiority of the homogeneous French army over a German force divided into "shock" and "occupation" components—served to validate the army's contemporary doctrine.

Doctrines imposed from above were not meant to be dissected below: "The junior officers refrained from discussing the fundamental problems because such discussion might have entailed criticism of their superiors, and that might have been interpreted as a violation of discipline."[46] French soldiers were not encouraged to try new ideas. On the contrary, some new doctrinal concepts were labeled "experimental," which meant not that subordinates were invited to test them empirically but rather that, because they had not yet been defined by the general staff, their unsupervised use was proscribed. Thus, Gen. Maurice Gamelin forbade maneuvers by medium tank units except in the presence of a member of the Conseil Supérieur de la Guerre because no official doctrine on the subject existed.[47] To allow no time for unauthorized maneuvers the high command formed the experimental armored division that was authorized for exercises from 30 August to 3 September 1937 only immediately before the test period began.[48] Gamelin also silenced the prevailing "widespread discussion of motorization and mechanization" with a stiff admonition that "the sole authority for the establishment of doctrine is the General Headquarters of the Army" and warned that no articles or lectures on doctrine were to be published or delivered without official authorization.[49]

Hostility to doctrinal experiment indicated not an unreflecting conservatism but a reasoned belief that the known benefits of reinforcing the existing correct doctrine outweighed the dubious advantages offered by innovation. Nothing was more frightening to French commanders than the possibility that, time having dulled institutional memory, the army would abandon tried and true methods and be forced to relearn the bloody lessons of 1914 to 1918. As the veterans of the Great War were replaced by men younger and more naive, it became the explicit purpose of the regulations to preserve from oblivion "certain lessons that the war had impressed so vividly on their hearts and spirits."[50]

By 1936, when these words were written, unorthodox ideas existed within the French army, and one can even find the elements of a reform school taking shape. During the 1920s, however, what stands out is the uniformity of views. Major debates occurred on such matters as the relative merits of linear versus deep fortifications and on how best to integrate the automobile and the tank into existing military institutions, but no one suggested that French military institutions were fundamentally unsatisfactory.

Motorization and Mechanized Cavalry

The prevailing notion within the army of the 1920s—that there was no need to reform an army whose mobilization arrangements suited an era of "total war" and whose defensive doctrine matched the technological conditions of the era—rested, of course, on an incomplete view of French strategy. The strategy and doctrines derived from the experience of the Great War prepared France only for the long defensive war that would arise in the event of a German attack to the west. France based her national security, however, not on her armed forces alone but also on a set of alliances with Germany's eastern neighbors; if France expected aid against Germany from Poland, Czechoslovakia, Yugoslavia, or Rumania, she had to be able to reciprocate should Germany move eastward. Until 1930 the contradiction between the demands of French alliance obligations and the military forces that were intended to support them had no practical consequences. That the French army lacked an offensive doctrine hardly mattered as long as the three corps it maintained on German soil sufficed to deter the small army allowed to Germany under the provisions of the Treaty of Versailles.[51]

The new decade saw a new situation. Early withdrawal of the army of occupation from the Ruhr in 1930 ended the French presence in Germany. Deterrence now rested on France's willingness and ability to strike eastward. In principle Germany could now launch an attack against Poland or Czechoslovakia, either of which would then demand from France offensive action for which neither her doctrine nor the reserve-based army created by the 1927–28 army laws was suited.[52] Or Germany could attack France herself, crossing the Belgian plain to reach a Franco-Belgian frontier invitingly bereft of fortifications. Because France intended to fight her long war north of that vulnerable frontier, even her defensive strategy demanded a mobile army that could reach the Belgian battlefields before the Germans did.[53] While the French army never effectively addressed its alliance obligations to an eastern offensive, it worked hard in the early 1930s on the reforms necessary to acquire the ability to beat the German army to Belgium.

The key reform was the equipping of certain infantry divisions with trucks and tractors for the rapid transport of troops and artillery. This motorization program demonstrated both the French army's receptivity to reforms that met its strategic needs and its care to avoid hasty and ill-considered action. Mobility was an attractive asset, but one that came with disadvantages as well. Motorization represented a huge financial investment that would impose a new set of operational supply problems and increase the nation's dependence on imported petroleum. Because it could not be achieved uniformly throughout the entire army, motorization promised a medley of wheeled, tracked, horsed, and foot-slogging formations moving at different speeds, equipped for different kinds of terrain, and requiring different fuels.[54] By increasing the number of technically trained specialists needed to meet army requirements, motorization complicated the induction and training of recruits and the distribution of reservists among regiments. Motorization enhanced operational mobility, the ability to move to the battlefield, but it reduced a division's organic artillery and increased its vulnerability while in transit. French commanders entertained nightmares about German aircraft making target practice of long, road-bound columns.[55] In addition, of course, both the trucks and their drivers of the late 1920s left much to be desired.[56] At the end of 1931 the cost of motorizing the cavalry and two corps reconnaissance groups was estimated to be 1,126 million francs, more than twice the annual materiel budget for the whole army.[57] Given these reasons for caution it is remarkable how quickly the French moved from the experiments with trucked movement in the late 1920s to the decree of 4 July 1930 which, by expanding the French motorization effort to encompass five infantry divisions, made the French army the world's most mobile.[58]

Creating motorized infantry formations that were capable of shifting the war's scene from France to Belgium was a reform that could not take place in isolation. Because such units could not afford to meet the enemy while still loaded in their trucks, they had to be protected by forces that combined rapid movement with firepower. Providing screening for conventional infantry divisions was a cavalry mission, but mounted units could not cover motorized troops. To protect the fast-moving new infantry divisions the French army saw the need for a new kind of cavalry as well, and the July 1930 decree motorizing five infantry divisions also authorized the transformation of a cavalry division into an experimental light mechanized division (Division Légère Mécanique, or DLM) and the "mechanization" of one brigade from each of the other five cavalry divisions.[59]

The DLM initially appeared in 1933 as an assortment of wheeled armored cars equipped with machine guns (*automitrailleuses de cavalrie*), trucks, motorcycles, and horses. The appearance of a purpose-built light tank, the Renault model 1935 *automitrailleuse de combat*, hardly improved the situation since the new machine proved to be underpowered, under-armored, and undergunned.[60] The division was no better served by its ill-matched reconnaissance teams of poorly armored cars and vulnerable motorcycles, and the DLM could not do its job in combat until its divi-sional artillery—two groups of 75mm guns and one group of 105mm howitzers—was tracked.[61] In fact, as of 1936 the DLM could not even protect itself let alone protect the motorized infantry it had been created to screen.[62] But French cavalry reform did not stop there. Even if the original DLM promised more than it could deliver, by the end of the decade France had four such units whose SOMUA cavalry tank made them full-fledged armored divisions comparable in equipment to the German panzer division.[63]

The teething troubles of the DLM were remedied with relative ef-ficiency because the unit's utility was undisputed. Far less consensus existed, however, on two other matters—the role of light tanks in the methodical battle and the role of medium (or battle) tanks in French doctrine. Here reform proceeded with an incoherence strikingly at odds with the relatively smooth adoption of motorized infantry and mecha-nized cavalry.

There was never any prospect that the French infantry would abjure the tank, and throughout the decade after the end of the Great War France both maintained a large arsenal of 1918 vintage machines and began planning for their future replacement.[64] As Gen. Maxime Wey-gand pointed out, "We had won the war thanks to the tanks, whose use had transformed the tactics of our attacks in 1918, and we were not stupid enough to forget it.[65] French leaders knew that regardless of how much the tanks cost, how awkwardly they meshed with the methodical battle, or how problematic their survival on battlefields dominated by artillery and antitank guns was, the machines were indisputably necessary. French infantry had become accustomed to close tank support in 1918; attacking infantry could not, or at least would not, advance without it.[66] Armor development proceeded at a glacial pace during the 1920s, however, for the perfectly sensible reason that the thirty-five hundred existing Renault FTS sufficed against an enemy who had nothing better.[67] Moreover, the FTS represented a large financial investment and served as a reminder that any replacement tank would be an expensive and ephemeral asset. If investing vast sums to build machines whose very nature rendered them obsolete at the moment mass production began was a dismaying prospect for an underfunded French army, the difficulties of producing tank crews from one-year conscripts were equally so. The most difficult problem of all, however, was not material but theoretical: how to integrate infantry tanks into the doctrine of the methodical battle.[68]

Able to take ground but not to hold it and happier in motion than stationary, even slow tanks fit badly into the methodical battle.[69] While advancing with the infantry, the tanks could provide immediate fire support against enemy strongpoints in return for the infantry's assistance in locating and destroying antitank weapons. During the halt at the end of each of the short bounds of methodical battle the large machines would act as magnets, drawing artillery fire upon themselves and the foot soldiers nearby. If stationary machines would be obvious targets, tanks that failed to halt would outrun the infantry and find themselves at the mercy of enemy positions they were too blind to see.[70] The result would be everything the methodical battle was designed to avoid: while the over-extended armored vehicles were picked off by antitank guns the infantry following close behind would be held up by concealed strongpoints that had been overlooked during the tanks' precipitous advance.[71] Eliminating such strongpoints had been the artillery's responsibility, but now the gunners had to worry about hitting friendly tanks.[72] In the absence of reliable communications tanks did not promise to open the battlefield to fluid, independent operations but intensified the need for disciplined adherence to prearranged plans. For the tank to introduce a new element of surprise into battle, artillery preparation had to be shortened, with larger numbers of guns massed to achieve the required impact. Thus tank attacks required not *less* artillery support but "as many guns as possible" and therefore increased the material requirements of the methodical battle.[73] In 1926, with these considerations in mind the infantry branch, which was responsible for using tanks, called upon the tank inspectorate to produce a machine suitable to a rigidly controlled battlefield.[74] It was to weigh no more than 13 tons, be too slow to escape the infantry, and "faire cavalier seule" (operate independently).

From these specifications the tank inspectorate produced in 1929 the Renault DI—a 13-ton machine with a top speed of 18 KPH, a radio set designed to talk to other tanks (but not to the infantry), a 47mm gun (and two machine guns), and an engine proportionally less powerful than that of the FT.[75] This ill-favored tank baffled the infantry branch and embarrassed the tank inspectorate. The former objected that the DI would outrun the methodical battle and the latter, secretly desirous of a tank capable of independent action, responded by offering the more powerful D2—which weighed 18.5 tons and had a top speed of 23 KPH. At this point the infantry branch redefined its objective. It now wanted a 6-ton tank armed with either a single machine gun or a 37mm cannon yet simple enough to be used by short-service conscripts. In response the government authorized on 2 August 1933 an infantry tank program that resulted in the R35 light tank, the FCM36 infantry tank, and the H35 and H39 Hotchkiss light tanks. The Renault R35 became the infantry's standard accompaniment tank, although discouraging trials in 1937 aroused complaints that the infantry might as well have stuck with the D2.[76] When the new tank came into service the type Ds were reclassified as medium tanks.[77]

Obstructing the development of a proper infantry support tank was not so much the tank inspectorate's purpose as it was a by-product of that agency's pursuit of a medium tank suitable for independent maneuver. The originator of the original French tank program, Gen. Jean-Baptiste Estienne, had from the very beginning conceived of massive "land battleships" armed with heavy ordnance and designed to operate independently of the traditional arms. The end of the war left Estienne unshaken in his commitment to the liberation of the tank from the infantry. Almost alone in an army whose Renault light tank was "l'enfant cheri de la victoire," he urged that "the idea and the label 'accompaniment tank' should be abandoned. . . . Motorization consists solely and essentially of putting at the disposition of the commander the largest and most powerful reserve of battle tanks possible."[78] As postwar inspector general of tanks, Estienne held a purely advisory position but made up in energy what he lacked in authority. Even though he could not promise that the French army would purchase enough machines to make up for research and development costs, Estienne negotiated his own scheme with five leading armaments firms to design and build a 20-ton "battle tank." Three prototypes were offered in 1925, of which the most promising was the Renault company's Char B.[79]

Thanks to Estienne's initiative the Conseil Supérieur de la Guerre recommended in March 1926 the purchase of three prototype 20-ton medium tanks and decided to abandon the Char c heavy tank program.[80] When the machines finally appeared for testing in 1930, however, the army had no conception of their purpose. Army doctrine asserted that tanks (other than breakthrough tanks) were a tool to assist the infantry, a role for which the B1 was excessively fast and too heavily armed.[81] Perhaps, as Gen. Henri Giraud had suggested in 1926, they could be used to support the cavalry.[82] In the wake of the unsuccessful performance of a "détachement mécanique de combat" of forty-five DI tanks and the three existing B1s at Mailly Camp in September 1932, few voices could be heard in favor of maneuvers by independent tank formations.[83] The demonstration at Mailly and subsequent experiments provided little stimulus for a reform movement based on the battle tank.

During the first half the 1930s the story of French armor has three major themes: the search for an effective cavalry tank with which to equip the DLMs, the difficult incorporation of the tank into the methodical battle, and the development of a medium tank. In the first case strategic and operational missions, doctrine, and technology were compatible and the French army took pride in the result.[84] In the second case the problem forced an important new technological tool—the tank—to fit into a doctrine—the methodical battle—with which it was largely at odds. Further impeding any successful resolution of this conundrum was the tank inspectorate's lack of enthusiasm for the enterprise. Though the inspectorate was called upon to create an infantry tank, it instead produced a series of tanks that were better suited to independent maneuver: the DI, the D2, and the B1. These detours by the inspectorate detracted attention from the much-needed infantry tank, which appeared late in the form of the unimpressive R35. Thus reform (in this case the development of a useful infantry support tank) was hampered by the failure of the tank inspectorate to heed the requirements of the infantry branch and, on the other hand, by the infantry's failure to impose its own vision on the tank's design.[85] The third story, that of the development of the B tank even in the absence of doctrinal imperative for a medium tank, was a victory for individual energy over institutional procedures. General Estienne and his heirs managed to provide the French army with an unwanted medium tank even though they failed to impose a new doctrine along with the machine. Like the "cult of the offensive" before 1914, the battle tank was developed largely without official support. This time, however, the mavericks had done the army a service. Without their efforts there would have been no maneuver tank available in 1936 when the French army suddenly discovered a pressing need for one.

Reserve Armored Divisions

By the mid-1930s the French were committed to the use of armor for cavalry functions, for local counterattacks in support of infantry formations, and for mobile firepower during the methodical battle. Within the cavalry they had created mechanized divisions but they saw the other functions as best carried out by single battalions that could be assigned as needed to infantry units. The rival notion of consolidating the armored battalions into armored divisions had few adherents. While General Estienne criticized the notion of infantry support tanks until his death in 1936 and Inspector General of Tanks G. M. Velpry continued to press the claims of medium tanks against light ones, both said little about unit organization above the battalion level.[86] While the tank enthusiasts were hesitant to press for armored divisions, the bulk of the French army deemed such units to be completely impractical. As the 1936 armor instructions claimed, "In the offensive, it cannot be emphasized too strongly that today the antitank weapon is to the tank what the machine gun was to the infantry during the World War."[87] Under such circumstances, expensive tanks could survive on the battlefield only with powerful artillery support and with the infantry's assistance in locating and destroying hidden antitank guns. Antitank developments over the course of the decade reinforced the need to retain the increasingly vulnerable tank within the protective framework of the methodical battle. As an American observer noted, since 1918 "nothing has developed . . . to change the situation except considerable improvement in antitank weapons and training in antitank defense."[88]

The one vocal exception to the pre-1936 consensus that French tanks were best employed by the DLM and the independent tank battalions was a certain Maj. Charles de Gaulle of the Secrétariat Général de la Défense Nationale, who began in 1932 to publicize a radically unorthodox proposal for a new shock force of six mechanized infantry divisions, a light division, an armored brigade, a heavy artillery brigade, and an air observation group.[89] In terms of armored organization the call for a single brigade was none too radical; what distinguished (and anathematized) de Gaulle's plan was his insistence that the new units had to be manned by one hundred thousand professional soldiers. No civilian or military leaders expended much energy debating the military merits of an organization so clearly opposed to the traditions of the Republic. The government had no desire to hand the army a force so suitable for a coup d'état, and most generals astute enough to have reached the upper echelons of the army knew better than to lobby for one.

The combination of German tank successes against France and de Gaulle's meteoric career have fostered exaggerated respect for a proposal that might otherwise have been judged merely a youthful indiscretion. Even had de Gaulle's mobile force fit French visions of a long defensive war, the proposal to recruit additional professional soldiers ignored the army's inability to retain its existing cadres.[90] A jejune proposal became a pernicious one because de Gaulle's insistence that only professionals could handle the demands of mechanized war led republican politicians to suspect the army of seeking to create a praetorian guard whose tanks would bring a new Bonaparte to power. Since plots against the Republic had existed in the 1930s and often included soldiers, the hysteria aroused by de Gaulle's inopportune proposal was not entirely paranoid.[91] By leading political leaders to associate armored divisions with a professional army, de Gaulle significantly hampered the army's ability to press for such units within the existing military structure.[92]

De Gaulle's poorly timed proposal kindled civilian fears of the army and reinforced soldiers' caution about politically sensitive reforms just as the high command was about to undergo a conversion experience on the subject of armored divisions. Proposals for offensively oriented armored forces that had previously been dismissed with predictions such as, "we will have a brilliant communiqué at the outset and, a few days later, a useless sos," found champions in 1936 at the very highest levels.[93] General Gamelin, who had told the Conseil Supérieur de la Guerre in April 1936 that "the development of the antitank weapon has caused the renunciation of [large tank units]," now instructed it to study the creation of armored divisions.[94] The man who had once rejected such units on the grounds that "just because the Germans have committed an enormous error does not mean we must do the same. . . . [These divisions] may accomplish small tasks such as reducing a pocket, but are incapable of offensive actions," had changed his mind in response to new conditions.[95] The creation of the first panzer divisions in 1935 would not have posed a threat to French operational conceptions had the new unit been intended as a screening force for infantry, like France's similarly equipped DLMs. French leaders recognized, however, the possibility that the Wehrmacht would choose to use its new armored force to launch a powerful surprise attack.[96] The horse-drawn artillery upon which French antitank doctrine depended would be too slow and the independent tank battalions too weak to offer an effective response against an offensive by a highly mobile army.

Suddenly the French army saw the need for the very organization that it had consistently rejected. From October 1936 on the question was not whether France would acquire armored divisions but how soon and in what form. The first point depended in part on French industry's ability to produce the necessary tanks, but large-scale production could not begin until the army had resolved the second point through a lengthy debate over the composition of the proposed units. Mere conviction that France needed to counter new German capabilities did not provide much guidance as to how the units would look. Nor did the simple phrase "armored division" (Grande Unité Cuirassée) solve the problem. In the DLM France already possessed an armored division very similar to the German panzer division.[97] In fact, a 1937 war game between a light mechanized division and a notional "German" armored division led Gamelin to praise the French unit as "a fortunate solution, more fortunate than the panzer division."[98]

As Gamelin told the Conseil Supérieur de la Guerre in October 1936, the French army was not seeking to copy the Wehrmacht. Because it was not designed to operate on its own, the proposed French armored division would rely on other units to provide it with supporting infantry, artillery, and reconnaissance.[99] By depriving it of such ancillary forces Gamelin ensured that the armored division would not *faire cavalier seul* but operate within the framework of the methodical battle.[100] He envisioned a powerful force of six battalions of B1 and B1bis tanks capable of handling any German attack; the problem, however, was lack of materiel. France produced 27 B tanks in 1936, 35 in 1937, 25 in 1938, 100 in 1939, and 187 in the first six months of 1940; the 198 machines necessary to create six 33-tank battalions were finally available in January 1940.[101] On 2 December 1938 the CSG reduced the number of battalions in the proposed armored division from six to four, but that concession to the realities of French production proved insufficient.[102] The three divisions activated in January and March of 1939 each combined only two battalions of B1 and B1bis machines with two battalions of H39s, while the Fourth Reserve Armored Division (formed in May 1940) was composed of two battalions each of B1bis and R35 infantry tanks.[103]

Although the slow rate of tank production blocked armor development in France, that is not to say that factors such as the forty-hour work week (established in June 1936), a strike-prone labor force, or artisan holdovers in French production are entirely to blame for the slow emergence of a French reserve armored division.[104] Many of the production delays were created by the army, whose bureaus slowly ground out demands for minor modifications of prototypes while plants awaited orders.[105] French industry did not build tanks in the speculative hope of being able to sell them once the army got round to shopping, and the French army did not order mass production of extraordinarily expensive battle tanks in the absence of a confirmed doctrine for their use. Complicating this impasse was the impossibility of formulating doctrine without conducting field tests with the sorts of tanks envisioned for the eventual armored units. Rather than risk deriving misleading results by testing an armored division with the available light tanks, the general staff replaced the field exercises scheduled for the summer of 1937 with map exercises.[106]

There is an instructive difference between the French army's refusal to pretend to work with materiel that it did not yet have and German willingness to do war games with plywood "tanks." The Wehrmacht treated such exercises as learning opportunities and used the results to guide further doctrine. The French, on the other hand, sought impressive demonstrations of approved methods of fighting. Reservists were not to be sent home from maneuvers with memories of ersatz weapons or experimental doctrines.

Without the machines for realistic exercises the French groped slowly toward solving doctrinal questions. Behind their hesitation to invest in large numbers of battle tanks lay the fear of diverting resources into a costly mistake. From the experiments done in 1937 came a tentative set of armor regulations, the "Notice provisoire sur l'emploi des chars modernes" of 15 December 1937, which began with warnings about the limitations of the new weapon.[107] Because tanks could neither hold terrain nor clear it completely of enemy positions, they could operate "only in close collaboration with other arms, especially infantry." The machines had a limited range of action and required six hours of daily maintenance and an additional full day of attention after three or four days of operation. Tank mobility was not what it might have been; to minimize wear on treads the machines were to be transported by train whenever possible. Accompaniment tanks were to remain close to the infantry and to concentrate on neutralizing the enemy's automatic weapon fire. Although advancing independently, companies and battalions of maneuver tanks were to maintain the closest possible contact with the mixed groups of infantrymen and accompaniment tanks. Like infantry attacks, advances by maneuver tanks were to be directed at a specific objective or a series of objectives that required precise artillery support. In essence this was the methodical battle with the maneuver tank as an added element, an effort to exploit the tanks' tactical possibilities without releasing them from a rigidly centralized command.

Tests of an experimental armored brigade scheduled for 1938 were canceled because of the Sudetenland crisis, but paper exercises under Gen. Julien Martin produced some useful results. Martin reported difficulties in handling a division of four tank battalions and recommended dividing the unit into two brigades, each consisting of two tank battalions and one battalion of infantry. He also argued that the division required additional elements: a reconnaissance group, air support, and an anti-aircraft unit.[108] Martin's proposal to equip the armored division with the tools for independent operation placed him in a small minority within an army where the conventional wisdom was that tanks had to be deprived of the ability—and therefore the temptation—to run amok. The majority position in the 2 December 1938 meeting of the Conseil Supérieur de la Guerre and the official statement on armor doctrine issued by General Gamelin on 18 December 1938 took a more conservative line.[109] Gamelin's note specified that armored divisions were only useful against materially inferior enemy forces that were not yet organized for defense or were already undermined by French actions. The armored unit could not protect its own movements nor provide its own reconnaissance and therefore had always to be part of a corps or mechanized group.

The Gamelin note gives a sense of the limited role of armored divisions in French thinking, as does the title chosen for the new formation. It was called the Division Cuirassée de Réserve because the Division de Cavalerie already owned the acronym of "Division Cuirassée." In addition, the title reinforces the image of a unit designed to exploit a victory already won by the artillery and the infantry. Regardless of how useful they were when their special attributes—speed, power, and mass—allowed them to contribute to operations, armor divisions were not central players and were certainly not to be unshackled from other units or from the confines of the methodical battle. Never does Gamelin's note or any other recorded statement on French doctrine treat armored divisions as essential weapons rather than as desirable adjuncts, nor suggest that any conceivable operational problem could exceed the combined defensive resources of France's infantry, cavalry, mechanized cavalry, and independent tank battalions. But what to make of Gamelin's 1936 argument that France needed armored divisions as the specific antidote to German developments, that only this type of unit had the speed and firepower to block a German panzer penetration? If the special virtue of the armored division was not defensive power (arguably less defensive than that of an infantry division) but rather the speed with which it could parry and riposte German thrusts, surely it could not be tied by its lack of reconnaissance elements to the pace of slower formations. Nor could an armored division without combat engineers move across blocked terrain or unbridged rivers.[110] Here doctrinal problems could not be solved within the framework of the methodical battle and, therefore, for the French army could not be solved at all.

The story of the development of the Division Cuirassée de Réserve is the story of French reform as a whole. The French army came out of the Great War with a winning doctrine which it saw no reason to change in the following decades. Faced at the end of the 1930s with the prospect of war against an army that had made a different set of doctrinal choices, French commanders continued to believe that theirs was the better understanding of modern war. On the whole, studying German doctrine reinforced French confidence in their own methods. Similarities were stressed, perhaps even wishfully invented, and discrepancies that could not be attributed to German miscalculation (like those arising from conflicting judgments of the relative effectiveness of the tank and of the antitank gun) were explained by differences in the two armies' composition and mission. Before May of 1940 it was not clear how wrong the French army had been. A German officer comparing French and German doctrine concerning the use of armor in 1937 "sincerely believed that his army might learn some important points about the employment of tanks from the French, who, as he pointed out, had more experience in war and peace with the tank."[111]

Even after the Polish campaign the French had no doubts that their theories were, if not abstractly superior to that of the Germans, at least appropriate to their own abilities and requirements. The valiant Polish effort had failed because their strategy was erroneous and their defensive fortifications inadequate. But France did not offer a countryside as hospitable to the panzers as the flat plains of eastern Europe; French and British generals were pleased to note that, even employed in inadequate numbers on unfavorable terrain, Polish antitank guns took a high toll on German tanks and blocked a direct German assault on Warsaw.[112]

Historians tend to correlate the stunning disparity between French and German battlefield performance in 1940 with the two armies' relative degree of military reform after the Great War.[113] Before dismissing French tactical doctrine out of hand, however, one does well to remember that the movement of the French left wing deep into Belgium, which was exacerbated by the failure to take simple defensive measures in the Ardennes sector, were free gifts to the Wehrmacht. The strategic dislocation of the French army in 1940 was such that its tactics were tested—and found wanting—only under thoroughly disadvantageous conditions.[114]

The primary explanation for the absence of military reform in France between the two world wars is that French soldiers believed their doctrines would be able to deal with the existing threat satisfactorily. When developments in Germany began to shift the military balance the French army, fearing any admission of uncertainty, chose to reaffirm rather than reevaluate its doctrines. Behind this explanation lies the army's understanding that any call for structural reform would have been futile and dangerous. The history of the Third Republic had irrevocably committed France to a conscript army. It had imbued in politicians a general suspicion of a professional army and created in generals a fear of civilian intervention. By the end of the Great War, old civil-military feuds had been, if not resolved at least suppressed within a system that sought in its military commanders not military brilliance but absolute loyalty to the Republic. An adroit politician, General Gamelin knew better than to ask more of the French government than it was willing to give.[115]

To say that politics created the framework within which the French army evolved between the wars is not to suggest, however, that a French army freed of political constraints would have acted differently. Although many French soldiers were hostile to the political culture of the Third Republic they were, nonetheless, its products. They offered no alternative to existing military institutions nor to the long war strategy that those institutions demanded. They undertook gradual reforms to improve the army's ability to execute the strategies and doctrines vindicated by French victory in the Great War, but these were introduced with delicate concern for the cohesion of the conscript-reserve army and for the soldiers' confidence in their commanders. In preparing for the next war French military leaders acted soberly, cautiously, and in accordance with their interpretation of professional subordination to the state. Ironically, caution in redesigning doctrine proved to have been imprudent, and refusal to pressure civilian authority came to be seen as an abdication of duty. Caution and concession to political constraint were, however, convenient postures. The French army would enter the next war ready to claim credit for victory or, if necessary, to shift to the Republic's leaders the responsibility for defeat.

Notes

1. The École Supérieure de Guerre was founded in 1875 and the general staff in 1890. For the army of the early Third Republic, see Col. André Paoli, *La Réconversion*, vol. 1, *L'Armée française de 1919 à 1939* (Paris: Ministère des Armées, 1969–71), 8–10; Douglas Porch, *The March to the Marne: The French Army 1871–1914* (Cambridge: Cambridge University Press, 1981); David B. Ralston, *The Army of the Republic: The Place of the Military in the Political Evolution of France, 1871–1914* (Cambridge: MIT Press, 1967); and Allan Mitchell, *Victors and Vanquished: The German Influence on Army and Church in France after 1870* (Chapel Hill: University of North Carolina Press, 1984). For the doctrine prescribed by the infantry regulations of 1875, see Michael Howard, "Men against Fire: The Doctrine of the Offensive in 1914," in *Makers of Modern Strategy: From Machiavelli to the Nuclear Age*, ed. Peter Paret (Princeton: Princeton University Press, 1986), 513.

2. For the impact of the Dreyfus Affair, see Ralston, *Army of the Republic*, ch. 5; Porch, *March to Marne*, ch. 4; and Paul Marie de la Gorce, *The French Army: A Military-Political History*, trans. Kenneth Douglass (New York: George Braziler, 1963), chs. 3 and 4.

3. See Porch, *March to Marne*, chs. 5 and 6; Ralston, *Army of the Republic*, ch. 6; and Jan Karl Tanenbaum, *General Maurice Sarrail 1856–1929: The French Army and Left-Wing Politics* (Chapel Hill: University of North Carolina Press, 1974), 4–9, 15–17.

4. Sources of military resentment included orders prohibiting military cadets from joining Catholic clubs. Tanenbaum, *Sarrail*, 19.

5. Messimy became minister of war on 27 July 1911, and Millerand held the portfolio from 15 January 1912 to 12 January 1913.

6. Millerand's policy was "to follow the directives of the General Staff, without seeking either to control it or to correct those ideas where it was wrong." Ralston, *Army of the Republic*, 339.

7. Until 28 July 1911, republican fears of military rule had dictated that the

commander in chief designate for the next war was virtually powerless in time of peace. Gen. Joseph Joffre, whose claims to be "above prejudices of caste, religion, and party" were taken at face value, held the unified appointment from 1911 until 1916. Ralston, *Army of the Republic*, 334.

8. For details, see Porch, *March to Marne*, ch. 9. The army restored three-year service in 1913 in an effort to increase the number of men available to stop a German surprise attack and because of the weakness of the French army's poorly trained reserve units. Tanenbaum, *Sarrail*, 27; Porch, *March to Marne*, ch. 10.

9. Porch, in *March to Marne*, 170–92, persuasively argues for military un-happiness against Ralston's picture of an army satisfied with the new tone of civil-military relations. Ralston, *Army of the Republic*, 40.

10. Howard, "Men against Fire," 513–14, 516, 520.

11. Ferdinand Foch taught at the staff college from 1895 to 1901 and was its commander from 1908 to 1911. Loyzeaux de Grandmaison, head of the operations bureau of the general staff, proclaimed that "Imprudence is the best security" in a pair of lectures he gave in 1911. Ralston, *Army of the Republic*, 351.

12. For a detailed study of one attempt to achieve reform through official channels, see Robert M. Ripperger, "The Development of the French Ar-tillery for the Offensive, 1890–1914" (unpublished essay, United States Military Academy, 1994). The heavy artillery issue is also addressed in Porch, *March to Marne*, ch. 12.

13. For a different analysis, see Porch, *March to Marne*, 213–15. Porch treats the adoption of the "cult of the offensive" not as a calculated change in French doctrine but as evidence of a doctrinal vacuum in prewar France.

14. For the generals' hostility to parliamentary investigation of French mil-itary weaknesses and failures, see Jere Clemens King, *Generals and Politicians: Conflict between France's High Command, Parliament and Government, 1914–1918* (Berkeley: University of California Press, 1951), ch. 3.

15. The radical infiltration tactics proposed in 1915 by French Capt. Paul Laffargue appear to have had more influence in Germany than in his homeland. Porch, "The French Army in the First World War," in *Military Effectiveness* vol. 1, *The First World War*, ed. Allan R. Millet and Williamson Murray (Boston: Allen & Unwin, 1988), 216; Timothy T. Lupfer, *The Dynamics of Doctrine: The Changes in German Tactical Doctrine during the First World War* (Fort Leavenworth KS: U.S. Army Command and General Staff College, 1981), 38–39.

16. The defining example of the methodical battle was the attack by Gen. Marie-Eugène Debeney's First Army at Montdidier on 8 August 1918; Gen. Marius Daille, *La Bataille de Montdidier* (Paris: Berger-Levrault, 1922) was the standard description. For the methodical battle see Robert A. Doughty, *The Seeds of Disaster* (Hamden CT: Archon Books, 1985), ch. 5.

17. For French war plans see Henry Dutailly, *Les Problèmes de l'armée de terre française (1935–1939)* (Paris: L'Imprimerie Nationale, 1980), 91–114.

18. The six hundred thousand figure omits forces overseas and men assigned to the air arm or to the *gendarmerie*. See Paoli, *La Phase de fermeté*, vol. 2, *L'Armée française*, 169. For more on the equipment involved see Philippe Pétain, "Note du 3rd Bureau de G.Q.G. au date du 24 February 1919 sur l'Artillerie et les Chars de l'avenir," quoted in Paoli, *La Réconversion*, 151–70.

19. For the continuing importance of horse cavalry, see a note on 8 July 1919 by General Robillot, quoted in Paoli, *La Réconversion*, 116.

20. General Régnier, "L'Étude sur l'Organisation des Unités de Chars Blindés," 16 February 1919, quoted in Paoli, *La Réconversion*, 125.

21. Paoli, *La Phase de fermeté*, 90–92.

22. Paoli, *La Phase de fermeté*, 128.

23. Law of 1 April 1923, quoted in Paoli, *La Phase de fermeté*, 119. Excluding officers and native troops, the French army had 472,000 men in 1923 and 457,000 in 1924 (p. 211). By 1930 the number had fallen to 351,000. See Paoli, *Les Temps de compromis*, vol. 3, *L'Armée française*, 141. By 1933 it had decreased even further to 339,000. Paoli, *La Fin des illusions*, vol. 4, *L'Armée française*, 59.

24. Paoli, *La Phase de fermeté*, 94. For the consensus within the army about resource mobilization, see Richard D. Challener, *The French Theory of the Nation in Arms, 1866–1939* (New York: Russell and Russell, 1955), 143–46.

25. *Procès Verbaux* (hereafter pv), csdn study commission (second section), 31 March and 7 April 1922, Service Historique de l'Armée de Terre (hereafter shat) 2N201. All references to documents at shat are by carton number. A detailed account of the national organization law appears in Eugenia C. Kiesling, *Arming against Hitler* (Lawrence: University Press of Kansas, 1996), 12–40.

26. See the summaries of the chamber debates of 28 February, 2, 10, 16, 22, 29 March, and 20, 27 June 1922 prepared by the National Defense Secretariat in shat 2N201/1.

27. Deputy Henri Lafonte, *Débats, Chambre des députés, Journal officiel de la république française 1870–1940*, first session, 4 March 1927 (Paris: Chambre des Députés), 488–90.

28. The versions passed by the Chamber and the Senate in 1927 and 1928, respectively, were irreconcilable on this point.

29. The key dates were 10 January 1924 (first presentation of the bill to the Chamber of Deputies), 17 February 1928 (Senate passage of a version irreconcilable with that passed by the Chamber), 12 June 1934 (Prime Minister Doumergue's call for the composition of a revised version), and 11 July 1938 (promulgation of the final law).

30. Of the 240,000 men in an average conscript class only 51.2 percent (122,880) were destined for the infantry—enough to fill the 56 authorized metropolitan infantry regiments only by ignoring the needs of the 21 battalions of *chasseurs à pied*, 6 regiments of zouaves, 29 regiments of *tirailleurs Nord-*

Africains, 10 tank regiments, and other similar formations (Paoli, *Les temps de compromis*, 65–66).

31. General Staff, *Monthly Intelligence Summary* (Great Britain War Office [hereafter War Office, MIS], March 1936), 148. In the active divisions mobilized in September 1939, 33 percent of the officers, 67 percent of the noncommissioned officers, and 55 percent of the enlisted men were professionals. For "A" divisions, professionals comprised 23 percent of the officers, 17 percent of the noncommissioned officers, and 2 percent of the enlisted men. "B" divisions contained three professional officers. See Jeffrey A. Gunsberg, *Divided and Conquered: The French High Command and the Defeat of the West, 1940* (Westport CT: Greenwood Press, 1979), 88; and Guy Chapman, *Why France Fell* (New York: Holt, Rinehart, and Winston, 1968), 339.

32. General Brindel, "La Nouvelle organisation militaire," *Revue de Deux Mondes* 51 (May–June 1929): 487; Challener, *French Theory*, 179–81.

33. The army's concerns are detailed in "Note au sujet de l'Organisation Générale de l'Armée," 6 November 1925, in Paoli, *Les Temps de compromis*, 56–61.

34. The "professional" cadres included both career soldiers and men who, after completing their obligatory service, reenlisted for a fixed period of time. Seventy-five thousand of the professionals were destined for the metropolitan army and thirty-one thousand for the colonial army. Paoli, *Les Temps de compromis*, 69.

35. On these points see I/EMA, "Note au sujet de l'Organisation Générale de l'Armée," 6 November 1925, quoted in Paoli, *Les temps de compromis*, 359 (I/EMA is the first section of the *État-major de l'armée*); "Instruction générale pour la convocation des réservistes en 1927," SHAT 7N2333/11; Stanley H. Ford, "Active Duty Training Periods for Reserve Enlisted Men, Non-commissioned Officers and Officers," 26 November 1930 (G-2 16,893-W), United States National Archives (hereafter USNA), Record Group 165 carton 2015–928/15; James B. Ord, "Training Instruction for Reservists French Army (Effective 1931)" (G-2 17,436-w), USNA RG 165, 2015–928/19. (Material from the National Archives of the United States is identified by USNA, RG 165, and carton number.)

36. I/EMA, "Note au sujet de l'Organisation Générale de l'Armée," 6 November 1925, quoted in Paoli, *Les Temps de compromis*, 59.

37. The reforms encompassed three laws: the *Loi sur l'organisation générale de l'armée* (13 July 1927), the *Loi des cadres et effectifs* (28 March 1928), and the *Loi de recrutement* (31 March 1928). With the establishment of twelve-month service the age of recruitment was raised to twenty-one years. Christophe Prochasson, "Les grandes dates de l'histoire de la conscription," *Revue Historique des Armées* 9 (1982): 67–69, provides a useful chronology of the laws' adoption.

38. The structural impediments to the creation of stable, well-trained reserve units appear in Kiesling, *Arming against Hitler*, 85–100.

39. See Gen. Paul Emile Tournoux, *Haut Commandement: Gouvernement et défense des frontières du nord et de l'est, 1919–1939* (Paris: Nouvelles Éditions Latines, 1960), and Anthony Kemp, *The Maginot Line—Myth and Reality* (London: Frederick Warne, 1981).

40. For the effective duration of the French training year, see Kiesling, *Arming against Hitler*, 66–68.

41. Touchon, Riom Testimony, 24 March 1942, SHAT 1K224 carton 2, dossier 3.

42. See Doughty, *Seeds*, 75, for the narrow focus of the historical articles published in the *Revue d'Infanterie* from 1928 to 1938, and see Kiesling, *Arming against Hitler*, 118–30, for official efforts to inculcate and reinforce doctrine.

43. Ministry of Defense, *Centenaire de l'École Supérieure de Guerre 1876–1976*, 22 (hereafter *Centenaire*).

44. Gen. Paul Azan, "But et programme de la Revue Militaire Générale," *Revue Militaire Générale* 1 (1937): 7.

45. Marius Daille, *La Bataille de Montdidier* (Paris: Berger-Levrault, 1922). For the importance of Montdidier in the War College curriculum, see Doughty, *Seeds*, 81–83.

46. Stefan T. Possony, "Organized Intelligence: The Problem of the French General Staff," *Social Research* 8 (1941): 231.

47. The order appeared in Gamelin, "*Directive sur l'instruction*," 25 January 1937, 52, quoted in Dutailly, *Problèmes*, 232.

48. "Note au sujet de la Division Cuirassée à expérimenter en 1937," 28 November 1936, SHAT 1N36/4.

49. Gen. André Beaufre, *Memoires 1920–1940-1945* (Paris: Presses de la Cité, 1965), 47.

50. Ministry of War, EMA, *Instruction sur l'emploi tactique des grandes unités* (Paris, 1936), preface.

51. For the composition of the French Army of the Rhine, see Paoli, *Les Temps de compromis*, 295–96.

52. For the argument that Poland was more likely to attack Germany see Robert Citino, *The Evolution of Blitzkrieg Tactics: Germany Defends Itself against Poland, 1918–1933* (Westport CT: Greenwood Press, 1987).

53. For the details of the 1933 Plan D calling for French penetration into Belgium or Luxembourg (at the invitation of the respective governments) see Paoli, *La Fin des illusions*, 48–49.

54. For General Brécard's argument that the mixture of mounted and mechanized units was an advantage, see "The Motorization of Cavalry," 29 June 1933 (G-2 19,477-W), USNA RG 165, 2015–827, 23.

55. These concerns are skeptically reported in Paoli, *La Fin des illusions*, 78.

56. See the comments of the British military attaché who attended Twentieth

Corps maneuvers in the Vosges in September 1928: War Office, MIS, October 1928, 257.

57. See Paoli, *La Fin des illusions*, 78–79, for the cost of motorization and 32–33 for budgets.

58. For an example of one early exercise see Debeney "Instruction générale sur la manoeuvre de Mailly," SHAT 7N4023/11, and General Maurin, "Rapport sur la manoeuvre de Mailly, 7–13 août 1928," SHAT 1N93/5, 12–13. On French motorization see Kiesling, *Arming against Hitler*, 144–47.

59. For the DLM's partnership with the motorized infantry see Gen. Maxime Weygand, "Note pour le Général Chef d'État-Major Général de l'Armée relative à l'organisation d'une division légère motorisée," 26 October 1933, quoted in Paoli, *La Fin des illusions*, 80–83, and War Office, MIS, July 1936, 109–10. The terms "motorized" and "mechanized" were at first used unsystematically, but, by the end of the decade, motorization came to refer to the use of wheeled vehicles for rapid road movement while mechanized units moved and fought in armored all-terrain vehicles. For more on the DLM, see Kiesling, *Arming against Hitler*, 147–48.

60. The AMC 35 (Renault ACG1 Light Tank) weighed 14.5 tons, carried a 47mm gun (25mm in one version) and a 7.5mm coaxial machine gun, had 25mm of armor, and traveled at a top speed of 40 KPH. Weygand admitted that the AMC was obsolete even at the moment of production. Contr. Gén. des Armées Pierre Hoff, *Les Programmes d'armement de 1919 à 1939* (Vincennes: Ministère de la Défense, 1972), 277; J. A. Lester, "Maneuvers, Field Exercises, Reviews and Inspections: French Maneuvers at Mailly-le-Camp," 28 October 1935 (G-2 21, 950–2), USNA RG 165, 2015–1195/4.

61. With 13mm of armor and a machine gun or 25mm gun, the 6.5 ton 1933 and 1935 Renault AMRS were very light tanks masquerading as armored cars.

62. War Office, MIS, July 1936, 109–10.

63. The SOMUA, a 20-ton machine armed with a 47mm gun and a machine gun and capable of traveling 45 KPH, has been called the best tank on the battlefield in 1940. Doughty, *Seeds*, 170. For the DLM's 1939 table of organization see Dutailly, *Problèmes*, 151. For a comparison of the DLM with the panzer division in doctrinal terms, see Jeffrey A. Gunsberg, "The Battle of the Belgian Plain, 12–14 May 1940: The First Great Tank Battle," *Journal of Military History* 56 (1992): 207–44. For the superiority of French tanks see Russell H. Stolfi, "Equipment for Victory in France in 1940," *History* 55 (1970): 1–20.

64. The tank program promulgated in the summer of 1921 by the artillery branch's *section technique des chars de combat* called for the development of a thirteen-ton infantry tank and a heavy "breakthrough tank" designed to deal with fortified positions.

65. Gen. Maxime Weygand, *Memoires* (Paris, 1957), 2:352.

66. See Jeffrey J. Clarke, "Military Technology in Republican France: The

Evolution of the French Armored Force, 1917–1940" (unpublished dissertation, Duke University, 1969), 28; Heinz Guderian, *Die Panzertruppen und ihr Zusammenwirken mit den anderen Waffen*, 2nd ed. (Berlin: E.S. Mittler, 1938), 14; and Weygand's testimony in France, Assemblée Nationale, Session de 1947, No. 2344: *Rapport fait au nom de la commission chargée d'enquêter sur les événements survenus en France de 1933 à 1945, Annexes, Témoignages et documents recueillis par la commission d'enquête parlementaire*, 9 vols. (Paris, 1951), 1:249 (hereafter *Événements*); General Marie-Eugène Debeney, "Les exigences de la guerre de matériel," *Revue des Deux Mondes* 40 (15 March 1933): 276; War Office, MIS, August 1934, 67; Gen. T. Delelain, "Étude sur l'emploi des chars moderns," 20 November 1931, SHAT 9N157/2; Hoff, *Programmes*, 318–19.

67. See J. Perré, "La Refont de la réglementation relative aux chars de combat," *Revue d'Infanterie* 75 (November 1929): 666, for the adequacy of the FT. The original Renault FT model 1917 light tank weighed 6.5 tons and carried a machine gun. It had a maximum *road* speed of 4.8 miles per hour and a range of 25 to 30 miles. The versions used in the 1930s carried a 37mm gun.

68. The integration of the tank into the methodical battle is discussed in Kiesling, *Arming against Hitler*, 140–43.

69. Even the ponderous tanks of the Great War had proved too fast for the infantry they were meant to support. Clarke, "Military Technology," 25.

70. The point that even fast tanks required supporting infantry is made by Gen. T. Delelain, untitled document, SHAT 9N157/2.

71. To send tanks without infantry support into even lightly fortified areas was to invite catastrophe. Daladier, PV, Cham. Army Comm., 1 December 1937, 15–16.

72. For more on the problem of damage received from French artillery among rapidly advancing B tanks, see *Événements* 5:1184.

73. For the importance of harnessing the tank to the methodical battles see R. Martin (détachement d'expériences d'emploi d'engins blindés), "Rapport du Colonel commandant le détachement, camp de Coëtquiden," 23 July 1922, SHAT 9N164, 31, 33, 37; Doughty, *Seeds*, 145–46, 211 n.28; "Provisional Memorandum Concerning the Employment of D Tanks in Liaison with Infantry (translated from French)," 13 July 1934, USNA RG 165, 2015–1223/7, 4. If tanks would not reduce the number of artillery tubes required, they might economize on shells by providing accurate close fire support and increasing the overall tempo of the battle. Sumner Waite, "The Tactical Employment of Divisional Artillery in Support of Tank Action," 13 May 1938 (G-2 24,266-w) 2, USNA RG 165, 2015–1245/2.

74. Originally part of the artillery, tanks came under the *direction de l'infanterie* on 28 March 1928. The *section des chars de combat* was created on 9 August 1929. Paoli, *Les Temps de compromis*, 164.

75. For more on tank radios see Gen. Maurice Guerin, "L'Evolution des

matériels de transmissions de 1920 à 1939," *Revue Historique de l'Armée* (1967): 61; and "Provisional Memorandum Concerning the Employment of D Tanks in Liaison with Infantry," 13 July 1934 (G-2 23,176-w) USNA RG 165, 2015–1223/7, 21. For a description of the engine see Hoff, *Programmes*, 326.

76. PV, CSG, 23 May 1934, SHAT 1N34/1, and Martin S. Alexander, *The Republic in Danger: General Maurice Gamelin and the Politics of French Defence, 1933–1940* (Cambridge: Cambridge University Press, 1992), 123. The R35 weighed 10 tons, had a top speed of 20 KPH and a range of 8 hours. It had no radio and poor cross-country speed, and carried a Puteaux 37mm gun cannibalized from the FTS. The diesel FCM36 proved too expensive for mass orders, and the two Hotchkiss machines, deemed too fast and too complicated for the infantry, found a home in cavalry units that were not yet equipped with the SOMUA.

77. The 150 D1s were shipped off to North Africa. Fifty D2s were produced in 1936 and into 1937, when production ceased because the D2 required special steel needed for the SOMUA. Manufacture of the D2 resumed in 1940 as a substitute for the ever-so-slowly produced B1bis medium tank.

78. General Estienne, "Résumé de mes convictions sur la politique des chars de combat exposée hier au Générale Corap," 20 October 1933, SHAT 9N157/2.

79. For Estienne's activities see Clarke, "Military Technology," 77–79.

80. Minutes of meeting of 19 March 1926, quoted in Paoli, *Les Temps de compromis*, 163; see also Doughty, *Seeds*, 141.

81. Thus the 1929 regulations on combat tanks described tanks as "only the supplementary means of action placed temporarily at the disposition of the infantry. They considerably reinforce the action of the infantry, but they do not replace them." Quoted in Doughty, *Seeds*, 142. The B1 tank's top speed was 28 KPH, and it carried a 75mm hull-mounted gun as well as a 47mm gun and a machine gun in the turret.

82. Paoli, *Les Temps de compromis*, 164.

83. Weygand, *Memoires*, 2:407; Doughty, *Seeds*, 145.

84. Doughty, *Seeds*, 174–75 points out that the cavalry adopted armor smoothly because it reflected a general consensus within the arm.

85. The infantry's quiescence up to this date can be deduced from Renault's manifest surprise, as described by Clarke in "Military Technology," 147, at the news that the D tank program was to be abandoned in favor of the development of a light tank.

86. Doughty, *Seeds*, 150–52.

87. Sumner Waite, "Organizational and Unit Training," 15 March 1937 (G-2 23,273-w), USNA RG 165, 2015–1179/4, 3. When it suited his purposes, however, Gamelin insisted that "Just as the bullets did not kill all of the infantry, the antitank gun will not demolish all of the tanks." PV, CSG 23 May 1934, SHAT 1N34/1, 10.

88. Smith, "501st R.C.C.," USNA RG 165, 2015–1213/1. For the efficacy

of French antitank guns see René R. Studler, "Armament and Equipment—Organizational Standard," 18 September 1938 (G-2 24, 525-W), USNA RG 165, 2100–106/4; Waite, "Anti-Tank Defense," USNA RG 165, 2015–1126/2; Stolfi, "Equipment," 17; and Trichel, "Armament and Equipment," USNA RG 165, 2281-c-162/2. This discussion of French armor derives from Kiesling, *Arming against Hitler*, 161–67.

89. De Gaulle's scheme appears in three works: *Le Fil de l'épée* (Paris: Berger-Levrault, 1932), "Vers l'armée de métier," *Revue Politique et Parlementaire* (1933), and *Vers l'armée de métier* (Paris: Plon, 1934). See the discussion in Brian Bond and Martin Alexander, "Liddell Hart and De Gaulle: The Doctrines of Limited Liability and Mobile Defense," in *Makers of Modern Strategy*, ed. Peter Paret (Princeton: Princeton University Press, 1986), 613–16. De Gaulle became a lieutenant colonel on 25 December 1933.

90. Alexander notes that only 70 percent of the professionals eligible to reenlist in 1936 did so. See his "Liddell Hart and de Gaulle," 616.

91. For soldiers' dabblings in conspiracy, see de la Gorce, *The French Army*, 216–51.

92. As Gamelin stated, "At bottom, it was the conjunction made between the issue of large armored units and the issue of the professional army that was detrimental in parliament and within a section of military opinion to the creation of tank divisions." See Bond and Alexander, "Liddell Hart and de Gaulle," 615.

93. De la Gorce, *French Army*, 273.

94. See Doughty, *Seeds*, 163, and, for a sympathetic interpretation of Gamelin's attitude toward the use of armor, Alexander, *Republic*, 121–24, 243–78.

95. Gamelin quoted in Adolpe Goutard, "La Bataille pour les divisions cuirassées," *Revue de Paris*, 66 (1959): 30–31.

96. For French thinking about such matters see PV, CSG study session, 14 October 1936, SHAT 1N36, 13; "Le Problème militaire français," 1 June 1936, SHAT 7N3697 as quoted in Dutailly, *Problèmes*, 326; C/EMA note no. 366 of 8 October 1936, quoted in 2/EMA "Avis du 3e Bureau sur L'étude de la division cuirassée," 4 February 1937, SHAT 7N3421; and "Note relative aux possibilités de création de 2 D.CR," 23 July 1936, SHAT 7N2293/3, as quoted in Dutailly, *Problèmes*, 155.

97. The CSG authorized a second DLM on 29 April 1936. Gamelin asked for three mechanized cavalry divisions, but the necessary materiel did not exist until 1939. The DLM was also lightened in 1936 by the elimination of its two truck-borne battalions, leaving two battalions in all terrain vehicles. See Clarke, "Military Technology," 192.

98. Doughty, *Seeds*, 174. Stolfi agrees with Gamelin that the DLM "can be considered to have been as powerfully equipped as any of the famed German panzer divisions." See "Equipment," 11. A comparative table of organized information

about the panzers produced by French intelligence in 1935 appears in Dutailly, *Problèmes*, 318–19.

99. PV, CSG study session, 14 October 1936, SHAT 1N36.

100. For six different opinions on the use of armor see EMA, "Note au sujet des divisions nouvelles," November 1936, SHAT 1N36/4.

101. These numbers can be found in Hoff, *Programmes*, 329. Stolfi claims that in May 1940 the four French armored divisions contained a total of 274 B1bis tanks.

102. PV, CSG, 2 December 1938, in Dutailly, *Problèmes*, 158.

103. The 10-ton H39 was an up-gunned version of the H35 whose 35 KPH speed and complex engine made it no friends in the infantry branch.

104. For more on the delays see Alexander, *Republic*, 116–20.

105. For a graphic depiction of the process of acquiring new materiel, see Dutailly, *Problèmes*, 127–29.

106. The general staff argued that substituting light tanks would lead to misleading results. See Maurice Gamelin, *Servir—Les Armées Francises de 1940*, 3 vols. (Paris: Plon, 1946–47), 2:290.

107. SHAT 9N157/1.

108. Doughty, *Seeds*, 165; Dutailly, *Problèmes*, 156–57.

109. Gamelin's "Secret Note No. 4617 on the Employment of Large Armored Units" is described in two reports by U.S. Assistant Military Attaché Sumner Waite: "Tactical Doctrine—Theories of Mechanization and Motorization: Organization, Characteristics and Employment of Large Armored Units," 20 December 1939 (G-2 25,406-w), 165, 2015–1223/14, and "Tactical Doctrines—Theories of Mechanization and Motorization: French and German Armored Units," 8 August 1939 (G-2 25,173-W), USNA RG 165, 2015–1223/12.

110. For more on the delays of the Third Reserve Armored Division by the lack of engineering troops to clear roads during the critical fighting south of Sedan, see Robert A. Doughty, *The Breaking Point: Sedan and the Fall of France* (Hamden CT: Archon Books, 1990), 287.

111. Doughty, *Seeds*, 160.

112. See Alexander, *Republic*, 346–47. *Le Temps* of 12 November 1939 reported that Gen. Georg-Hans Reinhardt's tanks were forced to withdraw before the barricades established by the capital's defenders. See Sumner Waite, "Limitations of the Armored Division," 22 November 1939 (G-2 25, 350-W) USNA RG 165, 2015–1223/13.

113. See, for example, Williamson Murray, "Armored Warfare" in *Military Innovation in the Interwar Period*, ed. Williamson Murray and Allan R. Millett (Cambridge: Cambridge University Press, 1996), 6–49.

114. For a nuanced explanation of Germany's tactical success in 1940 see Doughty, *Breaking Point*, 323–32.

115. For Gamelin's political adroitness see Alexander, *Republic*, 392–96.

2. A COMPREHENSIVE APPROACH TO CHANGE

Reform in the German Army in the Interwar Period

James S. Corum

In the modern era there have been sufficient examples of comprehensive military reform undertaken by various nations to provide a basis for the study of such change as a major military theme. Several fundamental questions must be answered, however, regarding such reform. First, what generates the necessity for a comprehensive program of military reform? Second, what is the context of the change—are the reforms undertaken by the military institution an appropriate response to the situation? Third, how is doctrine developed and modified within the bureaucratic organization and how is this process sustained over a long period? Finally, what is the relationship between doctrine and the organization of the army, the training of that army, and its technology?

The German army of the interwar period provides one of the best historical examples of a successful program of military reform. During the twenty years preceding World War II the small Versailles Treaty army of a defeated Germany—limited to one hundred thousand men and four thousand officers, bereft of tanks and heavy equipment, and denied an air force—was transformed into the most effective, efficient, and combat-capable force in the world. From 1939 to 1940 the German army and air force were able to defeat, in succession, Poland, Denmark, and Norway and, eventually, the Low Countries, the French, and the British Expeditionary Force (BEF) in rapid and effectively conducted campaigns of maneuver. Moreover, the early German victories of World War II, particularly the campaign of 1940, were not carried out under circumstances of overwhelming German superiority. Indeed, the Germans in 1940 had numerical equality with the Allied troops but had fewer tanks and artillery pieces than the Allied forces in the west.[1] German victories in the early part of the war were largely due to having a more effective operational doctrine and a more effective training program to implement that doctrine. While this chapter will focus heavily upon reform that was made in German army doctrine, the process of reform, particularly as found in Germany, was a comprehensive one that included not only doctrine but also extensive reform of the army organization and its training and military education process.

Catalyst for Reform

World War I saw the longest and most dramatic period of sustained change in all aspects of warfare in the entire twentieth century. No nation or any group of military leaders in 1914 could have predicted what actually occurred during the four years of the war. World War I was the first truly industrialized war, with multimillion-man mass armies consuming virtually the entire financial and industrial output of their respective nations. An enormous number of new weapons were developed and fielded during the course of the war. World War I saw the introduction of light machine guns, submachine guns, flamethrowers, rifle grenades, and light mortars for the infantry. World War I also saw gas warfare become an important part of combat operations. The tank was developed during the course of the war and by 1918 thousands of tanks were serving on the front lines. The airplane evolved from a new, relatively primitive weapon into a powerful combat-effective weapon by the end of the war. Fast, all-metal aircraft supporting ground operations were also introduced in 1918. Strategic air bombardment was born as both sides were able to use aircraft to bomb deep into the enemy homeland. The submarine became one of the primary weapons of naval warfare and was used as a strategic, almost a war-winning, weapon. World War I also saw such organizational changes as integrated air defense systems employing ground-based observers, flak, and fighter squadrons to defend the homeland. Every army involved in the conflict developed its tactics, its military organizations, and even its uniforms. The French replaced their bright red trousers and blue coats of 1914 with their horizon-blue uniforms and steel helmets of 1918.

Even the most obtuse officer or military commentator of 1918 could note that World War I had dramatically and permanently changed the nature of warfare, tactics, and military technology. Any infantry company of 1914, when compared to an infantry company of the same army in 1918, was virtually unrecognizable as even being from the same era much less from the same army in the same war. Indeed, immediately following World War I the French army demonstrated this point dramatically by parading a company in the uniforms and equipment of 1914, followed by an infantry company in the uniforms and equipment of 1918, with their steel helmets and gas masks, as well as light machine guns, light cannon, and tanks.

Some military commentators have pointed out that a nation that loses a war has more incentive to reform than a nation that wins.[2] The professional German officers certainly understood this, and understood as well that Germany had been defeated militarily on the battlefield. Postwar writings by professional German officers provide extensive commentary on the numerous strategic, operational, and technological mistakes made by the German armed forces during World War I.[3] While Hitler and the Nazis may have used the "stab-in-the-back" legend as a main pillar of National Socialist ideology, the professional soldier who had experienced World War I overwhelmingly rejected this legend and was fully aware of the military's failures during the war.[4]

But military collapse was not the only reason the German officer corps initiated a thoroughgoing process of study and reform in the post–World War I period. For more than a century the general staff of the German army had built up a strong tradition of carefully examining military operations and conducting historical study and analysis of war campaigns and battles. Of all the general staffs of the era the German general staff had perhaps the strongest tradition of studying war in a critical fashion while providing objective analysis of military operations. This tradition of critical thought and debate within the general staff corps was essential in directing the process of analysis and reform undertaken during the interwar era.

The Role of Vision

A perceived need for a program of reform in a military organization does not mean that the process of reform will in fact lead to the right solutions. Indeed, the rational and sensible direction for military reform in the period after World War I would have been for Germany to adopt the military system, tactics, organization, and doctrine of the victorious army—namely, to adopt the system the French army developed at the end of the war of methodical advance using heavy firepower. Many sensible observers in 1918 might have concluded, as did the French, that World War I had proved that the defense was the stronger form of warfare. These individuals argued that the defense could only be overcome by massive firepower and that to overcome a moderately well-trained militia army in defensive positions would require enormous expenditure of men, materiel, and firepower.[5]

All of these sensible conclusions were, in fact, reached by the first commander in chief of the Versailles Treaty army, General der Infanterie Walter Reinhard, who was relieved as army commander in chief in 1920. Reinhard and some other German generals of the immediate postwar period were strong advocates of the power of the defense. Reinhard argued that firepower was the primary factor in offense and that mobile war had become a thing of the past.[6] Reinhard also argued that modern technology favored the defender over the attacker.[7] A frank admirer of the French army, Reinhard praised the French innovation of the Maginot Line when it was constructed in the late 1920s.[8] Additionally, Reinhard praised the World War I mass army, declaring in 1930 that Germany should establish a national militia force similar to Switzerland's.[9] Reinhard's enthusiasm for the mass army was such that he even argued in 1919 that "front officers" should be selected over general staff officers or other highly trained professional officers for the new German officer corps as men who would work to bring a more democratic style of leadership to the army.[10]

That the German army after World War I did not adopt the fairly commonsensical solutions provided by General Reinhard is primarily the work of one man of vision: Col. Gen. Hans von Seeckt. Chief of the general staff and the Truppenamt (literally, "Troops' Office," a shadow general staff) from 1919 to 1920 and commander in chief of the army from 1920 to 1926, von Seeckt dominated the thought and organization of the German army more than any other military figure of the interwar period. Hans von Seeckt was an effective operational and strategic-level commander as well as an efficient army administrator. He was a sound military thinker highly respected by his fellow officers. Most of all von Seeckt was a man of vision and it was his vision that came to dominate the nature, direction, and form that the German army took immediately after World War I.

During the course of the war, on both the western and eastern fronts von Seeckt had demonstrated his ability as an innovative tactician and operational thinker. He planned the German-Austrian Eleventh Army's breakthrough at Gorlice on the eastern front in May 1915, an offensive that drove the Russians out of Poland and netted four hundred thousand Russian prisoners in only a few weeks. Von Seeckt had spent most of the war on the eastern front where he had clearly experienced considerably more maneuver than the war in the west involved. He also planned the operation that overran Serbia in 1915 and was an army group chief of staff during the campaign in 1916 that rapidly conquered Romania. At the end of the war von Seeckt's reputation and prestige within the officer corps made him the obvious choice for chief of the general staff.[11]

As von Seeckt prepared himself for his duties as chief of staff and his concurrent duty as German army senior representative to the Peace Conference of Versailles, he wrote a memorandum in February 1919 that was circulated within the general staff.[12] The subject of the memorandum was a proposed program of comprehensive reform in the postwar German army based upon his own vision of future warfare. Von Seeckt argued that the primary lesson of World War I was not of the superiority of defense over offense but the superiority of maneuver over firepower. This implied that the increase in mobility brought about by mechanization and other forms of technology would lead to a future war of maneuver.

Von Seeckt argued that the era of the mass infantry army was over and that the greater tempo of maneuver warfare would require the creation of a professional German army that would be manned by long-service soldiers with much higher standards and superior training and led by a highly educated officer corps and general staff. The professional army, smaller than the opposing mass army, would, by using technology more effectively, be able to out-maneuver its less well-trained enemy. The small professional army would be backed up by a larger reserve/militia force, men who had undergone basic military training who would serve as a manpower pool for the field army. By itself, however, the reserve force would not engage in maneuver warfare. This highly trained and well-equipped professional army would be supported by an independent air force capable of striking deep into the enemy's homeland and disrupting the enemy's transportation and mobilization systems as the field army drove rapidly around its opponents.[13]

Von Seeckt took on the personal mission of reorienting and re-educating the German army toward the doctrines of modern maneuver warfare. This was not an easy task, for four years of combat on the western front had instilled a deep-seated preference for trench warfare within much of the German officer corps. His efforts to reorient the German army are best seen in his annual remarks as the army chief which were published and distributed throughout the army. During his six-year command of the army von Seeckt was highly critical of the trench warfare mentality and constantly emphasized the need to practice maneuver warfare. He also stressed the need for flexibility in the army's plans and operations, recommending in 1921 that as training for the offense the army should practice attacking from the march while emphasizing its "elastic spirit."[14] In 1922 von Seeckt urged the infantry to concentrate unit training on mobile warfare and the conduct of flank attacks. At the same time he urged the artillery to stop practicing trench warfare tactics and to reorient its training toward fire support for maneuver warfare.[15] In 1925 von Seeckt recommended that officers should practice giving short clear orders in a form suitable for maneuver warfare.[16] By this time von Seeckt could see considerable progress in his program to reform army doctrine and training: "The field maneuvers show that finally the army is succeeding in loosening the still-binding chains of trench warfare. Mobility is a primary necessity of the army."[17]

The Process of Doctrinal Development

Hans von Seeckt was a firm believer in the tradition and methodology of the old imperial general staff, and he used the general staff corps as the primary tool for effecting doctrinal and organizational change in the German army. In the immediate postwar period when the German army was reduced to one hundred thousand men with an officer corps of only four thousand, von Seeckt fought hard to ensure that a disproportionate number of officers having general staff education and experience were retained to form a core of leadership for what was, essentially, a new army. Von Seeckt used the general staff corps and expert officers from throughout the army during this period to inaugurate a comprehensive study of all the lessons from World War I in order that a new organization and operational doctrine, based upon the broadest possible military scholarship and analysis, would be implemented throughout the army.

In December 1919, von Seeckt directed the Truppenamt to form committees of officers to write "short, concise studies on the newly gained experiences of the war and consider the following points:

What new situations arose in the war that had not been considered before the war?

How effective were our prewar views in dealing with the above situations?

What new guidelines have been developed from the use of new weaponry in war?

Which new problems put forward by the war have not yet found a solution?"[18]

Von Seeckt followed up his directive with a list of fifty-seven aspects of the war to be examined, including issues of military leadership and equipment, tactical subjects such as river-crossing operations, and organizational questions such as the proper use of the weather service.[19] By 1920 over four hundred general staff officers were at work researching and writing reports on the experience of the war. Additional committees were soon created that were staffed with general staff officers and technical specialists. For example, a committee on tank warfare was created and manned by officers who had served with the tank force in the war. In addition, the "shadow Luftwaffe," an air staff which von Seeckt had hidden within the army staff, went to work on a parallel program of analysis following von Seeckt's directive, putting another 130 officers to work analyzing all aspects and lessons of the air war.[20]

The committee reports that were submitted in 1920 and 1921 are models of clear, concise, critical military analysis. Many of these reports are still extant. This large body of scholarship was turned over to the Truppenamt staff, was carefully edited and subsequently became the basis for a new operational doctrine for the German army. This new operational doctrine, *Army Regulation 487, Leadership and Battle with Combined Arms*, was issued in three parts between 1921 and 1925.[21]

The Content of Reform

The very title of the new operational doctrine, *Leadership and Battle with Combined Arms*, tells much of the actual nature and content of the doctrinal reforms of the German army. The principle of combined arms was stressed throughout. In order to function effectively in an atmosphere of maneuver warfare each officer was required to have the flexibility of mind and breadth of experience to understand much more than the mere function of his own particular branch of the service. Officers were to be cross-trained as much as possible.[22] Thus infantry officers were trained to handle an artillery gun section while cavalry officers were trained to fight as infantry. Motor transport officers were expected to be familiar with both infantry and artillery operations while all ground officers were to have a fundamental understanding of air operations.

All of the primary aspects of what we now call maneuver warfare (the Germans used the term *Bewegungskrieg*) are clearly elucidated in the 1921 regulations. The importance of mobility and maneuver is stressed throughout *Army Regulation 487*. Flexibility and tempo were emphasized as primary principles. In order to maintain a rapid tempo of operations officers at the lowest possible level were required to assume responsibility and decentralize command so that the combat leader at the front would have the ability and the authority to concentrate the available forces at the point of decision. The World War I obsession with maintaining a continuous front was rejected; the new doctrine stressed the importance of maintaining the offense even if it meant not securing the flanks. The use of combined arms became a major new principle of war as did the importance of joint air-ground operations. The new doctrine created a vision of a strong air-ground partnership and gave airpower considerable emphasis in the conduct of army operations.

The new operational doctrine stressed many of the traditional principles of the German way of war. A number of these principles, however, were given new emphasis. For example, the correct determination of the *Schwerpunkt* (point of decision) was strongly emphasized in the doctrine of the 1920s. In maneuver warfare operations conducted with a relatively small army it was more important than ever to determine the most crucial point in time and space for the employment of force. Airpower, mechanized forces, artillery support, and reserves were to be concentrated and employed en masse at the *Schwerpunkt*—even at the risk of severely weakening other sections of the line. The new technology that came out of the First World War was given a primary place in the new operational doctrine; the relatively large-scale armor operations, that is, tank attacks in regimental strength, were foreseen as being an important part of the new maneuver war.[23] Airpower, in both its strategic and tactical support forms, was seen as a major new addition to military doctrine. Although the German army was denied an air arm by the Treaty of Versailles, a secret air staff was maintained within the Reichswehr in order to create and update doctrine for aerial warfare.[24]

It is a common belief that blitzkrieg—the concept of modern mechanized warfare with combined arms—was developed by the Nazis after Adolf Hitler became chancellor in 1933. Such a position stands in clear contradiction to the historical evidence. Except for the creation of armored and paratroop divisions in the 1930s, all of the primary doctrinal operational concepts that came to be known as blitzkrieg during World War II had been developed and were well in place as part of the mental equipment of the German army by the mid-1920s. What occurred from that period onward was a constant refinement and evolution of essential principles that had already been worked out.

Organizational Influence upon Doctrine

The organization of an army has a profound influence upon the development and evolution of operational doctrine. The German army was inadvertently granted a tremendous benefit by the Allied powers in the Versailles Treaty when it was forced to fundamentally change the structure of its military organization.

In many respects the pre–World War I German army organization was inefficient. First, the imperial constitution allowed for the constituent kingdoms of the empire to maintain their own armies, even to include individual war ministries and general staffs. In the pre–World War I army, for example, Saxony and Bavaria maintained their own war ministries, their own systems of military regulations, and indeed their own systems of budgeting and equipment procurement for their forces. At the top level the central direction of the army was split between the Prussian War Ministry and the general staff. The general staff had control of war plans, the creation of doctrine, and command of the field armies in time of war. The War Ministry, however, controlled the budget and equipment procurement. This meant that while the general staff could request equipment and develop a doctrine requiring new equipment, the final decision was in the hands of the War Ministry, which would decide whether or not to provide the funds to develop equipment or to fund new military units and organizations that the general staff deemed necessary. This system led to considerable fragmentation within the military in the pre–World War I army and to constant bickering over issues of funds and organization. For example, the prewar chief of the general staff, the young Helmuth von Moltke, had to fight with the War Ministry to obtain funds for a modern military aviation arm while the War Ministry—against the wishes of the general staff—preferred to fund the airship development of Count Ferdinand von Zeppelin.[25]

The demise of the imperial system in 1918 allowed a far more rational system of military organization to be developed. The Weimar constitution swept away all of the small armies and war ministries and left behind a single national army under a unified command. The German navy and army were, in turn, answerable to a single defense ministry that in turn was answerable to the president of the republic. Within the army the functions of the general staff were taken over by a reorganized general staff and renamed the Truppenamt in deference to Allied sensibilities. The Truppenamt continued to perform all of the previous functions of the general staff including controlling the military's organization, determining doctrine and training for the army, creating war plans, and directing army operations in wartime. Next to the Truppenamt a parallel organization called the Waffenamt (weapons office) was created and made responsible for the research and development of weaponry and the coordination of the manufacture of military armaments. In addition, each major branch of the army—the infantry, the artillery, the cavalry, the motor transport troops, the medical corps, the veterinary corps, the signal corps, and the engineers—had its own branch inspectorate. These inspectorates were responsible for branch-specific training and for developing equipment coordination with the weapons office. By 1925 the branch inspectorates were actually incorporated into the jurisdiction of the weapons office. Above these two equal agencies, the Truppenamt and the Waffenamt, stood the army commander in chief who had full control over the subordinate agencies and had his own military budget office that was answerable to him.[26]

Having the general staff and the weapons office answerable to a single military commander meant that the efforts of the two agencies could be effectively coordinated. This simplified system was far superior to the old system; the constant interchange of officers transferred from the general staff to the weapons office and vice versa ensured that the two agencies worked together in fairly close coordination. In effect the Truppenamt developed ideas and doctrine while the Waffenamt conducted research and developed weaponry to suit this doctrine. Neither the sections of the Waffenamt nor the branch inspectorates were allowed to become compartmentalized or work alone on their own projects since virtually all the major weapons projects of the 1920s required the coordinated efforts of several sections of the Waffenamt as well as the branch inspectorates. An early example of this is the tank development program initiated by von Seeckt in the mid-1920s. In contrast to the French, whose infantry and cavalry inspectorates conducted independent tank development programs, the Waffenamt was directed to oversee one tank program that combined the efforts of several departments. While the motor vehicle section of the Waffenamt was the primary office overseeing development of tanks, the artillery inspectorate was given guidance on the development of appropriate tank guns and the communications inspectorate was directed to coordinate its efforts with the other branches to develop appropriate radios for armored vehicles.[27]

This system for procurement and development continued throughout the entire interwar period. A fairly simple system, it enabled the German army to efficiently and quickly manufacture entire series of new weapons in the 1930s. For the most part these weapons were of very high quality and were generally suited to the kind of war the German army planned to fight.

Reform of Army Personnel and Education

Some of the most dramatic reforms made by the German army in the interwar period were those effected in the officer and noncommissioned officer (NCO) education system. Because von Seeckt believed that the requirements of modern warfare necessitated a well-trained and educated officer corps, the postwar period saw a remarkable increase in the standards required for officer candidates. In 1920 the requirement was laid down that all officer candidates had to have completed the Abitur (university matriculation certificate). In other words, all officers had to be eligible to undertake a university education.[28] Immediately after the war the one-year cadet schools of the Prussian army, which had provided a large number of the old army's officer corps, were abolished; a new three-and-a-half-year officer training program was then instituted. The new officer training program was perhaps the most rigorous and thorough in the world at the time. Upon his acceptance into the army each officer candidate had to undergo basic training then spend several months as a private soldier, living in the barracks and performing basic military duties. From there he moved up into the NCO ranks; while undergoing additional training courses he also served time in troop units, acting as a junior NCO.[29] Aspiring officers from every branch of the army, including doctors and veterinarians, were required to serve for six months as officer candidates in a combat branch before being fully accepted as officers. This policy ensured that every officer in the army was familiar with at least the rudiments of combat leadership.[30]

In the prewar army the voluntary examinations for the general staff course were usually taken when the officer was a senior first lieutenant or junior captain. By 1919 the general staff examination was made mandatory for all officers of the army when they reached the level of senior first lieutenant. The general staff examinations were comprehensive, emphasizing military subjects such as leadership and military tactics at battalion and regimental levels. Officers were also required to pass tests in chemistry, civics, economic geography, mathematics, physics, and a foreign language.[31] Failure to pass the general staff examination resulted in the officer's elimination from the service. This examination virtually mandated that all officers undergo a continuing program of academic and military education. The intermediate and senior commanders of the army were required to ensure that regular lecture programs and academic courses were available to the officers at the regimental and garrison levels. Throughout the 1920s and early 1930s a very strong education ethic was built into the German army. Officers were encouraged to attend local civilian universities when possible. A number of officers obtained university degrees and some even earned Ph.D.s while serving in the Reichswehr.

The new education ethic of the German army partly resulted from a realization that the prewar general staff had been deficient in its understanding of technology. This deficiency had caused the general staff to underestimate the importance of the tank so that only a handful of German tanks were deployed on the battlefield at the end of World War I. This failure by the Germans to grasp the possibilities of the tracked and armored vehicle on the battlefield handed the Allied forces a distinct advantage during the last year of the war. Col. Kurt Thorbeck, an armaments expert who wrote a critique of the general staff's performance shortly after the war, argued that it had failed miserably when it came to understanding technology and its role in warfare. The general staff had been composed of tacticians and had provided no place for engineering expertise. Thus, despite the fact that Germany had possessed the necessary industrial resources and technological expertise, the army had failed to develop a tank in time to use it in quantity on the battlefield and had also failed to develop an effective light machine gun.[32]

There was widespread agreement with Thorbeck's critique within the general staff, and von Seeckt himself argued that the officer corps required a better understanding of technology.[33] Out of this realization a new form of general staff education was created. Officially, the old Kriegsakademie of the general staff had been eliminated along with the old general staff corps. In its place the "Leadership Assistant" course was created, a three- to four-year program conducted and directed from the headquarters of the seven military districts of the Reichswehr. The program provided a general staff education for top-scoring officers who took the military district examinations. In this fashion the old Kriegsakademie course, with its emphasis upon military history, analytical thought, war games, and military theory, was effectively replicated and carried on under a new name.[34] One real major reform of general staff education was, however, initiated by von Seeckt. Each year the Reichswehr selected a dozen or more officers to be sent to civilian universities in order to obtain engineering degrees. Upon completion these men would return to the general staff and function as staff officers without having undergone the regular general staff course.[35] Many officers who received high rank in the Wehrmacht, most notably Field Mar. Wolfram von Richthofen, entered the general staff this way. In 1929 Von Richthofen received his Ph.D. in engineering at the Reichswehr's expense. This education program ensured that when rearmament came a solid corps of officers highly familiar with technical matters would be available within the general staff.[36]

Several other innovative programs designed to encourage officer development were put into effect in the 1920s. To ensure that the officer corps was not solely composed of small unit tacticians or purely military operational thinkers, officers who completed the full three- to four-year general staff course were in many cases allowed to spend a year at the University of Berlin taking courses in politics and economics.[37] The study of foreign languages was encouraged throughout the Reichswehr, and every officer was required to have at least a reading knowledge of one foreign language.[38] Reichswehr officers were encouraged to study foreign military journals and literature and to visit foreign countries in order to observe their armed forces. In the 1920s the Reichswehr encouraged officers to travel abroad for one to three months, even providing a special allowance for this purpose. Some German officers went to Italy and Spain; a large number traveled to the United States, where they could observe the conduct of training and maneuvers that employed modern equipment. Each officer, upon his return, was required to write an extensive report detailing the thought, equipment, and tactical ideas of the foreign army he had visited.[39]

Partly due to this program the Reichswehr of the 1920s and early 1930s was a very outward-looking force. In the area of foreign military affairs its officer corps was as well educated as any officer corps in the world. The encouragement to travel abroad also meant that the Reichswehr was able and willing to understand, borrow, and modify foreign ideas and equipment and to apply them to the German army. For example, in the 1920s German officers appreciated the American programs for early motorization of the military.[40] British experiments with motorized forces were also watched and reported upon in great detail.[41] German officers' observations of foreign equipment had a direct impact on the development of German equipment. For example, the French Citröen company and the French army had pioneered the use of effective half-track technology in the 1920s; a favorable assessment of this technology eventually led German firms to license the French half-track technology and to begin production of half-tracks for the German army. By the outbreak of war in 1939, half-tracks (a French idea that had languished in France) played an important part in the development of effective motorization and mechanization in the German army.[42]

Testing and Developing Doctrine

Any large professional officer corps is capable of producing a wide variety of useful ideas—one need only look at the numerous proposals made by career officers for modernizing doctrine, organization, and equipment that came out of the British, French, American, and Italian military journals of the interwar period. However, for a theory to make the jump to effective doctrine requires a rational and objective methodology for testing theories, which is where the Germans had a distinct advantage.

The Germans had created an effective process for examining doctrine during the nineteenth century. The German general staff had a long tradition of war gaming in which plans and operational concepts were played out against a simulated opposing force. The war gaming system forced a scrutiny of plans and operational doctrine against a competent and realistic opponent. The Reichswehr carried on the war gaming tradition and intensified the process. Every year major war games were held in Berlin in which the navy, air arm, and even the diplomatic service were included in the play. General staff officers and specialists from throughout the army played the roles of army staffs and major unit commanders.[43] Foreign operational doctrine was translated and studied so that officers playing the roles of that nation's force commanders in war games and maneuvers could act realistically and not simply "mirror image" German doctrine.[44] Realistic problems were posed in major maneuvers—for example, a war with Poland or France. Modern forms of ground and air forces were simulated and new ideas for German doctrine and organization were first tried out in these games. In the 1926–27 army-level war games, which postulated a future war with Poland, the Reichswehr staff included the use of simulated motorized divisions and brigades in the play on both sides. It was in these war games that the Germans first developed a detailed organizational model for motorized brigades and divisions.[45]

The shadow Luftwaffe within the general staff also used war games to test new concepts. The Reichswehr air staff conducted war games in 1924 that postulated France as the enemy. As part of the German response to a French invasion, the Reichswehr air staff drew up an outline for a strategic bombing campaign against vital French defense industries. Target lists were made of the most vital munitions factories, primary aircraft and engine factories, and France's most important motor vehicle factories.[46]

Even more important than war gaming was the German method of testing organizations and operational concepts using large-scale maneuvers. Of all the major powers the German army had the strongest tradition of conducting maneuvers. Prior to the Franco-Prussian War of 1870 the Prussian army had formalized a system for conducting and evaluating large-unit exercises. Corps and divisions would maneuver against each other, often in free play, while a corps of specially trained NCOs and officers would serve as umpires to adjudicate results of the action and provide operational parameters.[47] After World War I the Germans placed even greater stress upon the use of large-scale maneuvers to test operational concepts. The 1926 maneuvers, the first multidivision exercises held by the German army after World War I, served as a field test of the new operational doctrine of maneuver warfare that was expounded in *Leadership and Battle with Combined Arms*. Tactics borrowed from foreign armies were tried out and, if shown successful, adopted. In the 1926 maneuvers the Reichswehr conducted tank attacks using mock tanks under the cover of an artillery-fired smoke screen to study a tactic first used by the Allies in the latter part of World War I.[48]

The German army used large-unit maneuvers to test organizational concepts before adopting any new sort of organization as part of operational doctrine. The maneuver system, which employed a ruthlessly honest evaluation process, ensured that flawed concepts were discarded before they became doctrine. This testing process worked to help critique even concepts that had support at the highest levels of the army.

One of the most popular operational concepts of the 1920s and 1930s was the idea of employing mixed horse cavalry and motorized divisions. On the surface the notion seemed sound and made sense to nations such as Germany, France, and the United States that all had strong horse cavalry arms. The horse cavalry, it was argued, could operate effectively in rough terrain while armored car and motorized infantry units could move quickly along road systems. Theoretically there was almost no

terrain in and through which such a division could not operate. Hans von
Seeckt himself was a strong advocate of creating such units and wrote
extensively about this subject. Future cavalry divisions, he reasoned,
would be composed of horse units, motorized infantry and artillery
units, and armored car formations. He argued that such divisions could
play a major operational role by conducting deep strikes and operating
up to one hundred kilometers behind the enemy lines.[49] Officers of
the Reichswehr cavalry also supported the idea of the mixed cavalry-
motorized force.[50]

The new cavalry concepts were specifically tested in the first motorized reconnaissance exercises conducted in 1932 and sponsored by
the inspectorate of motor troops. The 1932 maneuvers featured the
employment of a motorized infantry unit, armored cars, and horse
cavalry units. The maneuver results were disappointing for advocates
of adopting the cavalry-motorized division. It was found that mixing
horse cavalry and vehicle-mounted troops was unworkable because the
horse cavalry were unable to keep up with the motorized forces.[51] The
operational tests of 1932 not only killed the mixed cavalry-motorized
troops concept in the German army but also convinced the cavalry that
horses could no longer compete with motorized troops. Prior to the
1932 maneuvers the cavalry had been, by far, the most conservative
branch of the army. After the maneuver results the cavalry came to this
obvious conclusion and enthusiastically embraced motorization of the
cavalry force. By the outbreak of World War II the German cavalry had
been almost completely converted into a mechanized force. The use of
maneuvers to test motorization and cavalry concepts in the early 1930s
caused the German cavalry to adopt mechanization before the cavalry
arms of the other major powers did. The mixed horse-motorized division
was a feature of the French army system in 1940, and as late as 1942 the
U.S. cavalry still persisted with the horse-motor troops concept.[52]

Heinz Guderian has been given credit for the creation of Germany's
panzer divisions in 1935. Prior to this time German operational doctrine considered the employment of tank regiments essentially as breakthrough and infantry support units only.[53] Guderian conceived of a large
self-contained tank division of all arms of the military including its own
logistics and support troops. Such a division would be more than a
breakthrough force—it would be a force capable of sustained offensive
action and deep penetration of enemy lines.

However, in many respects Guderian's original concepts were flawed.

The first organized panzer division was a very tank-heavy force with relatively few infantry. Field exercises showed that this organization contained too many tanks and not enough infantry and support troops, so the panzer division was modified before the war to increase the number of support troops (engineers, logistics, etc.) and to change the ratio of tank companies to infantry companies from 16:9 to 12:12.[54] By 1940 the panzer division had evolved into a true combined arms organization capable of gaining decision on the battlefield. While Guderian played a central role in championing the creation of panzer divisions in the early stages of rearmament, it must also be noted that the evolution of the panzer division concept was the result of the combined effort of many talented officers who conducted exercises, analyzed the results, and made constant and sensible modifications to the organization, equipment, and tactics of the units.

All the innovative unit designs and tactics employed by the German army in the blitzkrieg campaigns of 1939 and 1940 had been thoroughly tested and modified during large-scale maneuvers before the war. The Luftwaffe began creating a small airborne force in 1935. The initial German airborne concept organized the paratroopers into commando units that could raid and destroy vital targets deep behind the enemy lines. In the 1937 Wehrmacht maneuvers a new idea was tested in which paratroop companies were dropped behind enemy lines in order to seize and hold such vital objectives rather than destroying them. When tried out in exercises this innovation proved to be successful.[55] The Wehrmacht decided in 1937 to expand the airborne force rapidly so that by the start of the war both a paratroop and an air-landing division had been created. By helping to defeat Holland in five days, the German airborne operations in 1940 played a significant role in the success of German operations in the west.

The Concept of Joint Operations

The creation of an operational doctrine that stressed close coordination and cooperation between air and ground forces was one of the most significant reforms carried out by the German military in the interwar period. The Germans carried the idea and spirit of joint operations to a much higher level than any other major power prior to World War II, and the effectiveness of its joint operations is one of the primary reasons for the German victories of 1939 to 1941.

When one compares the German situation with that of the British,

French, or American armed forces the German army and air force had a discernible lack of interservice rivalry. Little rancor existed within the German armed forces on the roles and missions of airpower. The primary reason for the good relationship between the air force and army was the willing and enthusiastic support the army gave to the establishment of an independent air force as an equal branch of the armed forces. As early as 1916 the army general staff had recommended that the imperial air service, the Luftstreitkräfte, a branch of the army at the time, be established as a separate military service.[56] That recommendation was stymied due to the navy's opposition and imperial politics. However, when the war ended von Seeckt, the general staff's representative to the Versailles conference, argued forcefully that Germany should be allowed to have a strong and separate air force in the postwar period.[57] Even though Germany was denied the right to have an air force by the Versailles Treaty, von Seeckt nevertheless built up a significant secret air arm within the army. He also insisted that all army officers were to be "air minded" and consider the operational use of airpower in their plans and exercises.

Because it was generally understood that when rearmament came Germany would create a strong, independent air force, the aviation officers within the general staff and Reichswehr felt no compunction to create an air doctrine that justified service independence. This is in contrast to the situation in the United States where the air corps promoted a doctrine of strategic bombing in order to justify a separate air force.[58] In Britain the Royal Air Force (RAF) was an independent service but saw its independent status challenged after the war by the other services. Thus the RAF also turned to a strategic bombing doctrine as the reasoning behind maintaining a separate status.[59] Both the American army air corps and the RAF were reluctant to work closely with ground forces or create an army support doctrine lest the airmen lose their independence and be made to serve under the command of ground officers.[60]

In Germany the army lived up to von Seeckt's requirement to be air-minded. Von Seeckt himself wrote knowledgeably about airpower and its operational use. Contrary to popular belief the German air force, when it was officially reborn in 1935, was not expected to be a tactical or army-support air force. In the 1920s von Seeckt had argued that the primary mission of the air force was to achieve air superiority over the enemy air force; air superiority was to be gained by first attacking the enemy air force. Once air superiority was gained von Seeckt believed that the best use of the air force was to bomb the enemy transportation and military centers in order to paralyze enemy movement and mobilization as the rapidly moving motorized forces carried the battle deep into the enemy heartland.[61] It was a concept of warfare that acknowledged the air force as an equal partner in the campaign rather than as a supporting arm.[62] German airmen generally had no major objections to operating within such a conceptual framework.

The attitude that the army had toward the importance of airpower is illustrated by the action of Hitler's first defense minister, Army General Werner von Blomberg. As rearmament began in earnest in 1934 and the creation of a large air force was envisioned, Blomberg saw that there were simply too few aviation officers with general staff experience to provide an adequate general staff for a large air force. Blomberg directed army headquarters and the general staff to transfer well-qualified and experienced general staff officers to the Luftwaffe. Soon some of the most highly regarded officers of the army general staff—men such as Walter Wever, Albert Kesselring, and Hans-Jürgen Stumpf—were transferred to the Luftwaffe. Upon their transfer the former army officers tended to become enthusiastic aviation advocates; many, such as Kesselring, learned to fly (at age forty-nine) in order to gain a practical understanding of airpower.

German air doctrine of the 1920s and 1930s did not suffer from the single-minded focus on strategic aviation that was the norm for the RAF and the U.S. army air corps. To be sure, strategic bombing of enemy industrial centers, ports, and transport networks was a major focus of the Luftwaffe's operational doctrine as expressed in *Luftwaffe Regulation 16, Luftkriegführung* (Command in the air war) issued in 1935. However, the German concept of airpower was more comprehensive than either the British or the American view. Under the German doctrine the air force's responsibilities also included command of the anti-aircraft artillery and full control over all civil defense activities, as well as control of the bomber and fighter forces. Indeed, the airborne forces of the Wehrmacht also came under Luftwaffe command, which was consistent with the broad view of airpower held by the German armed forces.

While the operational doctrine of the German army in the interwar period emphasized the vital role of the air force, the primary doctrine of the Luftwaffe emphasized the common purpose of all branches of the armed forces in military operations.[63] "The Luftwaffe, even if it is not in direct proximity to the army and navy, must remember that it is part of the whole *Wehrmacht*. The Luftwaffe must remain aware of the unity of all parts of the *Wehrmacht* in the common struggle."[64] From the time of the Luftwaffe's establishment in 1935 the army and the Luftwaffe commanders stressed joint training and operations. In 1935 Gen. Walter Wever, chief of staff of the Luftwaffe, directed that: "Army training exercises should be used as much as possible as Luftwaffe exercises in order to deepen our understanding of inter-service cooperation . . . direct coordination of air unit commanders with the army saves unnecessary paperwork, and is useful for the units that take part in exercises."[65] Both services worked hard to achieve a basic familiarity with close support operations. The newly established panzer troops stressed army-Luftwaffe cooperation. In 1936 the commander of the panzer troops, Gen. Oswald Lutz, ordered his panzer divisions to train with Luftwaffe units and include them in communications and reconnaissance exercises.[66] The level of Luftwaffe-army training increased in degree and complexity from 1936 to the start of the war. The Wehrmacht maneuvers of fall 1937 contained a variety of air-ground operations, including interdiction attacks and close air support provided for the army by the Luftwaffe.[67]

While the Luftwaffe developed into a bomber-heavy force that emphasized strategic and deep interdiction operations, its effectiveness in conducting close support and interdiction operations in support of the Nationalist ground forces during the Spanish Civil War (1936–39) caused the Luftwaffe high command to form a special air corps to support army operations.[68] This "special operations force" was composed primarily of dive-bombers and ground attack aircraft and was soon renamed the Eighth Air Corps and placed under the command of Gen. Wolfram von Richthofen, who had just returned to Germany after having served as the last commander of the Condor Legion in Spain. This force soon showed its effectiveness in conducting joint operations with the army in Poland in 1939 and in France in 1940. In their capability to conduct joint air-ground operations the Germans were years ahead of the other major powers that frantically worked to develop a similar capability in the first years of World War II.

The Attitude of Critical Thought

Perhaps the most important single reason for the German army's ability to reform its doctrine and organization after World War I was the officer corps' spirit of critical analysis. German officers had free rein to publish their ideas on military affairs and doctrine and to critique the ideas of other officers—even to criticize established doctrine.

The German army had long had a tradition of scholarship by officers who carefully analyzed the lessons of military history. The military history series published by the general staff before World War I covered in detail most of the major European conflicts of the era, even those wars in which Germany took no part such as the Russo-Turkish and Russo-Japanese wars. The general staff history books had detailed and perceptive analyses of tactics and operations and were written for the education of officers at the tactical and operational levels of war. After World War I the general staff historical section continued its work. Officially it had been disbanded at the same time as the general staff had, in 1919; in reality it had merely been transformed into the military history section of the Reich's Archives. The military historians of the Reich's Archives were mostly former general staff officers.[69] From 1920 to the mid-1930s, when the historical sections of the general staff were officially revived, the military historians of the Reich's Archives worked closely under the Truppenamt's direction to conduct historical studies of the battles and campaigns of World War I. For the most part, the historical studies produced by the Reich's archives were some of the most critical and objective studies of wartime operations written in the interwar period.[70] Moreover, the Truppenamt used these studies to help shape operational doctrine.

In the postwar period a defeated German army looked to its own history for a source of inspiration. This was found in the example of Generals Gerhard von Scharnhorst and August von Gneisenau who had led the reform of the Prussian army a century before. Scharnhorst and Gneisenau had introduced fundamental reforms in the training and education of officers after Napoleon's defeat of the Prussian army in 1806. The creation of a true general staff and the establishment of the Kriegsakademie come from these reformers. The Prussian army was reorganized and a modern and comprehensive reserve system complete with reserve training was introduced. From 1813 to 1815 the reformed Prussian army was put to the test and played a central role in the defeat of Napoleon.[71] The German officer corps, stung by defeat in the World War, consciously tried to imitate the spirit of Scharnhorst and Gneisenau in preparing the ground for the time when Germany could rearm and become once again a major military power capable of defeating its enemies, just as the Prussians had done a century earlier.

Like the Prussian army of the 1807–13 period, the interwar German army was reduced to the status of a small cadre army. However, with the thought of greatly expanding the army in the future, von Seeckt turned the entire army into a *Führerheer*, an army of leaders. Each officer was expected to be able to serve and command effectively at two levels above his current position. A similar ethic was expected of the enlisted force. Virtually the entire enlisted force of the one hundred thousand–man army was composed of career NCOs who were also expected to be able to serve at two ranks above their own.[72] The most senior NCOs were expected to be able to serve as junior officers. Furthermore, every German soldier was expected to embrace an ethic of personal development—to learn, to study, and to be able to perform at a higher level of responsibility.

The spirit of *Ausbildung*, or professional development, was already a part of the ethic of the professional German officer; it was, however, taken to a much higher degree than it had been in the prewar era. For example, part of this ethic was to develop the ability to think critically and objectively. The "organization man" style of leadership was actively discouraged. Indeed, the small Reichswehr officer corps of the 1920s to the mid-1930s produced an enormous amount of critical writing on military history, technology, and doctrine. Many officers in this period wrote books and articles; most were fairly basic military texts, while many were original works in which new ideas of doctrine or operations were proposed.

The German army journals of the interwar period such as *Wissen und Wehr* (Education and defense) and the *Militär Wochenblatt* (Military weekly), the latter being the primary journal of the German army, allowed for a considerable degree of open debate and comment concerning all aspects of doctrine, organization, and technology. The *Militär Wochenblatt* of the 1920s contains hundreds of capably written articles by many authors about maneuver warfare, the role of mechanization, the role of airpower, and the like. Many of the writings of German officers in the interwar period were at the cutting edge of military innovation. For example, in 1929 and 1930 *Wissen und Wehr* and the *Militär Wochenblatt* published a series of articles discussing the possibility of the use of paratroop divisions at the operational level of war. One writer of 1929 proposed that large paratroop forces could seize vital objectives behind enemy lines in a future war and be resupplied and reinforced by airlift. It was the first detailed discussion of large-scale airborne operations to be found in western military literature.[73]

Much of the history of the German army in the interwar period has been influenced by the memoirs of Gen. Heinz Guderian.[74] Guderian described a German army that was led by traditionalists and reactionaries at the top who opposed concepts of mechanization. In Guderian's version it was primarily he who overcame strong opposition from a reactionary establishment to promote the concept of mechanization—and maneuver warfare—in the German army. For many years the attractive image of military reform that was being accomplished by the lone rebel fighting a traditionalist establishment was accepted by many historians as the explanation of Germany's remarkable achievements in mechanized warfare in the early years of World War II.[75] Another model of the German army proposed by political scientist Barry Posen is that military institutions are by nature bureaucratic and resistant to change. Posen argues that the German army did not make any fundamental reforms but merely grafted modern technology on to a traditional preference for the offense.[76] The problem with such descriptions of the reform process in the German army is that they fly in the face of fact.

The work of mechanizing the army and developing a doctrine for a war of maneuver was the product of the work of many officers, virtually none of whom get any credit in Guderian's self-serving memoirs. This effort was part of a long process that began in the 1920s before Guderian's involvement with motorized warfare. The German army had already developed tanks and an extensive body of literature on armored warfare before Guderian started writing.[77] The idea that the high command—men such as Generals Ludwig von Beck (army chief of staff, 1935–38) and Werner von Fritsch (army commander in chief, 1935–38)—were conservative traditionalists holding back innovation is also a pleasant fiction. With the beginning of rearmament the senior army leaders worked tirelessly to expand the armored and motorized force as fast as the German economy could provide the tanks and equipment. While von Beck and von Fritsch themselves were not especially original thinkers, innovative thinkers such as Guderian flourished and received rapid promotion and senior command under their tenure. As a result the German armed forces took the lead in the late 1930s in areas such as armored and airborne doctrine. This hardly fits with the description of the highly traditional military bureaucracy described by Posen: "Historians agree that Hitler played an important role in helping the advocates of Blitzkrieg to overcome organizational resistance . . . it does appear from the little evidence available that Hitler provided the essential political support for armor in the face of traditionalist resistance."[78] The officer corps of the Reichswehr and the Wehrmacht were granted wide latitude to discuss and debate ideas of military organization and doctrine. Debate on military issues was encouraged during the tenure of von Seeckt as army commander in chief. Albert Kesselring, later a field marshal, recalled the atmosphere of working on the army staff in Berlin during the 1920s. Kesselring and other officers would debate issues in his office, often with General von Seeckt present. Von Seeckt would carefully listen to all the arguments and "sum up in a way that always hit the nail on the head."[79] Kesselring remarked that the years spent on the army staff in this atmosphere "were a schooling for me."[80]

Within the general staff there was the tradition of the *Denkschrift* (idea paper), in which general staff officers would put their ideas and proposals for reform of army organization and doctrine into a formal paper then circulate the paper for comment among the general staff. Many of the most fundamental reforms of German organization and doctrine originated as *Denkschriften*. Von Seeckt originally circulated his ideas for an elite professional army wedded to a concept of maneuver war in a *Denkschrift* of February 1919. Colonel Thorbeck's *Denkschrift* of 1920, which ruthlessly criticized the lack of technical expertise within the general staff, led to the creation of a program that educated officers in engineering then brought them onto the general staff.

A *Denkschrift* written by Erich von Manstein in 1935 had a major impact on the operations of the German army and its combat effectiveness during World War II. As the panzer forces were being rapidly built up under Generals Oswald Lutz and Heinz Guderian, von Manstein circulated within the general staff a *Denkschrift* that argued for some armor support for the infantry divisions. Von Manstein proposed that a heavy gun armored and mounted on a tracked chassis could provide some limited armored support for the infantry in assaulting fixed enemy defenses. Because the assault gun would have no turret it would be cheaper and simpler to produce than a tank; and, though less effective than a tank, it would still be an invaluable weapon in defense or offense. Von Manstein argued that a detachment of such guns should be assigned to each infantry division.[81]

Guderian and the inspectorate of panzer troops strongly opposed von Manstein's concept. All armored vehicles should go to the panzer divisions, they argued. Building assault guns for the infantry would dilute the German armored forces. Von Manstein's proposals won support in the infantry and artillery inspectorates, however, who saw merit in the idea. Despite ardent opposition from the panzer forces the idea progressed; by 1937 the development and testing of the assault gun was underway. The first models had a 75mm gun mounted on a Panzer III tank chassis. A small number of these saw action in the 1940 campaign and proved their worth.[82] The assault guns, as von Manstein predicted, were cheaper and simpler to use than tanks and very effective on the battlefield. Tens of thousands were manufactured by the Germans in World War II and were regarded as among the war's most effective battlefield weapons.

The High Command and Strategy: Reform and Failure

When the Weimar Republic arose out of the defeat of the German Empire, the military leadership was faced with the novel prospect of determining its proper role as strategic advisors to a republican government. Since Bismarck's demise these leaders had become accustomed to dominating any considerations regarding the use of military power in the service of the state.[83] Throughout World War I they had dictated national strategy with little interference from political leaders. Men such as Generals Erich von Falkenhayn and Erich Ludendorff, both of whom were remarkably successful in the realms of tactics and operations, performed poorly, however, in the strategic domain. From the younger Moltke's demand for full mobilization in July 1914 to Falkenhayn's attrition strategy of 1915 to 1916, from Alfred von Tirpitz's program of unrestricted submarine warfare in 1917 to Ludendorff's abortive offensives of 1918, the chiefs of the imperial army and navy demonstrated a notable lack of understanding of the political and grand strategic elements of modern warfare.

During the period of the Weimar Republic, 1918 to 1933, the military leaders had to create a new relationship with the state, a relationship in which they would play a central but not sole or even dominant role in charting the state's strategic course. On the whole the armed forces leadership did an effective job in developing a new relationship with the government and in creating a process for developing a long-term military and national strategy. During these years the military side of the strategic planning process was dominated by two men: von Seeckt and Wilhelm Groener, a brilliant general staff officer who became army quartermaster general in 1918 and served as defense minister from 1928 to 1932.

As army commander, von Seeckt had close and immediate contact with the president, the chancellor, and the cabinet. His long-term plan for the armed forces, which the civilian leaders fully shared, was to erode and eventually revoke the disarmament provisions of the Versailles Treaty in order to build the Reichswehr into an expanded military force equipped with a full array of modern weaponry. Von Seeckt, the Social Democrat Friedrich Ebert (who served as president from 1919 to 1925), and the conservative Paul von Hindenburg (who served as president from 1925 to 1934) shared a common desire to see Germany again take its rightful place as a great power among the concert of nations. The development of a large and capable military force was accepted as an integral and necessary requirement of achieving this status. In the short term, however, Germany's military strategy was to avoid conflict at almost any cost because the small Reichswehr was scarcely capable of engaging in a war with Poland, much less France, with any real hope of success.[84]

Under these circumstances von Seeckt and Groener carried out programs of clandestine rearmament and reserve training as a defensive measure in case either France or Poland should invade Germany. The consistent military strategy of the Weimar era had been to assume the strategic defensive in case of invasion and to defend and delay any invasion in order to buy time for diplomatic intervention by the other major powers. It was a cautious and pragmatic military strategy that received consistent support from civilian governments that had funded the clandestine reserve forces and rearmament efforts. One aspect of the new strategic relationship between the civilian politicians and the soldiers was a mutual realization of Germany's dependence on a diplomatic solution in the event of war or invasion. Starting in the mid-1920s German foreign office personnel were invited to observe and participate in the yearly general staff war games, which were built around realistic scenarios such as an invasion by Poland.

Both von Seeckt and Groener had a sound grasp of grand strategy and the military's role in national defense. Von Seeckt initiated the policy of rapprochement with Russia, which led to the Rapallo Treaty of 1922 that broke Germany's diplomatic isolation and provided secret bases and facilities where the German armed forces could develop and train with modern weapons that the Versailles Treaty had denied.[85] The rapprochement with Russia not only strengthened Germany's hand in diplomacy and relieved tensions with a potentially dangerous enemy, it also served notice on Poland that any aggressive action against Germany could potentially involve Russia as well. Thus one can argue that during the Weimar era there was a relatively rational and useful connection between military strategy and the larger national purpose it was meant to serve. That was soon to change.

Hitler's accession to power in January 1933 was viewed with favor by most of the Reichswehr's officer corps. Some senior officers, such as Werner von Blomberg and Walter Reichenau, were openly enthusiastic about the new regime.[86] An ardently nationalistic officer corps saw in Hitler a man who would restore prestige to the military, abrogate the Versailles Treaty, and initiate rearmament. Once in power, Hitler instituted a national rearmament program that exceeded these officers' wildest dreams. Nazi ideology was attractive to the officer corps, and many of its members enthusiastically embraced the party in its first years in power.[87] Even the brutal murder of Gen. Kurt Schleicher by Hitler's henchmen during the bloody purge of June 1934 caused few to have second thoughts about the Nazi regime's propensity to violence against those who stood in its way.

Appointed as war minister in 1933, former chief of the Truppenamt Werner von Blomberg saw himself as a central figure in strategic development. Blomberg and other generals seem to have hoped for a return to the imperial relationship in which military expertise was the dominant factor in setting national strategy. Here they would be grossly mistaken. Hitler, while desiring powerful armed forces, had little use for strategic advice from his professional soldiers, preferring to rely upon his own intuition. As far as Hitler was concerned generals were little more than technicians appointed to carry out his bidding.

From the early days of the Nazi regime, Hitler refrained from confiding his strategic views to his senior officers or even allowing them a real voice in strategic decision making. When Hitler announced his decision to remilitarize the Rhineland in early 1936, War Minister von Blomberg and Army Commander Werner von Fritsch protested that the action could lead Germany into a war for which it was ill-prepared. Hitler ignored their advice and ridiculed them for their caution.[88] The decision to send military aid to Gen. Francisco Franco's forces that were rebelling against the Spanish Republic was taken without any prior consultation with military advisors.[89] Only rarely did Hitler discuss his strategic ideas with his top military officers and, on those rare occasions, was angered by the pleas of his soldiers to follow a more cautious policy.

In November 1937 Hitler broached the possibility of a war with Austria and Czechoslovakia in a meeting with Blomberg, Fritsch, and Foreign Minister Constantin von Neurath. All expressed reservations concerning Hitler's strategy. Three months later all had been replaced with more reliable men who could be expected to not question the Fuehrer's judgment.[90]

When Hitler reorganized the military command apparatus in early 1938 it spelled the end of any genuine role for the armed forces in the formulation of strategy. Hitler placed himself in direct command of the armed forces and reorganized the defense ministry into the Oberkommando der Wehrmacht (OKW, or High Command of the Armed Forces) which, despite its title had no authority over the armed services. In reality it functioned merely as the military extension of Hitler's personal staff. For the first time in the history of the modern general staff its chief lacked direct access to the head of state.[91] Gen. Wilhelm Keitel, known as a quiet functionary and yes man, became head of the OKW; Hitler could be assured of not having his strategic judgment questioned by the armed forces.[92] Essentially the general staff had, by its habit of blind obedience to Hitler in the early years of the Nazi regime, allowed itself to become relegated to the margins of strategic formulation. Rather than becoming the dominant voice for strategic decision making, the generals' uncritical acceptance of the "Fuehrer principle" allowed that very precept to be used against them when they attempted to criticize the Fuehrer's strategy.

Hitler's elimination of the defense department organization also insured that there was no authority in the Reich, other than himself, with the power to coordinate armaments production. Under the Nazis there was intense interservice rivalry for funding and limited resources as each service attempted to fulfill Hitler's grandiose production and expansion plans. At the same time the Nazis' chaotic system of government developed no process by which conflicts over resources and production could be effectively resolved. Moreover, Hitler did not provide the armed forces with any coherent strategic priorities by which resources could be allocated.[93] Through mismanagement and the lack of any coherent grand strategy, armament production was in disarray when Germany went to war in 1939. The Nazi system ensured that war production was inefficient and that few reserves of equipment and ammunition were available for the army and air force.[94] While the army may have been ready for war in terms of training and doctrine, poor strategic planning had left it no more ready than the western powers in terms of industrial preparation for war.

In carrying out a comprehensive program of military reform in the interwar period, the German army started with a number of significant advantages. It had an impressive and thorough system of officer training and general staff education. Germany had a superb and well-trained NCO corps, perhaps the best in the world. The German army had a long tradition of seriously studying military theory and military history. Added to all of this the German army, though defeated by the Allies on the western front battlefields in 1918, had some advantages in experience that the Allies did not. Virtually all the combat experience of the British, French, and U.S. armies had been gained in the trenches and on the fairly static battlefront of the west. A major part of the German army had, however, served on the eastern front where the war had taken a far more mobile form. While thousands died in 1916 to take or defend a few yards of earth in places such as Verdun and the Somme in the west, the Germans had orchestrated a mobile campaign in the east that overran all of Rumania in six weeks. This broader base of experience in mobile warfare paid off in the interwar period. While maneuver warfare was something of a theory to the British and French officer corps, many of the German officers who worked to perfect the doctrine of maneuver war, such as Erwin Rommel, had actually seen the potential of mobility and maneuver.

Of all the elements of German military reform discussed here, none stands out as being the single defining element. The leadership of the German army after World War I made a conscious decision to retain the best elements of the old military system. The general staff system and education were retained as well as the excellent system of large-unit maneuvers. The quality of the officer corps was maintained and even increased by new higher standards and longer training periods for officers.[95] The system of a highly trained NCO corps was retained and even strengthened by the imposition of higher standards and professional NCO schools.[96]

The content of the German army reform, however, entailed much more than the careful selection of the best elements of the old imperial army tradition. The program that created a corps of technically educated general staff officers was an innovation, as was the reorganization of the general staff and the creation of the Waffenamt. The interwar organization of the German army headquarters and staff made for clear and direct lines of communication, it enhanced staff cooperation and coordination, and it made it possible to design and build weapons and equipment that fit the new doctrine of the army. For all of the inefficiencies of military procurement—and under the Nazis there were many—the Germans were able to design a new family of maneuver weapons with considerably less duplication of effort and at a considerably faster pace than either the French or the British.

A relatively accurate and far-reaching operational vision on the part of the top military leadership certainly played a central role in reforming the German army. Alone among the army commanders in the immediate postwar period who believed so, German Army Commander in Chief Hans von Seeckt correctly surmised that the next war would be a war of maneuver in which mobility would be the predominant factor. As one of the most influential military thinkers of the century, von Seeckt was able to articulate clearly his vision of future warfare and to convince the officer corps to adopt his vision as their own. Even after his retirement in 1926 this vision continued to guide the army. The senior army leadership after von Seeckt—which included generals such as von Beck and von Fritsch, and Lutz of the panzer troops—were all protégés of von Seeckt and continued using the centrality of maneuver warfare as the army's doctrine.

Another significant factor in German army reform was the degree to which open discussion and debate were allowed within the officer corps. New ideas were subjected to intense critical thought. The intellectual tradition of the general staff and the culture of the German army, both of which emphasized the corporate nature of the general staff, probably gave officers more freedom to advance new ideas or to take issue with the majority view than the British, American, or French general staffs did. In the French and American military cultures general staff officers were seen as functionaries carrying out the will of the commanders rather than as an integral part of the army leadership. Such an approach resulted in efficient military bureaucracies but tended to dampen open debate. With its emphasis upon critical thought, the prevailing military culture allowed the Germans, of all the major powers, to conduct the most thorough examination of the lessons learned from World War I. Moreover, the process of subjecting doctrinal ideas to extensive field tests and the willingness to ruthlessly criticize even the ideas favored by the senior leadership resulted in a German army that developed doctrinal concepts and tactics for maneuver warfare several years ahead of its opponents. Under the Nazi regime, however, strategic concepts were not subjected to the same critical process that shaped operational doctrine.

Although the German process of reform in the interwar period generally put the German army ahead of the major Western armies, there were some notable failures experienced by the Reichswehr and Wehrmacht processes with respect to maneuver war doctrine, joint air-ground operations, and large-unit training that became evident with the onset of World War II. The general staff education of the army, while a superb system for teaching about large-scale operations, tended to ignore the logistical side of war. In the Kriegsakademie curriculum of 1934 to 1938, instructional hours were devoted almost exclusively to tactics, operations, and military history. While on average there were over six hours of instruction in tactics per week, less than one hour per week was devoted to logistics. The issues of supply planning and logistics operations received the same emphasis in the curriculum as military engineering.[97] As Martin van Creveld has pointed out, German operations even at the start of World War II, were hampered by poor logistics planning caused partly by a disjointed general staff logistics system: responsibility was divided between the army chief of transport and the army quartermaster general with no single coordinating authority.[98] The general staff's poor planning in logistics became very evident in campaigns from North Africa to Russia in the early part of the war.

Another deficiency of the German reform process was its failure to create a corps of officers specially versed in the intricacies of industrial war planning and industrial mobilization. General staff officers of the interwar period understood the lessons of World War I concerning the importance of mobilizing the economy for war. The Germans even had a model for an institution that could develop a corps of officers knowledgeable about military production. The American army, embarrassed by the failure of the country to mobilize industry for war production during World War I, set up the U.S. Army Industrial College in 1924 where officers underwent an intensive one-year course on procurement and national industrial mobilization.[99] The college certainly helped the American armed forces mobilize the industrial base in World War II.[100] The German army was familiar with this institution, for German officers had visited the Army Industrial College in the 1920s and submitted reports to the general staff expressing their admiration for the institution and the quality of its education and research.[101] Nevertheless, a German counterpart was never developed.

Surprisingly, the Nazi leadership played little role in the internal organizational and doctrinal reform of the German army in the 1930s. While the Wehrmacht expressed its public loyalty to the ideology of National Socialism, the only direct impact the Nazis had upon German military training and education in the interwar period was the addition of about four hours of lectures a year given to the general staff on the principles of National Socialism.[102] The primary principles of the blitzkrieg operations had been worked out long before the Nazis came to power. Hitler, in fact, coming from the lower middle class as he did, held a strong antipathy against the nobility-dominated general staff, remarking in the early 1930s that if he went to war he would prefer a new—and Nazi—general staff.[103] Hitler's major positive contribution to the German military was in granting his generals financial and industrial resources for rearmament beyond their wildest dreams. On the negative side Hitler fired some of his best strategists, such von Beck and von Fritsch, and deprived the military leadership of any significant role in the formulation of grand strategy. Moreover, Hitler denied his armed forces any coherent strategic guidance and even the apparatus for making long-term decisions concerning resource allocation and defense production. In the army of the Third Reich one can see the astounding combination of tremendous competence at the tactical and operational levels of war combined with profound incompetence and disorganization at the strategic level.

Nevertheless, the effectiveness of any program of military reform can best be measured on the battlefield. Possessing no significant advantage either in the number of troops or the number and quality of artillery and tanks, but with a better operational doctrine and a superior training system, the Germans managed to inflict catastrophic defeat upon the British and French armies in 1940.[104] Throughout World War II the German army managed to maintain a consistently high performance in battle. Indeed, while the army's most effective striking power was organized in a small number of armored and motorized divisions, the predominant force of infantry divisions relied largely on horse-drawn transport and artillery throughout the war.[105] Yet even when outnumbered and outgunned the German army, man for man, was superior on the battlefield.[106] Judging by its operational competence the German army's program of reform during the interwar period has to count as one of the most successful examples of military reform at the tactical and operational levels of war.

Notes

1. Alistair Horne, *To Lose a Battle: France, 1940* (New York: Penguin, 1969), 218–20.

2. Barry Posen, *The Sources of Military Doctrine* (Ithaca NY: Cornell University Press, 1984), 57.

3. Many of the postwar writings of German officers after World War I were openly critical of strategic mistakes made by the general staff, and of the failure of the military to adapt to tank technology during the war. See Lt. Gen. Wilhelm Groener, *Der Feldherr Wider Willen* (Berlin: E. S. Mittler & Sohn, 1931); Col. Max Bauer, *Der grosse Krieg in Feld und Heimat* (Tübingen: Osiander Verlag, 1921); Freiherr von Bernhardi, *Vom Kriege der Zukunft: Nach den Erfahrungen des Weltkrieges* (Berlin: E. S. Mittler & Sohn, 1920); and Gen. Max Schwarte, *Die Technik im Weltkrieg* (Berlin: Verlag Offene Worte, 1920). The failure of the Schlieffen Plan in 1914 alone generated a large body of critical writing within the officer corps concerning strategic and operational mistakes made in the war. For a list of works on this subject see Jehuda Wallach, *The Dogma of the Battle of Annihilation* (Westport CT: Greenwood Press, 1986), 209–28.

4. James S. Corum, *The Roots of Blitzkrieg: Hans von Seeckt and German Military Reform* (Lawrence: University Press of Kansas, 1992), 2–5, 22–23.

5. On French interwar doctrine see Robert Doughty, "The French Armed Forces, 1918–1940," in *Military Effectiveness*, ed. Allan Millett and Williamson Murray (Boston: Allen and Unwin, 1988), 2:39–69.

6. Herbert Rosinski, *The German Army* (New York: Praeger, 1966), 218–19.

7. General der Infanterie Walter Reinhard, *Wehrkraft und Wehrwille*, ed. Ernst Reinhard (Berlin: E. S. Mittler & Sohn, 1932), 152–53.

8. Reinhard, *Wehrkraft und Wehrwille*, 100.

9. Reinhard, *Wehrkraft und Wehrwille*, 103–4. See also Hans Meier-Welcker, "General der Infanterie a. D. Doktor Hermann von Kuhl," *Wehrwissenschaftliche Rundschau* 6 (1956): 595–610.

10. "Record of Conversation with General Groener," 1919, National Archives, German Military Records, file T-78, roll 25, item 111.

11. The definitive biography of von Seeckt is Hans Meier-Welcker's *Seeckt* (Frankfurt am Main: Bernard und Graefe Verlag, 1967). See also Hans von Seeckt, *Seeckt: Aus meinem Leben, 1866–1917*, ed. Lt. Gen. Friedrich von Rabenau (Leipzig: Hase-Koehler Verlag, 1938), and Friedrich von Rabenau's *Seeckt: Aus seinem Leben, 1918–1936* (Leipzig: Hase-Koehler Verlag, 1941).

12. Hans von Seeckt, "Report to the Army High Command," 18 February 1919, National Archives, von Seeckt Papers, file M-132, roll 21, item 110.

13. Most of von Seeckt's 1919 memo is reproduced in Hans von Seeckt, *Thoughts of a Soldier*, trans. Gilbert Waterhouse (London: Ernest Benn, 1930), 61–62. As early as 1919 von Seeckt outlined most of the characteristics of future warfare that would make such an impact on the battlefields of 1939 and 1940. He emphasized not only the idea that future warfare would include maneuver warfare, thus requiring an extensive mechanization of the military, but also that future operations would require a rapid tempo of operations, a preference for deep offensive operations, the need for combined arms, and close air and ground coordination.

14. Hans von Seeckt, "Bemerkungen des Chefs der Heeresleitung," 1921, Bundesarchiv/Militärarchiv/Reichsheer (hereafter BA/MA RH), 2/69, 5.

15. Hans von Seeckt, "Bemerkungen des Chefs der Heeresleitung," December 1922, BA/MA RH 2/2987, 4–7, 11, and 13.

16. Hans von Seeckt, "Bemerkungen des Chefs der Heeresleitung," 1925, BA/MA RH 2/70, 2.

17. Von Seeckt, "Bemerkungen des Chefs," 1925, 2.

18. Von Seeckt, letter to Truppenamt et al, 1 December 1919, BA/MA RH 2/2275.

19. Von Seeckt, letter to Truppenamt, 1 December 1919.

20. Flugmeisterei, letter of 13 November 1919, in BA/MARH 2/2275. See also Flugmeisterei, Abteilung II, letter of 4 December 1919, in BA/MA RH 2/2275.

21. *Heeresdienstvorschrift 487, Führung und Gefecht der verbundenen Waffen* (Berlin: Verlag Offene Worte, 1921–1925).

22. Hans von Seeckt, "Bemerkungen des Chefs der Heeresleitung, 1920," 7 January 1921, BA/MA RH 2/2963, 2–3.

23. See *Heeresdienstvorschrift 487*, part 2, paras. 524–65. The German regulations of the early 1920s not only set out some principles of armored warfare but also proposed a table of organization and equipment for tank battalions and regiments.

24. The army personnel office opposed keeping 180 aviation officers on the strength of an army denied an air arm. Gen. der Flieger Wilhelm Wimmer asserted that "Seeckt used all of his influence and ability to protect his group of fliers against attacks all the way up to cabinet level." See Richard Suchenwirth, *The Development of the German Air Force, 1919–1939*, USAF Historical Study no. 160 (New York: Arno Press, 1968), 5.

25. See Gen. Helmuth von Moltke, chief of the general staff, letter of 6 November 1912 in *Urkunden der Obersten Heeresleitung über ihre Tätigkeit, 1916–18*, ed. Erich von Ludendorff (Berlin: E. S. Mittler & Sohn, 1920).

26. A good description of the workings of the Truppenamt, the Waffenamt, and the defense staff is found in Harold Gordon's *The Reichswehr and the German*

Republic 1919–1926 (Port Washington NY: Kennikat Press, 1957). See also Wiegand Schmidt-Richberg, *Die Generalstäbe in Deutschland, 1871–1945 (Beiträge zur Militär- und Kriegsgeschichte 3)* (Stuttgart: Deutsche Verlagsanstalt, 1962).

27. James S. Corum, *The Roots of Blitzkrieg* (Lawrence: University Press of Kansas, 1992), 97–121.

28. Gordon A. Craig, *The Politics of the Prussian Army* (New York: Oxford University Press, 1955), 393–94.

29. A detailed description of German officer training in the interwar period is found in Hans Meier-Welcker's "Der Weg zum Offizier im Reichsheer der Weimarer Republik," *Militärgeschichtliche Mitteilungen* 19 (1975): 147–80.

30. Hans von Seeckt, letter to All Branch Schools, 8 November 1924, BA/MA RH 12–2/22.

31. Hans-Georg Model, *Der deutsche Generalstabsoffizier: Seine Auswahl und Ausbildung in Reichswehr, Wehrmacht und Bundeswehr* (Frankfurt am Main: Bernard und Graefe Verlag, 1968), 25–26, 28.

32. Col. Kurt Thorbeck, "The Technical and Tactical Lessons of the World War," *Reports of the German Army Inspectorates*, 12 April 1920, BA/MA RH 12–2/94.

33. Von Seeckt instituted bimonthly seminars for Truppenamt officers in which Waffenamt officers briefed them on the latest German and foreign technological developments. See Hans von Seeckt's letter to the *Waffenamt und Inspektionen*, 21 January 1924, BA/MA RH 12-2-21.

34. The best overview of general staff training in the interwar period is Model's *Der deutsche Generalstabsoffizier.*

35. Adolf Reinicke, *Das Reichsheer, 1921–1934* (Osnabrück: Biblio Verlag, 1986), 312.

36. For more on von Seeckt's initial program to send Reichswehr officers to technical colleges see Hans von Seeckt, letter to General Groener, 17 February 1919, National Archives, von Seeckt Papers, file M-132, roll 25, item 126.

37. Martin van Creveld, *The Training of Officers* (New York: The Free Press, 1990), 32.

38. Van Creveld, *Training of Officers*, 32.

39. Numerous surviving detailed reports from officers who conducted foreign travel are found in Reichswehr files. See, for example, "Report of Lt. Kurt Hesse's Trip to South America and the USA, 1924–1925" BA/MA RH 2/182, 144–45, 177, 184.

40. Colonel von Boetticher, "Report on Artillery Motorization in the U.S.," and Captain Speich, "Travel Report," 30 December 1924, both in BA/MA RH 2/1820. See also Major Radelmeier and Captain Austmann, "Travel Report on American Visit, 31 January 1929," BA/MA RH 2/1822.

41. Col. Werner von Blomberg to T-3, "Bemerkungen zu den englischen Manövern 1924," 1 December 1924, BA/MA RH 2/1603; also von Blomberg to Chef der Heeresleitung, 29 May 1926, BA/MA RH 2/2195.

42. Walter Spielberger, *Die Motorisierung der deutschen Reichswehr, 1920–1935* (Stuttgart: Motorbuch Verlag, 1979), 145–51.

43. The 1926–27 winter war games included a large contingent of aviation officers as well as representatives of the navy. See "Operatives Kriegsspiel 1926–27," November 1926, BA/MA RH 2/2822.

44. The primary interwar doctrine of the French army was translated into German and made widely available in the Wehrmacht. The foreword to the publication states that the doctrine was to be studied by officers playing the French side in exercises. See *Französische Truppenführung: Vorschrift für die taktische Verwendung der Grossen Verbände* (Berlin: Verlag Offene Worte, 1937).

45. Truppenamt Section T-4 (Training), "Operatives Kriegsspiel 1926–1927," November 1926, BA/MA RH 2/2822.

46. Luftschutz, "Übungsreise," 1924, BA/MA RH 2/2244 [microfiche].

47. The Prussian army had a detailed regulation for the conduct of large maneuvers. See Kriegsminister, *Verordnung über die Ausbildung der Truppen für den Felddienst und über die grösseren Truppenübungen* (Berlin: Verlag der königlichen geheimen Ober-Hofdrückerei, 17 June 1870).

48. Lt. Col. S. Boelcke (ret.), "Die Süddeutschen Reichsheer-manöver 1926," *Schweizerische Monatsschrift für Offiziere aller Waffen* 38 (November 1926): 364.

49. Col. Gen. Hans von Seeckt, "Neuzeitliche Kavallerie," *Militär Wochenblatt* 6 (1927).

50. Gen. de Kavallerie M. Von Posek (ret.), *Der Aufklärungsdienst der Kavallerie* (Berlin: E. S. Mittler, 1927).

51. Gen. Walther Nehring, *Die Geschichte der Deutschen Panzerwaffe von 1916 bis 1945* (Berlin: Propläyev Verlag, 1974), 67–69. See also Robert Citino, *The Evolution of Blitzkrieg Tactics* (Westport CT: Greenwood Press, 1987).

52. In May 1940 the French army had five light cavalry divisions (Divisions Légères de Cavalerie) each of which consisted of a mounted cavalry brigade and a motorized brigade. See Janus Piekalkiewicz, *The Cavalry of World War II* (New York: Stein and Day, 1980), 237–38. On the U.S. army cavalry see the same, p. 253–54.

53. *Heeresdienstvorschrift 487*, part 2, para. 535: "The high command will employ tanks where they seek the decision. They must achieve surprise, be used in mass on a wide front and be employed in deep columns."

54. R. M. Ogorkiewicz, *Armoured Forces* (New York: Arco Publishing, 1960), 72–74.

55. Volkmar Kuehn, *Deutsche Fallschirmjäger im Zweiten Weltkrieg* (Stuttgart: Motorbuch Verlag, 1993), 16–18.

56. For a collection of studies on the establishment of a separate air force in 1916, see "Die Luftstreitkräfte der Deutschen Reiches," ed. Dr. Klemp, ca. 1930, BA/MA Potsdam W-10/50845, 17–32.

57. Mathew Cooper, *The German Air Force 1922–1945* (London: Jane's, 1981),

379. In 1919, von Seeckt proposed that Germany be allowed a peacetime air force of eighteen hundred aircraft and ten thousand men. Von Seeckt also favored the creation of the air force as a separate branch of service, equal to the army. See von Rabenau, *Seeckt: Aus seinem Leben*, 529.

58. Frank Futrell, *Ideas, Concepts, Doctrine: Basic Thinking in the United States Air Force 1907–1960* (Maxwell AFB AL: Air University Press, 1989), 1:70–79.

59. Max Hastings, *Bomber Command* (New York: Simon and Schuster, 1987), 38–43.

60. Futrell, *Ideas, Concepts, Doctrine*, 1:83–84.

61. Hans von Seeckt, *Gedanken eines Soldaten* (Berlin: Verlag für Kulturpolitik, 1929), 93–95.

62. Von Seeckt, *Thoughts of a Soldier*, 61–62.

63. *Leadership and Battle with Combined Arms* had several large sections on airpower and gave far more emphasis to the role of airpower than the corresponding French operational doctrine of the period, *Instruction sur l'emploi tactique des grandes unités* (1922).

64. *Luftwaffe Dienstvorschrift 16, Luftkriegführung* (1935), para. 8.

65. Oberbefehlshaber der Luftwaffe, "Bemerkungen der Oberbefehlshabers der Luftwaffe zur Ausbildung und zu den Übungen im Jahre 1935," National Archives, German Military Records, T-177, roll 1 (4 January 1936), paras. 8–9.

66. Kommandeur der Panzertruppen, "Zusammenarbeit zwischen Panzereinheiten und die Luftwaffe," 9 December 1936.

67. *Anlagen zum Bericht über die Wehrmachtmanöver (Heer)* (1937), Anlage 48 and 64.

68. When Germany went to war in September 1939, the Luftwaffe had a total of 2,765 combat aircraft—bombers, fighters, ground attack aircraft, and dive-bombers. Of these, 1,180 were bombers and 366 were dive-bombers. See Williamson Murray, *Strategy for Defeat: The Luftwaffe 1933–1945* (Maxwell AFB AL: Air University Press, 1983), 32–33.

69. For example, Archivrat Wilhelm Liesner, who served as editor for many of the military history monographs produced by the military history section of the Reich's Archives, had served as a general staff captain in World War I (From Wilhelm Liesner's personnel record).

70. At the request of the Truppenamt, the Reich's Archives military historians conducted an extensive study of "People's War" (Volkskrieg) to determine German capability to use guerrilla war as a defensive measure. See *Volkskrieg, Reichsarchiv, Kriegsgeschichtlich Forschungsamt*, ed. Archivrat Liesner (1930), MA/DDR W10/S0203. The Reich's Archives also conducted a detailed study on the use of bombers in tactical air support in 1918. See *Reichsarchiv, Abteilung B, Referat Luftstreitkräfte*, study, 2 April 1926, BA/MA RH 2/2195.

71. See Walter Goerlitz, *History of the German General Staff 1657–1945* (New York: Praeger, 1953), 15–49.

72. On the concept of the Führerheer and the NCO training of the German army, see Harold Gordon, *The Reichswehr and the German Republic 1919–1926* (Port Washington NY: Kennikat Press, 1957).

73. See Friedrich Borgmann, "Vertikale strategische Umfassung," *Wissen und Wehr* (10 December 1929), and the commentary in *Militär Wochenblatt* 28 (1930): 1087–90.

74. Heinz Guderian, *Erinnerungen eines Soldaten* (Heidelberg: K. Vowinckel Verlag, 1950). See also the English translation with a foreword by B. H. Liddell Hart, *Heinz Guderian, Panzer Leader*, trans. Constantine Fitzgibbon (New York: Dutton, 1952).

75. See Charles Messenger, *The Art of Blitzkrieg* (London: Jan Allan, 1976), 79–81; Field Mar. Lord Carver, *The Apostles of Mobility* (London: Weidenfeld and Nicolson, 1979), 55–59; and Kenneth Macksey, *Guderian: Creator of the Blitzkrieg* (New York: Stein and Day, 1976).

76. Barry Posen, *The Sources of Military Doctrine*, (Ithaca NY: Cornell University Press, 1984), 215–19.

77. The first two major German books on armored warfare were written by a serving officer, Lt. Ernst Volkheim: *Die deutschen Kampfwagen im Weltkriege* (Berlin: E. S. Mittler & Sohn, 1923), and *Der Kampfwagen in der heutigen Kriegführung* (Berlin: E. Mittler & Sohn, 1924). In 1924 and 1925, the *Militär Wochenblatt* published a monthly journal on armored warfare called *Der Kampfwagen* (The tank). By the time Guderian became prominent there was already an extensive body of German literature on armored war.

78. Posen, *Sources of Military Doctrine*, 210–11.

79. Albert Kesselring, *The Memoirs of Field Marshal Kesselring* (Novato, CA: Presidio Press, 1989), 20.

80. Kesselring, *The Memoirs of Field Marshal Kesselring*, 20.

81. Erich von Manstein, *Aus einem Soldatenleben* (Bonn: Athenaeum Verlag, 1958), 246–49.

82. Walter Spielberger and Uwe Feist, *Sturmartillerie* (Fallbrook CA: Arco Press, 1967), part 1.

83. Wilhelm Deist, "The Road to Ideological War: Germany 1918–1945," in *The Making of Strategy: Rulers, States and War*, ed. Williamson Murray, MacGregor Knox, and Alvin Bernstein (New York: Cambridge University Press, 1994), 352.

84. A useful overview of the military strategy of the Weimar Republic is found in Deist, "Road to War," 361–71.

85. Gaines Post, *The Civil-Military Fabric of Weimar Foreign Policy* (Princeton: Princeton University Press 1973), 110–29. See also Craig, *Politics of the Prussian Army*, 408–15.

86. Telford Taylor, *Sword and Swastika: Generals and Nazis in the Third Reich* (New York: Barnes and Noble, 1952), 77–81.

87. Taylor, *Sword and Swastika*, 117.

88. Craig, *Politics of the Prussian Army*, 486–87.

89. James Corum, *The Luftwaffe: Creating the Operational Air War 1918–1940* (Lawrence: University Press of Kansas, 1997), 182–83.

90. Norman Rich, *Hitler's War Aims* (New York: W. W. Norton, 1973), 51.

91. Walter Goerlitz, *History of the German General Staff* (New York: Praeger, 1953), 342–43.

92. Goerlitz, *History of General Staff*, 320–23.

93. Manfred Messerschmidt, "German Military Effectiveness between 1919 and 1939," in Millett and Murray, *Military Effectiveness*, 223–27.

94. Messerschmidt, "German Military Effectiveness," 227.

95. The German army maintained a four-year training program for commissioning until 1937, when it was shortened to two years. Even at the height of World War II and under a subsequent officer shortage, the officer training period was still eighteen months (in contrast to a nine-month training period for U.S. officers to be commissioned in World War II). The Germans made few compromises in maintaining a high quality officer corps. See Martin van Creveld, *Fighting Power* (Westport CT: Greenwood Press, 1982), 137–41.

96. Van Creveld, *Fighting Power*, 121–24.

97. Messerschmidt, "German Military Effectiveness," 244.

98. Martin van Creveld, *Supplying War* (London: Cambridge University Press, 1980), 145–47.

99. Van Creveld, *Training of Officers*, 63–66.

100. Van Creveld, *Training of Officers*, 63–66.

101. Cpt. Kurt Hesse, "Report on U.S. Military Power," February 1925, BA/MA RH 2/1820, 177–82.

102. The Luftwaffe general staff curriculum, which paralleled the army's in many ways, included National Socialist ideology in the curriculum as part of the administration course. This amounted to about two percent of the total instruction, or about four lectures a year. See Generalstab der Luftwaffe, Section 3: Training, Generalstabsoffizier: Erziehung und Ausbildung auf der LuftKriegsakademie. Richtlinien, 5 July 1937, BA/MA RL 2 II/164, 2.

103. Harold Deutsch, *Hitler and His Generals* (Minneapolis: University of Minnesota Press, 1974), 41–49.

104. For comparisons of troops, equipment, tanks, and aircraft in 1940 see Karl-Heinz Frieser, *Blitzkrieg-Legende: Der Westfeldzug 1940* (Munich: Oldenbourg Verlag, 1995), 41–70.

105. For more on the German army's dependence on horses see Richard DiNardo's excellent work, *Mechanized Juggernaut or Military Anachronism?* (Westport CT: Greenwood Press, 1991).

106. Col. Trevor Dupuy, *A Genius for War* (Englewood Cliffs NJ: Prentice Hall, 1977), 234–35.

3. TANKS, VOTES, AND BUDGETS

The Politics of Mechanization and Armored Warfare in
Britain, 1919–1939

Harold R. Winton

Writing in the *Journal of the Royal United Service Institution* in 1930,
Brig. A. P. Wavell observed that the situation facing the reformers of
armies in peacetime could be likened to "that of an architect called on
to alter and modernize and old-fashioned house without increasing its
size, with the whole family still living in it . . . and under the strictest
financial limitations."[1] Wavell's reminder that finances play a large part
in any military reform movement is a fact of which more contemporary
military leaders, laboring to recast their forces in the light of rapidly
changing circumstances and declining revenues, are painfully aware. And
because in democratic societies politicians make the major decisions on
how resources are to be expended, it is not at all surprising that the
success of many military reform movements depends at least in part on
the ability of the reformers to garner support for their plans among
individuals outside their service. An examination of the British army's
experience between the Great War and World War II may shed some
light on the dynamics of this process.

This study examines the political and economic implications of the
British army's effort between the wars to develop programs of mechanization and armored warfare. Mechanization may be defined as the
substitution of mechanical power for human and animal power mostly in
the form of transportation. Armored warfare, on the other hand, signifies
the development of army units in which the tank is the central element
and around which the other arms (such as infantry, artillery, engineers,
etc.) are organized. These distinctions, however, were not always clear
during the period under consideration. In fact, it took a number of years
to develop a common lexicon to describe the army's modernization.
These basic definitions will, however, allow analysis to proceed with
some degree of precision in order to answer the following questions:

What foreign and domestic political and economic conditions affected the fate of mechanization and armored warfare?

What steps did the advocates of mechanization and armored warfare take to garner support for their reforms among constituencies external to the uniformed members of the army?

What were the results?

What does this study tell us about the role of external constituencies in influencing the military reform process?

Before proceeding, a brief review of some recent literature on the dynamics of military reform is in order. Two of the most interesting works published on the reform process are Barry Posen's *The Sources of Military Doctrine* and Stephen Rosen's *Winning the Next War*.[2] Posen's work assesses changes in the military doctrines of Britain, France, and Germany during the interwar years and the early years of World War II. His primary purpose is to examine the relative explanatory power of balance of power and organizational behavior theories regarding why military institutions do or do not amend their doctrines. Posen concludes that both theories are operative but that the former is somewhat more important than the latter. For our purposes, however, Posen's most significant argument is that organizational tendencies within military institutions make them relatively impervious to change and that reform comes about most often as a result of external political pressure, frequently applied in alliance with military "mavericks."[3] Rosen's work draws on evidence from twenty-one British and American cases ranging in time from 1918 to 1967. These studies are categorized into peacetime, wartime, and technological examples of innovation. Rosen derives from these cases a much different and more sophisticated view of the reform process than does Posen. He concludes that military reform movements generally succeed when a small group of relatively senior military professionals redefines the fundamental manner in which its service will conduct operations and advances the careers of like-minded younger service members who implement the new design.[4] Because this study will focus on the efforts to win external support for reform, it will not conclusively settle the issue of the relative significance of internal versus external impetuses to change. Nor will it examine in detail the debates about the possible forms of armored warfare that took place among the reformers themselves.[5] It may, however, shed some light on the issue and offer some general food for thought to both political and military leaders who are struggling today to adapt to very rapidly changing realities.

Armored warfare and mechanization developed in four fairly distinct periods between the wars. From 1919 to 1926 the army demobilized and a small group of thinkers sketched out the opening tactical and operational concepts. Actual field trials with an experimental force were conducted on Salisbury Plain from 1927 to 1928. From 1929 to 1933 the results of these trials were codified in army doctrine; other trials were carried out with various mechanized units; and the army, like all other institutions in British society, dealt with the painful effects of economic depression. Beginning with an ad hoc armored force exercise in 1934, the next five years were spent in a long and agonizing effort to develop a single armored division. At the end of this period the army possessed one embryonic armored division that was in such a state of disorganization it did not even participate in the disastrous Flanders campaign of May 1940.

Demobilization and Early Thoughts, 1919–1926

Britain's demobilization began even before the treaties ending World War I were signed. When the armistice went into effect on 11 November 1918, the army's strength stood at 3,500,000; two years later it had been reduced to 350,000.[6] This rapid melting away was not, however, accompanied by a reduction in its responsibilities. 1922 found British soldiers stationed in Gibraltar, Malta, Egypt, Aden, India, Singapore, Hong Kong, China, and the Caribbean. As before the war, these overseas responsibilities were managed using the Cardwell system, named after Edward Cardwell who became secretary of state for war in 1868. Cardwell rationalized the army's structure so as to provide for regular relief of units abroad, usually every seven years. This system dictated, however, that the home army be organized according to imperial requirements, thus severely limiting its ability to prepare for continental warfare. Lord Richard Haldane had partially resolved the imperial-continental dichotomy by organizing the battalions of the home army into divisions whose subordinate infantry, cavalry, and artillery units were still linked to units policing the empire. As long as the types of units required for overseas service were roughly compatible with those required for the continent, this modification to the Cardwell system functioned smoothly. However, when the requirements of continental warfare and imperial policing began to diverge significantly, the army was placed squarely on the horns of a dilemma: whether to organize primarily to police the empire or to intervene on the continent.

Britain demobilized politically as well as militarily. Prime Minister David Lloyd George, the dynamic Welshman who had galvanized Britain for the Great War, was removed from office in October 1922 when Conservative members of his coalition government revolted and forced him to tender his resignation.[7] His ouster clearly signified Britain's return to "normalcy." Lloyd George was succeeded by Andrew Bonar Law, newly elected leader of the Conservative party. Bonar Law quickly dissolved Parliament and remained head of the government when the Conservatives won a sizable majority in the general election that followed. This election also hinted at a significant change in party politics. With the Liberals split between those following Henry Asquith and those following Lloyd George, the political rivalry between conservatives and liberals that had dominated nineteenth-century politics was clearly about to dissolve. It was replaced by a split between Conservatives and the newly emerging Labor party, which increased its representation from 59 to 142 members. Bonar Law resigned for reasons of health in 1923 and was succeeded by Stanley Baldwin, who dominated British politics for the next twelve years. Baldwin had steadily worked his way up through party ranks since his election to Parliament at age forty.[8] A man of common sense, gentility, and manners, Baldwin was the personification of normalcy. He had earned fame when, at a critical meeting to decide Lloyd George's fate, he had denounced the fiery Welshman as "a dynamic force" and added that a dynamic force was "a very terrible thing."[9] Baldwin called for a new general election in late 1923 in which the Conservatives lost more ground to Labor and were subsequently defeated on a no-confidence motion. Ramsay MacDonald's first Labor government lasted only ten months, felled by MacDonald's insistence on regarding a Liberal motion for a committee of inquiry as a measure of confidence. Baldwin's Conservatives, with the tight-fisted Winston Churchill as chancellor of the exchequer, returned to power with a huge majority in November 1924 and remained in government until 1929.[10]

Britain also demobilized economically. Having accumulated a large war debt, it was obvious that government expenditures in general would be low and that money for the armed services would be particularly tight. Army funds decreased from £93,714,000 in 1921 to £62,300,000 in 1922 and to £42,500,000 by 1926.[11] This shortage of funds was exacerbated by the pervasive system of "treasury control" by which the chancellor of the exchequer maintained very tight reins on national expenditures.[12] Each ministry, including the War Office, was required to submit its "estimates" or budget requests to the Treasury Office, where they were reviewed in detail. The guiding philosophy at the Treasury was that each increase over the previous year's expenditure required explicit justification. Upon Treasury approval the estimates were printed and sent to Parliament. Favorable votes were the norm because the government in office always had a majority in Commons. Individual members did, however, frequently attempt to influence army policy by debating specific provisions of the estimates. Treasury sanction was required for any expenditure not specifically included in the estimates, and all funds not spent at the end of the fiscal year reverted to the Treasury. While this system admirably fulfilled its accounting purpose and discouraged excess expenditures, it was overly rigid, it placed too great a premium on precedent, and it was actively hostile to innovation. Declining revenues and treasury control were supplemented by a particular cabinet policy to keep military expenditures low, known as "the ten-year rule." This budgetary guideline, formulated in 1919 and reaffirmed in 1925 and 1926, stipulated that "It should be assumed, for framing the revised [defense] estimates, that the British Empire will not be engaged in any great war during the next ten years, and that no expeditionary force is required for this purpose."[13]

It was thus within a venue of declining resources and increasing responsibilities that the interwar reformers first articulated their thoughts on mechanization and armored warfare.

The opening battle cry for a new approach to warfare came in a seminal article penned by Col. John Frederick Charles Fuller in response to an essay contest in the RUSI *Journal* that called on contestants to assess the implications of recent advances in science and mechanics for the conduct of future land warfare.[14] Fuller's central argument was that the Great War had shown that the specialist corps of machine guns, tanks, and infantry did not cooperate well and that the army's main task was therefore to "reduce the various arms to that common denominator, the tank, which more than any other arm, combines offensive and defensive power with mobility."[15] Fuller planned to accomplish this conversion to an "all-tank army" in three phases over the period of about a decade. The chief value of Fuller's scheme was that rather than looking at the Great War and asking how it could be fought better it asked how, given advancing technology, a future war might be fought more rationally.

The plan's chief deficiency was the ultimate conclusion that the primary land combat functions could be performed by three classes of mechanical vehicles. These same strengths and weaknesses were evident in a follow-up article in which Fuller argued that the development of the tank presaged an era in which land maneuver would closely resemble the fluidity of sea warfare.[16]

Fuller was soon joined in his efforts to spread the armored gospel by a young infantry officer, Capt. Basil Henry Liddell Hart. Liddell Hart had served as a company commander on the western front, had been gassed while there and was subsequently posted as the training officer in a volunteer infantry battalion.[17] This experience led him to publish several articles, one of which he sent to Gen. Sir Ivor Maxse, late inspector of training in France.[18] Maxse liked what he read and in 1920 chaired a RUSI lecture that allowed Liddell Hart to expound his ideas in a highly visible forum. A portion of Liddell Hart's remarks, entitled "The Expanding Torrent System of Attack," contained portent for armored warfare.[19] His analysis suggested that the fundamental problem of the Great War had been that of bad timing when exploiting gaps. Fresh troops that were pushed through too quickly got cut off while those brought up too late lost the initiative. The solution, he said, lay in imitating the natural way in which flowing water broke down successive earthen obstacles: automatically widen each breach as the penetration deepened. The military manifestation of this phenomenon would mean that each penetrating unit would move forward as long as it had a reserve behind it while units that were held up would send their reserves to the flanks to widen the gaps. This system would be continued by each succeeding upper echelon in perfect imitation of nature's method.

While Liddell Hart's ideas did not incorporate the new technology of tank warfare, a synthesis of his ideas with Fuller's was clearly possible. That melding began in early 1922 when Liddell Hart sent Fuller a draft article on modern infantry he was preparing for *The Encyclopedia Britannica*. Fuller's comments and confirmation of a few technical details convinced him that tanks were, indeed, the wave of the future.[20] He attempted, however, to stake out a somewhat more moderate position than Fuller had by calculating the cost of mechanization and by amending the ultimate form of armored warfare to incorporate a group of specialized armor-accompanying infantry he referred to as "tank marines."[21]

Fuller and Liddell Hart both realized that their ideas could come to fruition only if some sort of experimental force were formed to test them. To plant the seed for this endeavor, Fuller arranged for Liddell Hart, who in July 1924 had been placed on half-pay because of his war wounds and had taken up work as a military correspondent for the *Morning Post*, to attend a lecture he gave in November of the same year on the progress of mechanization. At the end of the lecture Liddell Hart, surely with something of a gleam in his eye, asked Fuller how he proposed to test his ideas without some "picked body of troops."[22] Fuller specifically advocated the formation of such a unit in early 1925 when he concluded his book *Sir John Moore's System of Training* with a call for "a second Shorncliffe Camp, another Experimental Brigade, in which . . . once again will the Army be leavened and a new epoch in its history will be ushered in."[23] These efforts soon bore fruit. In his presentation of the estimates in March 1926, Secretary of State for War Sir Laming Worthington-Evans announced that the army would form a small experimental force in order to examine the issue of mechanization in a step-by-step manner.[24] This public commitment by the army's political leader seemed to indicate a clear victory for Fuller and Liddell Hart's campaign to create an experimental mechanized force.

Thus by 1926 the situation for the advocates of mechanization and armored warfare appeared to be relatively bright. Supporters were, to be sure, faced with daunting challenges brought on by the army's rapid demobilization, the expansion of its overseas commitments, and a radical reduction in financial resources. In the face of these obstacles, however, they had managed to get their message concerning the need for reform into the public view and to garner at least the qualified support of the army's political leadership. The task was to turn these advantages into reality and get on with the business of finding out what would work and what would not, determinations that could only be made with the benefit of actual field trials.

The Birth of the Mechanized Force and the Death of the Armored Force, 1927–1928

In May 1927 the world's first completely mechanized combat brigade was formed on Salisbury Plain. Out of this Experimental Mechanized Force grew many of the concepts that were to influence significantly the future conduct of land warfare. A year later it was renamed the Experimental Armored Force. The change in name seemed to suggest that the army was hoping this formation would provide guidance on the conduct of armored warfare as opposed to the mere mechanization of existing arms.

Although this was a noteworthy aspiration, the actual accomplishments of the force in 1928 did not live up to the expectations that had been set for it. Furthermore, at the end of the 1928 training season Gen. Sir George Milne, who in 1926 became chief of the imperial general staff (CIGS), decided to disband the force in order to concentrate the army's efforts on the mechanization of infantry and cavalry units. In attempting to understand this significant period in the army's history, it will be helpful to survey briefly the international and domestic events of the time.

Subtle alterations of mood and outlook were evident both overseas and at home. The "Spirit of Locarno," as reflected in Gustav Stresemann's policy of conciliation in Germany and Aristide Briand's policy of *apaisement* in France, kept the European situation relatively calm.[25] However, Nationalist riots at the British concession in Hankow in January 1927 were symptomatic of unrest throughout China, and a force of twelve infantry battalions was dispatched to Hong Kong to protect British lives and interests in Shanghai.[26] At home 1927 was the middle year of the period C. L. Mowat has called "Dead Centre." The general strike of 1926, which had briefly threatened to drive a deep ideological cleavage in the body politic, was over; Labor was too cowed to do much; the Liberals were still in disarray; and the Conservatives were faring badly with problems of unemployment. Churchill, in an attempt to keep government expenditures to a minimum, constantly badgered the services to reduce their budgets.[27] In response to this pressure for economy the War Office eliminated the enlistment bounty paid to territorial soldiers, a move that saved £64,000 per year but raised howls of protest in Parliament when Worthington-Evans presented the estimates.[28] During the debate following this speech a Labor member introduced a motion for the reduction of land forces in preparation for the upcoming disarmament conference. Tanks were a particular bone of contention; the Laborite raised a specter of "a new land super-Dreadnought" that would lead to an arms race in tanks similar to the pre–Great War naval race.[29] Although this motion was easily voted down, it reflected a wider trend toward popular pacifism that was also evident in the fifteen memoirs from the trenches published by Great War veterans in 1927.[30]

Alarmed by efforts to reduce the army, Milne prepared a comprehensive survey for Worthington-Evans that described the many demands being placed on the British forces: requirements of the Locarno agreement, which pledged Britain's aid to France or Belgium if either country's borders were violated by Germany; unrest in China; growth of the Swaraj movement in India; Britain's responsibility to police the mandated areas of Palestine and Iraq; and the political ambitions of an anti-British Egypt together were severely straining the force.[31] The pressure of these commitments was exacerbated by the fact that the number of infantry battalions had shrunk from 157 in 1914 to 136 in 1927. In short, the margin for error in simultaneously meeting the demands of the empire and preparing for a possible continental war had grown almost nonexistent.

Against this background of economic stringency, popular pacifism, pressing overseas commitments, and reduced forces, the effort to form the experimental force moved slowly through the bureaucracy. Worthington-Evans's 1926 estimates speech had clearly indicated that his concern was primarily an economic rather than a doctrinal one. "We are," he said, "already ahead of all other nations in mechanicalisation, and there is therefore no justification for uneconomic haste."[32] Apparently as a move to encourage forward thinking in the army, Milne had appointed Fuller as his military secretary, a kind of senior aide and executive assistant. The CIGS, however, ran into a number of roadblocks about the mechanized force from his military colleagues on the Army Council. The proposal to establish the force was undercut by questions about the cost and design of shelters for the vehicles (permanent or temporary) and the issue of command.[33] As a consequence, the formation of the experimental unit was held in abeyance as memoranda passed back and forth among the concerned agencies in the War Office.

A year after his original announcement Worthington-Evans reiterated his intention to form the experimental force and added that it would be commanded by "an officer who has made a specialized study of mechanical warfare."[34] Despite this obvious allusion to Fuller and Fuller's manifest qualifications, his command of the unit was in doubt. Milne had offered him command of the unit in December 1926, and Fuller had accepted.[35] However, in the intervening months he had begun to sour on the opportunity when he learned that this experimental force was to be formed around a regular infantry brigade and that, in conjunction with command of this brigade, he would also have administrative responsibility for the garrison at Tidworth. Fuller then presented Milne with a series of requests for amendment to his appointment including authority to delegate to other officers the responsibility for the brigade's three infantry battalions and the garrison and to have a stenographer and staff captain added to his staff to assist in the experimental work. These requests lay dormant until Fuller read Worthington-Evans's estimates speech and pressed the issue with Milne. When Milne refused to accommodate him Fuller walked out of the CIGS's office and penned his resignation, stating that he could not assume responsibility for a command that was so misrepresented.[36] Fuller was subsequently persuaded to withdraw his resignation but he had forfeited his one great opportunity to make a substantial contribution to the development of armored warfare.

The formation of the experimental force was ultimately precipitated by a bombshell in the press. In 1925 Liddell Hart had moved from his position at the *Morning Post* to become the *Daily Telegraph*'s chief military correspondent. This position gave him, in his own words, a "platform for launching a campaign for the mechanisation of the Army."[37] Thus, when the War Office announced on 21 April that Col. R. J. Collins would command the Seventh Infantry Brigade but made no mention of the experimental force to which Worthington-Evans referred in Parliament, Liddell Hart was in a perfect position to influence events. His article, "An Army Mystery—Is there A Mechanical Force?" was a masterpiece of journalistic intervention in bureaucratic affairs. After reviewing the various official pronouncements on the issue since 1926 he asked, "has the scheme broken down, or was the formation of such a force no more than a figure of speech? Parliament and the public . . . have a right to enlightenment."[38] The desired effect was soon achieved. On 27 April the War Office announced the definite formation of the experimental force; on 12 May Colonel Collins was gazetted to command both the experimental force and the Seventh Brigade, with priority to the former.[39] Although one cannot say with a high degree of certainty what would have happened had Liddell Hart not intervened, the fact that Milne was allowing events to drift after Fuller's resignation strongly suggests that were it not for Liddell Hart's surgically precise strike, the experimental force might have been stillborn.

Despite some initial disappointments attributable in part to Colonel Collins's methodical style of command, the 1927 field trials of the experimental force produced some useful results, particularly in the handling of light tank units.[40] In September Milne visited Salisbury Plain where he delivered his own thoughts on mechanization to an audience that included members of the press who had come at his specific invitation. Prefacing his remarks with caution regarding the stringency of finances and the effect of multiple overseas commitments, Milne went on to say that the advances made possible by the gasoline engine presaged the eventual formation of armored divisions and called for a whole new outlook on modern war.[41] Liddell Hart saw the speech as a clarion call for mechanization and, with Milne's permission, published a synopsis in the *Daily Telegraph*.[42] However, Maj. Gen. Archibald Knox, the director of military training, was horrified at its revolutionary import and persuaded Milne not to let it be circulated within the army.[43] One of the most balanced and comprehensive analyses of the 1927 trials was rendered by Maj. Gen. John Burnett-Stuart, commander of the Third Infantry Division, who had oversight responsibility for the experimental formation. In a lecture at the University of London in March 1928 Burnett-Stuart stated that the exercises on Salisbury Plain had demonstrated that the tank, hitherto a subordinate to the infantry soldier, had been developed to the point that it could "cut itself adrift from the infantry battle, and go into business on its own as a principal, not merely an assistant."[44] Burnett-Stuart also outlined a gradual program of conversion (beginning with the establishment of four tank brigades, two at home and two overseas) and concluded with the observation that "Mechanization, chemical warfare and scientific methods generally mean quicker and more decisive results, and therefore in the end less expenditure of life."[45] It was clear from Burnett-Stuart's remarks that the experimental force had converted a conventional but open-minded commander into a convinced advocate of armored units built around the tank and that he was looking forward to continuing the experimental work in 1928.

Both internationally and domestically 1928 demonstrated a continuation of the trends noted the previous year. Aristide Briand's crowning diplomatic achievement came on 27 August when representatives of fifteen countries, including Great Britain, France, Germany, and the United States, gathered to sign the Pact of Paris and renounce war as an instrument of policy.[46] British policy thus seemed to offer a convincing reason *not* to retain a standing army. Churchill continued his budget-cutting ways by convincing the Committee of Imperial Defense (CID) to add the phrase "at any given date" to the language of the ten-year rule, thus causing it to roll forward in seeming perpetuity.[47] Although the assumption that there would be no major war for ten years could be challenged at any time and was subject to annual review, the practical effect of Churchill's motion was to give the Treasury an even stronger position than it previously had vis-à-vis the armed services. This mood in the cabinet reflected an even larger outpouring of trench literature that in 1928 included, among many others, Robert Graves's *Good-bye to All That* and Siegfried Sassoon's *Memoirs of a Fox-Hunting Man*.[48]

The 1928 exercises of the newly redesignated Experimental Armored Force failed to live up to the potential that had been projected for it by Burnett-Stuart in his March lecture. Shortages of equipment, a concentration on conducting demonstrations designed to sell the concept of armored warfare to officers at the Staff College and members of Parliament, and a final exercise that divided the experimental force among two different units all combined to inhibit progress in the development of tactical ideas and their organizational implications.[49] Liddell Hart's analysis of these exercises noted that while the force had gained useful experience in driving and maintenance, the main lesson was a negative one: armored and unarmored vehicles could not work together effectively in one unit.[50] Burnett-Stuart's endorsement of the force commander's report on the 1928 exercises highlighted three requirements for the future of armored warfare: first, leaders whose mental pace matched the speed of the formation; second, the presence of accompanying arms and services with the same mobility as the tank; and third, the ability to operate on fronts wider than the limits of Salisbury Plain.[51] These three issues constituted his agenda for the presumed armored force exercises of 1929. Unfortunately the trials did not take place.

On 12 November 1928 Milne informed Worthington-Evans that he wanted to disperse the Experimental Armored Force for one year.[52] Citing the good progress that had been made in vehicle design and the probable organization of a future armored brigade, Milne argued that the important issues now were to determine the optimal grouping of tanks, machine gun carriers, and infantry units in infantry brigades and the correct mix of medium and light tanks in tank battalions. It would not be possible, he maintained, to study these issues and simultaneously continue trials with the armored force. Therefore he proposed to proceed with the infantry experiments in 1929 and to form a permanent armored brigade in 1930. However, in order to conduct the trials he proposed it would be necessary to place early orders for new equipment. He therefore sought authority to spend £150,000 in anticipation of the following year's estimates. Worthington-Evans supported Milne's unusual request and obtained the necessary authority from Churchill, who stipulated pointedly that "this part of your programme will be given absolute priority within whatever total is fixed when Estimates come to be considered."[53]

On 27 November 1928 the secretary of state announced in Commons that the armored force had fulfilled its purpose and would be dispersed, while two new mechanized units would be formed at Aldershot and Salisbury Plain in order to "extend the experiment."[54]

On the surface the dispersal of the armored force appears to have represented both progress and consensus. If one looks beneath the surface, however, it appears much different. Shortly after the 1928 trials had been terminated, Lieut. Gen. Archibald Montgomery-Massingberd, commander of Southern Command and the intermediate officer between Burnett-Stuart and the war office, had concluded that the armored force experiment was having an adverse effect on infantry and cavalry morale.[55] Based on this conclusion he had recommended to Milne that the proper course of action was to shift the focus of the trials so that the traditional branches could catch up with the armored force. Milne's decision thus represents the success of Montgomery-Massingberd's agenda of "evolution, not revolution."[56] This analysis and agenda were directly at odds with those of Burnett-Stuart, who had argued that the competition from the tank corps was a "healthy stimulant to progress" for the older arms and that it was vital to continue the armored force trials in order to work out the details of both its tactics and its composition.[57]

Liddell Hart's commentary on the decision is instructive. Responding to Worthington Evans's announcement in the *Daily Telegraph* he argued that while there was an urgent need to mechanize the existing arms there was an even greater need to create an armored division that operated as an independent striking force. He also warned that the policy of distributing mechanization across the entire army would require at least a decade to fulfill and that unless this program accelerated as it developed, the mechanized army would still not be a reality "before the youngest-joined subaltern of to-day is a permanent inmate of a bath-chair."[58] This time, however, the outside actor was powerless to influence the decision. Nineteen months earlier Liddell Hart had been able to use his journalistic vantage point to bring the experimental force to life when it was in serious danger of expiring in the womb of Whitehall bureaucracy. He could not, however, restore it to life on this occasion when it was killed by conservative opposition. In the former case he had highlighted an obvious discrepancy between War Office policy and War Office action. In the latter case, however, Milne had in effect declared victory in the armored warfare experiments and offered a professional judgment that it was time to move on to new horizons. Worthington-Evans's reaction was simply to accept Milne's professional military advice at face value and concern himself solely with the budgetary implications of the decision. All Liddell Hart could do was offer comment from the sidelines.

There is one final irony to this story. Milne's decision has been represented by Liddell Hart and others as one that gave undue weight to the opinions of conservatives such as Montgomery-Massingberd.[59] In a sense it was. Milne's critics do not, however, comment on his intention to form a permanent armored brigade in 1930, which he announced to Worthington-Evans in the same memo that proposed dispersal of the experimental force. We will never know how firm Milne's intention to establish a permanent armored force was because the worldwide economic depression that began with the American stock market crash of 1929 upset everyone's economic calculations, including the army's, and had a profound effect on the development of British mechanization and armored warfare.

Doctrine and Debate in the Depression, 1929–1933

In his 1929 estimates speech Worthington-Evans proclaimed proudly and accurately that Britain led the world "not only in our equipment of tanks but also in our ideas as to their use in war."[60] Although this assertion remained valid for several years, progress in armored doctrine during the depression was uneven. On the one hand the experiments with mechanized infantry units at Salisbury Plain and Aldershot proved disappointing. On the other hand, results of the 1927–28 trials were codified in a remarkable little manual drafted by Col. Charles Broad entitled *Mechanised and Armoured Formations*. Then Broad made even more progress in the command and control of armored formations when a tank brigade was temporarily assembled in 1931. During these four years there was a great deal of debate in the army concerning its future direction. Fuller contributed to this debate with a series of books on armored warfare, though his influence on the army was uneven. Liddell Hart shifted the focus of his thoughts from tactics and operations to military strategy and policy. These events took place, however, in an international environment marked by progressive unrest and a domestic environment characterized by popular revulsion to war and strict economic stringency.

The rise of National Socialism in Germany, the weakening of French defenses, and the failure of the American stock market were events of profound significance. Stresemann's death and the collapse of the

American stock market in 1929 led to the dissolution of the "Grand Coalition" in 1930 and ushered in a period of instability in German politics that ultimately resulted in Hitler's assumption of the chancellorship in January 1933. Although the depression did not reach France until 1931, France's military potential relative to Germany's was declining. The early withdrawal of Allied occupation forces from the Rhineland exposed the weakness of an army whose term of service was limited to one year, and French alliances with Poland and the so-called Little Entente of Czechoslovakia, Rumania, and Yugoslavia could not replace the loss of Russia as a counterweight to Germany in the east.

The general election of 1929 returned 288 Laborites, 260 Conservatives, and 29 Liberals. Policy differences over unemployment as well as continuing antipathy between Baldwin and Lloyd George ruled out the technical possibility of a Conservative-Liberal majority and subsequently led to MacDonald being asked to form a second Labor government.[61] Although MacDonald was again dependent on liberal support in Commons, his purging of Labor's left wing gave him a stronger political base than he had possessed five years earlier. MacDonald followed a policy of moderate socialism and strict economic conservatism at home while advocating conciliation, disarmament, and support for the League of Nations abroad. In its economic policy, however, the new government did not differ substantially from its predecessor regarding the size of the army. In his estimates speech of March 1930, Thomas Shaw, the new secretary of state for war, stated that while the government was willing to take the lead in international negotiations for disarmament it would not do so unilaterally.[62]

The continuing effects of economic depression ultimately forced the dissolution of the second Labor government in August 1931. It was succeeded, however, not by a Conservative or Liberal cabinet but by a national government headed by MacDonald, with Baldwin serving as lord president of the council (effectively deputy prime minister) and token Liberal participation. A general election in October returned the national government but in much different proportions. The Conservatives were triumphant, gaining over 11.8 million votes and 472 seats in Commons. Both the Liberal and Labor parties were split into factions that would or would not support the ruling government. Paradoxically, MacDonald remained prime minister but he was reduced to the status of a figurehead (with real power being exercised by the Conservatives), while Baldwin continued as lord president and Neville Chamberlain the newly appointed chancellor of the exchequer.[63] This anomaly in British governmental practice, which effectively created a government without opposition, produced not bold new action to solve the economic ills of the day but only drift and muddle. Its history has been aptly described by C. L. Mowat as "one long diminuendo."[64]

Much of the progress in mechanization and armored warfare during this era was attributable to Col. Charles Broad. Broad had originally served as an artillerist in the Great War. He transferred to the Royal Tank Corps (RTC) when he contrasted the results of the November 1917 British attack at Cambrai (in which tanks, infantry, and artillery had for the first time in the war acted in close cooperation) with those of the disastrous failure on the Somme in 1916.[65] Broad had been instructed by Milne to produce a manual on armored warfare drawn from his analysis of the 1928 trials. He quickly drafted a concise pamphlet, entitled *Mechanised and Armoured Formations*, that articulated the role of armored brigades in independent attacks whose exploitation would produce chaos in the enemy's rear and "create opportunities for decisive operations under mobile warfare conditions."[66] In 1931 Milne authorized Broad to assemble the four existing tank battalions into a provisional tank brigade for new trials on Salisbury Plain. In these exercises Broad developed a system of tank tactics that would be common among the various units and an accompanying series of two-letter codes to represent the different formations. These codes, which could be transmitted by flag, Morse code, or voice radio, added significantly to the flexible handling of tank units and contributed substantially to the success of the 1931 exercises.[67] Further exercises were held in 1932 that finally convinced Milne of the absolute necessity of forming a permanent tank brigade, which he announced in a lengthy and strongly worded memorandum of 15 September 1932.[68] Milne's proposal was endorsed favorably by the other members of the Army Council and subsequently approved by Viscount Hailsham, the new secretary of state.[69] Although a number of materiel problems still had to be worked out and little had been done to develop combined arms armored formations, this decision indicated that the momentum that had been lost with the dispersal of the armored force in 1928 had finally been recovered.

Fuller and Liddell Hart both continued to write on military issues during the depression era, but their foci began to diverge significantly. Fuller's aim was to work out in some detail his thoughts on mechanization and armored warfare. Unlike a number of his earlier works that had been aimed at both military and civilian audiences to convince them of the necessity for new forms of warfare, his publications in the late 1920s and early 1930s were aimed primarily at military readers to inform them of the ideas he had developed and the details of these new methods. The core of his ideas was contained in two extended articles in the *Army Quarterly* that provided an outline for two of his most significant works on armored warfare: *Lectures on F.S.R. II* (1931) and *Lectures on F.S.R. III* (1932). In these articles Fuller qualified his earlier notion of sea warfare on land by recognizing that the land environment would approximate "an ocean full of islands and shallows."[70] Fuller also broadened his concepts of the composition of armored formations, citing the necessity for armored cars, airplanes, self-propelled artillery, and antitank weapons to work together with tanks.[71] Although he was promoted to brigadier in 1929 and to major general in 1930, Fuller was becoming psychologically detached from the army. He declined command of a district in India and retired in 1933.[72] In the early 1930s Liddell Hart began to change his focus from tactical and operational matters to those of strategy. This was presaged in a 1931 RUSI lecture, "Economic Pressure or Continental Victories," in which he argued that the Great War had been an aberration from Britain's traditional strategy of using its sea power to exercise economic influence on continental adversaries, and that she tragically and mistakenly had "spent the strength of England, pouring it out with whole-hearted abandon on the soil of our allies."[73] Themes of wasteful sacrifice and the use of the navy in a strategy of "limited liability" began to appear with increasing frequency in Liddell Hart's writings and continued for the rest of the decade.

In late 1932 Milne, whose term as CIGS had been twice extended, was finally nearing retirement. Liddell Hart was among those consulted by Maurice Hankey, secretary to the cabinet and the CID, to comment upon the likely candidates to succeed him. Liddell Hart mentioned Generals Charles Harington, Cecil Romer, Philip Chetwode, and Montgomery-Massingberd, and Lieutenant Generals Burnett-Stuart, James Charles, and Edmund Ironside.[74] Although from Liddell Hart's account of the conversation it is impossible to determine the extent to which he commented upon the relative qualifications of the individuals involved, the inclusion of three relatively junior officers among his list may have represented an attempt on his part to suggest to Hankey the need for more pronounced reform in the army. If so it had little effect. Eventually Montgomery-Massingberd, who had been assigned to the War Office as adjutant general and, perforce, a member of the Army Council following his tenure at southern command, was chosen to replace Milne. On learning of the appointment Liddell Hart wrote Hankey that he fully anticipated that Fuller would be squeezed out of the army; that progressive soldiers such as Burnett-Stuart and Ironside would find their prospects impaired; and that the well-known conservative Harry Knox, who had dissuaded Milne from publishing his Tidworth speech, would find enlarged opportunities for resisting change.[75] Liddell Hart was right on all counts.

This episode provides some insight into the question of Liddell Hart's influence on army policy in late 1932. On the one hand he was sufficiently influential to be consulted by one of the men who would be involved in the decision. On the other hand the candidate he had obviously favored the least got the job. Several years later Liddell Hart's ability to influence army appointments increased dramatically, but the manner in which that influence was used undermined its effectiveness and led to an almost total separation between the reforming journalist and the War Office. This story was intimately intertwined with the issue of who was to command Britain's only armored division.

The Search for an Armored Division, 1934–1939

The mid- to late-1930s mark a distinctive period in British interwar history. Men at the top seemed paralyzed by the dilemma they faced between responding within the means of Britain's limited economic resources to an increasingly dangerous world versus ruling an electorate whose main concern appeared to be avoiding the repetition of another Great War. As Michael Howard has so aptly noted, the CID minutes and papers of the era begin to reflect the sound of a "heavy and ominous breathing of a parsimonious and pacific electorate, to the variations in which the ears of British statesmen were increasingly attuned."[76] The central manifestation of this dilemma was the army's role in national defense.[77] Two schools of thought prevailed. The first, known as the "blue water" or "limited liability" strategy, was to use Britain's geographic isolation from the continent as the basis for a plan that took a long view of a possible European war. Advocates of this concept intended to employ Britain's economy, navy, and air force as the primary instruments of power. The army would be used to police the empire; to mount such minor overseas expeditions as may be required; to furnish ground-based air defenses at home; and, only when all these tasks had been completely fulfilled, to develop a limited capacity to engage a continental adversary in conjunction with Britain's allies. The second school (which was never given a shorthand label) may be called "continental intervention." Advocates of this position argued that the blue water strategy was both politically and militarily bankrupt: if Germany invaded France and the Low Countries, Britain could not possibly ignore their ensuing calls for help, and, while splendid isolation may have been a viable military policy in the pre-airpower era, Britain simply could not afford to permit German airbases to exist immediately across the Channel. Given these strategic realities, interventionists argued passionately for a large, well-equipped, expandable army that could make a substantive military contribution to the defeat of German aggression. The debate over this issue raged back and forth, from the ambivalence of the hesitant rearmament actions of 1934 to 1936, to a decision completely in favor of limited liability in December 1937, and ultimately to a total reversal in favor of continental intervention in March and April 1939. The protracted uncertainty over the army's role produced by this debate significantly influenced its deliberations over mechanization and armored warfare.

The violent, unpredictable mood of the era was most clearly evident in Nazi Germany. Hitler's consolidation of power, his mobilization of the German *volk*, his stunning, bloodless diplomatic triumphs (that is, remilitarizing the Rhineland in March 1936, annexing Austria in March 1938, and occupying the so-called Sudetenland of Czechoslovakia in October 1938 and the rest of the state in March 1939), left the statesmen of Europe befuddled and confused. These threats to British security were compounded by Japan's growing aggressiveness in the Pacific, Italian adventurism in the Mediterranean, and a civil war in Spain that exacerbated tensions between the left and the right both internationally and domestically.[78] France, Britain's major potential ally on the continent, was rocked by internal dissent as well. A succession of governments, seriously divided over issues of party ideology, the distribution of domestic wealth, and the conduct of diplomacy abroad reflected an increasingly fractious body politic.[79]

At home domestic developments, economic developments, and renewed manifestations of pacifism conditioned the cabinet's response to the volatile international situation. MacDonald resigned in 1935 in favor of Baldwin, who called for a general election. Baldwin ran on an ambiguous platform that alluded to Britain's declining security but promised "no great rearmaments."[80] Although depression-generated unemployment began to decrease and industrial production slowly increased from 1934 to 1936, large pockets of unemployment remained in industrial Scotland, South Wales, west Cumberland, northeast England, Lancashire, and Northern Ireland.[81] The popular revulsion of war, previously reflected in the Oxford Union resolution not to fight for king and country, was reinforced by the publication of A. A. Milne's book *Peace with Honour* and the Peace Pledge Union's one hundred thousand signatories led by such notables as George Lansbury, Bernard Shaw, and Virginia Woolf.[82] When the Defence Requirements Committee, commissioned to survey the country's most pressing military needs, reported in early 1934 that the protection of Britain from air attack dictated the immediate dispatch of an expeditionary force to the continent, Chamberlain rejoined that the experience of the last war indicated that the majority of resources should instead be placed in the navy and the air force.[83] Chamberlain's view was also reflected in the Defence Committee's White Paper of 1936; therefore, when he succeeded Baldwin as prime minister in May 1937 it was almost axiomatic that limited liability would carry the day as national defense policy.[84]

While the strategic debate over the army's purpose proceeded in the cabinet, another debate was coming to the surface in the tank corps between two different concepts of armored warfare.[85] These two concepts can be referred to as the all arms concept and the tank brigade idea. The first visualized a balanced force of all arms and services that would be capable of executing a variety of operational and tactical missions, the most important of which was to penetrate deeply into the enemy's rear areas to disrupt its command and supply network. The second visualized the same purpose but held that the other arms, particularly the infantry, were unnecessary encumbrances that would only hinder tank units in the accomplishment of their missions. The primary advocate of the former position was Brig. George Lindsay, an early member of the tank corps who commanded the Seventh Infantry Brigade. The leading representative of the latter was Brig. Patrick Hobart, commander of the Tank Brigade, which had been permanently formed in 1933. At the end of the 1934 training season, an opportunity arose to test the overarching concept of armored warfare in an exercise that amalgamated Lindsay's and Hobart's units into a mobile force with Lindsay in overall command.

The exercise proved disappointing. The mobile force was stalemated in its attack against a series of closely grouped objectives approximately sixty miles behind the lines of an opposing infantry division. This defeat was brought about by a number of circumstances including an artificially constricted start time for the exercise; disagreements between Lindsay and Hobart on the tactical plan; inadequacies in the mobile force's staff and means of communications; audacity on the part of the infantry division commander; and, according to the tankers, bias on the part of the umpires.[86] Despite these particulars the exercise was a setback for the cause of armored warfare simply because the outcome showed a conventional infantry division defeating two of the army's most modern formations. The exercise also resulted in Lindsay's eclipse as a spokesman for the combined arms concept of armored warfare and Hobart's rise to prominence as the leading exponent of the tank brigade idea.

At the War Office Montgomery-Massingberd directed the policy of gradual mechanization that converted the cavalry mounts from horses to light tanks and provided trucks and lightly armored machine gun carriers to the infantry.[87] This policy was strongly opposed by tank corps officers who doubted that cavalrymen were capable of mastering the techniques of armored warfare and argued instead for the dissolution of cavalry formations and the expansion of the RTC.[88] As one of his final acts as CIGS, Montgomery-Massingberd drafted a memo outlining the composition and possible employment of a continental expeditionary force that would consist of a number of infantry divisions, augmented by tanks, whose forward movement would be covered by a mobile division containing a tank brigade and several mechanized cavalry units.[89] This memo constituted Montgomery-Massingberd's intellectual legacy to the army. His personal legacy was his successor, Gen. Cyril Deverell. Deverell was a competent tactician but more significantly he was a conservative and safe candidate for the position who perfectly complemented both Montgomery-Massingberd's plans for gradual mechanization and the national government's policy of muddling its way out of the depression and going slowly and circumspectly toward rearmament.

Accompanying Deverell's appointment was the appointment of Alfred Duff Cooper as secretary of state for war. Duff Cooper had served as the army's financial secretary in Baldwin's second Conservative government from 1928 to 1929 and in the national government under both Mac-Donald and Baldwin. In the latter instance he had appeared frequently in Commons in the place of the two secretaries of state, the Viscounts Hailsham and Halifax, both members of the House of Lords. A man who moved easily in literary circles (and the biographer of Douglas Haig), Duff Cooper was in many ways a natural for the War Office. Shortly after his appointment he approached Liddell Hart to obtain the journalist's views on military reform. The two worked out an arrangement to hold confidential discussions on military matters after which Duff Cooper would take care to protect Liddell Hart's identification as the source of any new ideas presented to the Army Council and Liddell Hart would retain the freedom to criticize War Office policy in his new position as defense correspondent for the *Times*.[90] Duff Cooper did not, however, have the stomach to force a confrontation with the Army Council. He recognized the need to reform and initiated a formal proposal to scrap the Cardwell system in order to break the stranglehold India had on the army. Duff Cooper retreated on this key issue, however, when Deverell said it could not be addressed until 1939 when the size and organization of the expeditionary force had been definitely determined.[91] In the cabinet and the CID, however, Duff Cooper was boldness personified. Throughout the early months of 1937 the cabinet stormily debated the role of the army, with Chamberlain the champion of limited liability and Duff Cooper the untiring advocate of the continental commitment.[92] In May, when Chamberlain succeeded Baldwin as head of the government, he eased Duff Cooper out of the War Office and into the Admiralty where, presumably, his advocacy of a strong national defense would be more in line with Chamberlain's strategic priorities.[93]

To fill the vacancy at the War Office Chamberlain selected the dynamic and ambitious young minister of transport, Leslie Hore-Belisha. As transport minister Hore-Belisha had combined zealous administration with a flair for publicity to tame the worst of Britain's chaotic highway conditions. He required that all new drivers be tested; he revised the highway codes; and he caused pedestrian crossings to be marked with striped poles topped by garish orange lights that quickly became known as "Belisha Beacons." Here was just the man, Chamberlain believed, to shake up an institution in which "the obstinacy . . . in sticking to obsolete methods is incredible."[94] Shortly before leaving the War Office, Duff Cooper arranged a meeting between Hore-Belisha and Liddell Hart.[95] Out of this meeting was born the Hore-Belisha–Liddell Hart "partnership." This combination of a dynamic secretary of state and a thoughtful, analytical adviser seemed to offer great promise for the army. Unfortunately, the temperamental blindnesses of both men, the aversion of senior military leaders to outside influence, and the imminence of war transformed the reform effort into a deeply passionate and naked struggle for power and doomed the partnership to defeat.

The most precise indication of the depth to which the lines were drawn between the army reformers and the old guard was the dispute over the composition and command of the Mobile Division.[96] The first question to be decided was whether or not the Tank Brigade would be included in the division. The directors of the general staff recommended that it should not. Hobart worried that omitting the brigade was intended to provide a pretext for emasculation of the RTC in favor of the newly mechanized cavalry. In response to a letter from Deverell on the subject, Liddell Hart said that he was withholding an article on the Mobile Division for publication in the *Times* pending the decision on the Tank Brigade issue. In a meeting with Liddell Hart on 18 November the CIGS argued that the brigade was "too precious" to be included in what was essentially a covering force. Liddell Hart countered with the argument that if the division did not contain a medium tank formation it would be defeated by a German armored division. Whether Deverell was impressed more by Liddell Hart's military logic or his journalistic clout is unclear. On the following day the War Office announced that the Mobile Division would consist of the First and Second Cavalry Brigades, the Tank Brigade, and supporting elements. This anomalous organization, suitable for neither imperial nor continental warfare, was obviously the product of a compromise between two competing power groups: the cavalry and the tank corps. The selection of a commander for the new formation was the product of a similar compromise. The War Office selection committee and Deverell put forward the name of a cavalryman based on the rationale that cavalry units made up the bulk of the division. Liddell Hart advised Hore-Belisha to hold out for an RTC officer, arguing that because the division was primarily a tank formation it required for its commander an individual with extensive tank experience. There followed a long impasse during which Deverell refused to submit a new nominee and Hore-Belisha insisted on an RTC officer. The typically British solution to this deadlock was the appointment of an artillery officer with absolutely no experience in armored warfare![97]

This prolonged controversy convinced Hore-Belisha that he needed a new Army Council if he were to carry out his reform program. With Chamberlain's backing, he moved quickly to put his handpicked people in place. On 3 December 1937 the War Office announced the retirement of Deverell, Knox, and Lieut. General Hugh Elles, master-general of the ordnance whose position was fused with the director of munitions production.[98] The new team was composed of much younger men:

Viscount Gort as CIGS, Ronald Adam in the newly created position of deputy CIGS, and Clive Liddell as adjutant general. Liddell Hart had lobbied hard to have Maj. Gen. Frederick Pile, who had commanded the light tank battalion in the experimental force, included in the new group, but Hore-Belisha believed Pile was too divisive.[99] With this group of senior officers in place, Hore-Belisha's victory over the old guard seemed complete. However, having picked his own team and traumatized the Army Council once he could not easily take such action again.

The next six months were marked by an almost constant struggle between the new Army Council on one side and Liddell Hart on the other, with Hore-Belisha caught in the middle. The main issue was the air defense of Great Britain, which Liddell Hart believed had to be the army's first priority and which Gort and the general staff directors saw as an impediment to other army missions. On 22 December the cabinet ruled in favor of air defense and relegated cooperation in the defense of allies (a euphemism for the continental commitment) to fourth of four among army missions.[100] In the ensuing analysis of just how many air defense weapons the army should produce Liddell Hart bombarded Hore-Belisha with papers of his own and scathing criticism of the general staff's appreciations.[101] Gort and his directors reciprocated with derision, calling Liddell Hart's missives the work of an amateur.[102] Hore-Belisha, who had conspicuously advertised his association with Liddell Hart in his early months in office, now began to dissimulate by pretending not to know him at all.[103] This charade fooled no one. Things finally came to a head in May 1938 when Liddell Hart advised Hore-Belisha to insist on the appointment of Pile to the newly created position of inspector general for air defense, even to the point of forcing Gort's resignation.[104] This, of course, was politically impossible for Hore-Belisha to accomplish. As a result, the Hore-Belisha–Liddell Hart partnership dissolved: Liddell Hart continued to use his position at the *Times* to criticize the inadequacies of the army's air defense efforts, and Hore-Belisha struggled on as best he could with an Army Council that turned out to be much less cooperative than he had anticipated.[105]

It is appropriate at this point to contemplate the differences of temperament and style between Duff Cooper and Hore-Belisha in their efforts to influence army policy. Both ultimately failed as reformers but for diametrically opposed reasons. Duff Cooper was too cautious, Hore-Belisha too impetuous. Duff Cooper was overly sympathetic with the high command and dealt with them too gently; Hore-Belisha was overly

unsympathetic and dealt with them too brusquely. Duff Cooper con-
sumed his political capital by defending the general staff; Hore-Belisha
appeared to be making political capital by attacking it. Duff Cooper used
Liddell Hart's advice discreetly; Hore-Belisha used it recklessly.

There is also a real dichotomy in their substantive records. Duff
Cooper did little to move reform forward. His main contribution to
British strategy, however, was to serve as the sole voice in government in
the mid-1930s that consistently recognized the inescapable necessity of
the continental commitment and the bankruptcy of limited liability. If
Duff Cooper failed to convince his political colleagues and superiors of
this unpalatable truth it was more their fault than his. Hore-Belisha was
only slightly more successful than Duff Cooper in advancing the cause
of armored warfare. At the outbreak of war in September 1939 the First
Armoured Division (a lineal descendant of the Mobile Division) was still
more an aspiration than a reality. Hore-Belisha was not, however, without
his successes. He ended the "Buggins' turn next" system of promotion
that had impeded progress for two decades; he significantly improved
conditions of army life for the private soldier; and he began to reduce
the garrison of India in a serious and responsible manner. However,
his most significant deficiency as war minister was the mirror image
of Duff Cooper's greatest strength. As a strategic dilettante, politically
beholden to a prime minister who was convinced of the viability of a blue
water strategy and the recipient of advice from a military critic who was
similarly persuaded, Hore-Belisha did nothing to disabuse the cabinet
of the error of its strategic calculations. When Hitler abrogated the
Munich pact and occupied the Czechoslovakian rump in March 1939,
the scales finally fell from Chamberlain's eyes concerning the nature of
his adversary.[106] The continental commitment became the army's top
priority, the Territorial Army was doubled, and peacetime conscription
was implemented.[107] The army could not, however, instantly reverse
its two decades of suffering as the Cinderella of the services. Thus
when Hitler invaded Poland six months later the minuscule two-division
expeditionary force dispatched to France was, in essence, an improvised
formation.[108] Sadly, Hore-Belisha had been part of the problem rather
than part of the solution.

Liddell Hart's role in this final act of the struggle for reform has
all the hallmarks of a Greek tragedy. Much of his advice was sound.
Frequently, however, he failed to consider the political realities that
influenced military decisions, particularly in his misunderstanding of

the role the government of India played in determining army policy. His advice on appointments had much to commend it because he was intimately familiar with the leading military personalities of the day. But his constant championing of tank corps officers gave the impression that he was attempting to maneuver his personal favorites into positions of responsibility. It was the form of Liddell Hart's advice, as much as its substance, that alienated him from the army.[109] His obsession with gaining acceptance for discrete, identifiable ideas may partly explain why Liddell Hart, who always emphasized the indirect approach in theory, was so startlingly direct in his one chance in life to *do* something.[110] It also led him to commit a fatal error. Throughout his "partnership" with Hore-Belisha he failed to appreciate how vehemently many senior officers resented the fact that a man with no formal responsibility in the army should have the power not only to influence army policy but also to determine their professional destinies.[111]

The evidence presented by this study is mixed. In the early era of mechanization and armored warfare (1919 to 1926) Fuller and Liddell Hart were able to create sufficient interest in the subjects to obtain support from the secretary of state for war to authorize the formation of an experimental force. From 1927 to 1928 Fuller's influence was cast aside by his refusal to accept command of this force without relief from responsibilities he considered diversionary. Liddell Hart's journalistic intervention in the form of his "Army Mystery" article in the *Daily Telegraph* was a triumph, rescuing the experimental unit from the suffocation of bureaucratic inertia. Liddell Hart was, however, unable to save it from dispersal a year later when conservatives in the army's upper ranks convinced Milne to shift the focus of experimentation from armored warfare to possible mechanization of the established branches. During the depression era, Fuller concentrated on perfecting the techniques of armored warfare, a necessary development in his writing but one not intended for an external audience. Liddell Hart, on the other hand, began to broaden his focus to issues of strategy rather than operations or tactics. From 1934 to 1939, as the army moved haltingly toward the formation of an armored division, Fuller's antidemocratic tendencies got the better of him; his endorsement of fascism removed him from serious consideration in British public affairs.[112]

Liddell Hart's championing of limited liability in the *Times* and elsewhere was enthusiastically noted by Chamberlain, who by the end of

1937 established it with a vengeance as national policy. We must not, however, mistake parallelism of ideas for influence. The minutes and memoranda of the CID indicate clearly that Chamberlain was completely convinced of the economic necessity of a blue water strategy based on his own analysis of the Great War and Britain's post-war economic condition. While Liddell Hart provided a convenient and perhaps even useful voice for this policy in the national press, there is absolutely no doubt that Chamberlain would have followed the dictates of his own internal logic concerning the foolishness of an expeditionary force for the continent no matter what defense policy Liddell Hart had advocated in the *Times*.[113] Regarding Liddell Hart's influence on armored warfare, the evidence here is ambiguous as well. On the one hand his intervention with Deverell may have kept the Tank Brigade as a constituent part of the Mobile Division. He was not, however, able to influence the more fundamental policy of expanding the armored component of the army by converting cavalry regiments to light tank units rather than disbanding them and expanding the RTC. Furthermore, his efforts to promote the careers of tank corps officers by lobbying Hore-Belisha for their appointment to senior positions generated a good deal of resentment among members of the Army Council. They also complicated Hore-Belisha's reform program sufficiently for the war minister ultimately to be forced to choose between Liddell Hart and his newly handpicked team of senior officers. On this issue there simply was no choice: Liddell Hart had to go.

What this all adds up to is that the ability of persons outside the army to bring about reform was limited. It was occasionally successful, as in the birth of the mechanized force in which Liddell Hart held up to public scrutiny an obvious discrepancy between previously announced army policy and existing reality. As head of the government in late 1937, Chamberlain was also successful in dictating the army's strategic priorities. These priorities, however, served to validate and reinforce rather than question the military conservatives' preference for mechanizing existing arms rather than expanding the tank corps. This points out one of the fundamental anomalies of the reform debate of the 1930s: the desire of the reformers for armored warfare was at loggerheads with their strategic preference for limited liability, while the preference military conservatives had for mechanization over armored warfare was directly at odds with their realization of the necessity for a firm continental commitment.[114] When we examine the efforts of political heads of the War

Office to induce reform we find similarly mixed results. Worthington-Evans was willing to support experimentation in new forms of war as long as such experimentation proceeded at an economic pace. He was not, however, capable of judging between the relative values of mechanization versus armored warfare when Milne recommended disbanding the experimental force in 1928. The distinctly different temperamental deficiencies of Duff Cooper and Hore-Belisha and the failure of each to bring about fundamental change have already been noted.

These gloomy reflections seem to indicate there is no hope for military reform. There are, however, instances in which outsiders have been able to bring it about. Viscount Haldane's rationalization of the prewar British army and Elihu Root's modernization of the American army following the Spanish-American War both indicate that military institutions *can* be transformed with the help of external actors. A comparative analysis of these efforts is well beyond the scope of this study. They both suggest, however, that successful reform is produced by men whose temperaments are sympathetic to the military's values and its role in society, whose intellects are capable of determining not only the need for change but also the general direction such reform must take, and whose constitutions are sufficiently robust to guide the course of events in the face of both active and passive opposition. Unfortunately for Britain and her interwar army, none of the significant outside players interested in its reform possessed this felicitous blend of human insight, intelligence, and determination.

Notes

1. A. P. Wavell, "The Army and the Prophets," *Journal of the Royal United Service Institution* (hereafter JRUSI) 75 (November 1930): 665.

2. Barry Posen, *The Sources of Military Doctrine: France, Britain, and Germany between the World Wars* (Ithaca NY: Cornell University Press, 1984), and Stephen Rosen, *Winning the Next War: Innovation and the Modern Military* (Ithaca NY: Cornell University Press, 1991).

3. Posen, *Military Doctrine*, 174.

4. Rosen, *Winning the Next War*, 251.

5. This subject is assessed at some length in J. P. Harris's *Men, Ideas, and Tanks: British Military Thought and Armoured Forces, 1903–1939* (Manchester: Manchester University Press, 1995). By explicitly examining diverging ideas among the reformers themselves, Harris makes an important contribution to our understanding of the dynamics of interwar armored development in Britain;

however, the analysis is largely divorced from the significant contextual element of British strategy.

6. Brian Bond, *British Military Policy between the Two World Wars* (Oxford: Clarendon Press, 1980), 21.

7. Charles L. Mowat, *Britain between the Wars, 1918–1940* (Boston: Beacon Press, 1971), 142.

8. Keith Middlemas and John Barnes, *Baldwin: A Biography* (London: Macmillan, 1969), 43–157.

9. Mowat, *Britain between Wars*, 142.

10. Remainder of paragraph based on Mowat, *Britain between Wars*, 143–200.

11. *Command Paper* (hereafter *Cmd.*) 2598, *Memorandum of the Secretary of State for War relating to the Army Estimates for 1926*, 1 March 1926, 2.

12. Description of the army's budget process based on a lecture by Sir Herbert Creedy found in Great Britain War Office, *Report on the Staff Conference at Staff College, Camberley, 14–17 January 1929* (London: HMSO, 1929), 69–84.

13. Peter Silverman, "The Ten Year Rule," JRUSI 116 (March 1971): 42. In a sophisticated and balanced appraisal of the operation of Treasury control of the defense services and the ten-year rule during the 1920s, John Ferris determined that this famous (or infamous) assumption did not operate evenly throughout the period or among the services. Ferris argues that Treasury did not achieve full control over all defense expenditures until 1925; it did, however, achieve control over army expenditures by as early as 1922. John Robert Ferris, *Men, Money, and Diplomacy: The Evolution of British Strategic Policy, 1919–1926* (Ithaca NY: Cornell University Press, 1989), 27, 158–78.

14. J. F. C. Fuller, "Gold Medal (Military) Prize Essay for 1919: The Application of Recent Developments in Mechanics and Other Scientific Knowledge to Preparation and Training for Future War on Land," JRUSI 65 (May 1920): 240.

15. Fuller, "Gold Medal Essay," 261.

16. J. F. C. Fuller, RUSI lecture, 11 February 1920, "The Development of Sea Warfare on Land and Its Influence on Future Naval Operations," JRUSI 65 (May 1920): 283.

17. B. H. Liddell Hart, *The Memoirs of Captain Liddell Hart*, 2 vols. (London: Cassell, 1965), 1:4–12, 18–26, 28–33.

18. Liddell Hart, *Memoirs*, 1:38–40.

19. Remainder of paragraph based on B. H. Liddell Hart, RUSI lecture, "The 'Man-in-the-Dark' Theory of Infantry Tactics and the 'Expanding Torrent' System of Attack," JRUSI 66 (February 1921): 1–22.

20. Liddell Hart to Fuller, 16 and 21 January 1922, quoted in Jay Luvaas, *The Education of an Army: British Military Thought, 1815–1940* (Chicago: University of Chicago Press, 1964), 382.

21. B. H. Liddell Hart, "The Development of the 'New Model' Army:

Suggestions on a Progressive but Gradual Mechanicalisation," *Army Quarterly* (hereafter AQ) 9 (October 1924): 37–50.

22. Liddell Hart's comments came following J. F. C. Fuller's RUSI lecture, "Progress in the Mechanicalisation of Modern Armies," JRUSI 70 (February 1925): 86–87.

23. J. F. C. Fuller, *Sir John Moore's System of Training* (London: Hutchinson, [1925]), 223.

24. *House of Commons Debates* (hereafter HC *Deb.*), 5th ser., 193 (15 March 1926): 78.

25. Erich Eyck, *A History of the Weimar Republic*, 3 vols., trans. by Harlow P. Hanson and Robert G. L. Waite (Cambridge: Harvard University Press, 1963), 3:127, and Gordon Wright, *France in Modern Times: 1760 to Present* (Chicago: Rand McNally, 1960), 427–28, 444.

26. William Louis, *British Strategy in the Far East, 1919–1939* (Oxford: Clarendon Press, 1971), 130, and "Army Notes," JRUSI 72 (February 1928): 208.

27. Stephen Roskill, *Hankey: Man of Secrets*, 3 vols. (London: Collins, 1970–1974), 2:416–19.

28. HC *Deb.*, ser. 5, 203 (7 March 1927): 876, 911–12.

29. HC *Deb.*, ser. 5, 203 (7 March 1927): 936, 939.

30. Correlli Barnett, *The Collapse of British Power* (New York: Morrow, 1972), 428.

31. Memorandum under cover of minute from Milne to Worthington-Evans, 2 November 1927, W.O. 32/2823.

32. HC *Deb.*, 5th ser., 193 (15 March 1926), 78.

33. The applicable correspondence begins with an undated Director of Staff Duties (organization) memo (circa early May 1926) entitled, "Scheme for Experimental Work with a Mechanical Force," and continues with comments from, among others, the inspector, RTC, the CIGS, the master-general of the ordnance (MGO), and the adjutant-general (AG). W.O. 32/2820.

34. HC *Deb.*, 5th Ser., 203 (7 March 1927): 887.

35. J. F. C. Fuller, *Memoirs of an Unconventional Soldier* (London: I. Nicholson and Watson, 1936), 434.

36. Fuller, *Memoirs*, 438.

37. Liddell Hart's diary note (later referred to as "Notes for History"), undated, Liddell Hart Papers, Liddell Hart Centre for Military Archives, King's College, University of London (hereinafter, LHCMA).

38. Anonymous [B. H. Liddell Hart], "An Army Mystery—Is there a Mechanical Force?" *Daily Telegraph*, 22 April 1927, 9.

39. Liddell Hart, *Memoirs*, 1:116–17.

40. Frederick Pile, "Liddell Hart and the British Army," in *The Theory and Practice of War*, ed. Michael Howard (Bloomington: Indiana University Press, 1975), 170.

41. Two accounts of Milne's speech are extant: in Liddell Hart, *Memoirs*, 1:128, and in Fuller, *Memoirs*, 441. Text of the speech is in Lindsay Papers, LHCMA.

42. Liddell Hart, *Memoirs*, 1:128.

43. Liddell Hart, *Memoirs*, 1:130.

44. J. T. Burnett-Stuart, "The Progress of Mechanization," AQ 16 (April 1928): 33.

45. Burnett-Stuart, "Progress," 49–51.

46. René Albrecht-Carrié, *A Diplomatic History of Europe Since the Congress of Vienna* (New York: Harper & Row, 1958), 442.

47. CID meeting 236, 5 July 1928, Cab. 2/5.

48. Correlli Barnett, *The Collapse of British Power* (New York: Morrow, 1972), 428.

49. B. H. Liddell Hart, *The Tanks: The History of the Royal Tank Regiment and Its Predecessors Heavy Branch Machine-Gun Corps, Tank Corps, and Royal Tank Corps, 1914–1945*, 2 vols. (New York: Praeger, 1959), 1:259.

50. B. H. Liddell Hart, "Armoured Forces in 1928," JRUSI 73 (November 1928): 723.

51. J. T. Burnett-Stuart, "Armoured Force Training Report—1928," W.O. 32/2828.

52. Milne to Worthington-Evans, 12 November 1928, W.O. 32/2825.

53. Churchill to Worthington-Evans, 11 December 1928, W.O. 32/2825.

54. HC *Deb.*, ser. 5, 223 (27 November 1928): 216–17.

55. Archibald Montgomery-Massingberd, "The Autobiography of a Gunner," unpublished memoir, n.d. [circa 1946], Montgomery-Massingberd Papers, LHCMA, 53.

56. Montgomery-Massingberd, "Autobiography," 53.

57. Burnett-Stuart, "Armoured Force Training Report—1928," 4–5, W.O. 32/2828.

58. B. H. Liddell Hart, "The War Office and the Mechanised Army," *Daily Telegraph*, 28 November 1928.

59. Liddell Hart, *Memoirs*, 1:135. The most unbalanced and unfair criticism of Milne is found in Shelford Bidwell and Dominick Graham, *Fire-Power: British Weapons and Theories of War, 1904–1945* (London: Arms and Armour Press, 1970), 154–55.

60. HC *Deb.*, ser. 5, 225 (28 February 1929): 2214–15.

61. Roy Douglas, *The History of the Liberal Party, 1895–1970* (London: Sidgwick & Jackson, 1971), 198–207; G. D. H. Cole, *A History of the Labour Party from 1914* (New York: A. M. Kelly, 1969), 196–233; and Middlemas and Barnes, *Baldwin*, 507–29.

62. HC *Deb.* ser. 5, 237 (24 March 1930): 82.

63. Mowat, *Britain between Wars*, 379–412.

64. Mowat, *Britain between Wars*, 413.

65. Shelford Bidwell, *Gunners at War: A Tactical Study of the Royal Artillery in the Twentieth Century* (London: Arms and Armour Press, 1970), 64–65; Liddell Hart, *The Tanks*, 1:227–28; and Kenneth Macksey, *The Tank Pioneers* (London: Jane's, 1981), 62.

66. See *Mechanised and Armoured Formations (Instructions for Guidance when Considering Their Action, 1929 [Provisional])* (London: War Office, 1929), 32.

67. Author's interview with Broad, 10 November 1972; Liddell Hart, *The Tanks*, 1:290.

68. Untitled minutes from CIGS to AG, Quartermaster General, MGO, and Parliamentary Under-Secretary, 15 September 1932, W.O. 32/2852.

69. PUS to CIGS, 23 September 1932, and Secretary of State to CIGS, 6 October 1932, W.O. 32/2852.

70. J. F. C. Fuller, "One Hundred Problems on Mechanization," AQ 19 (October 1929): 15.

71. Fuller, "One Hundred Problems," 18.

72. Fuller, *Memoirs*, 447–50.

73. B. H. Liddell Hart, RUSI lecture, "Economic Pressure or Continental Victories," JRUSI 76 (August 1931): 488. The fundamental flaw in Liddell Hart's strategic prescriptions for Britain in the 1930s was that the advent of airpower made control of the Low Countries and the French coast even more significant than it had been for the previous three centuries. However, his argument was also flawed historically. For a comprehensive review of the reciprocal relationship between British sea power and land power, see David French, *The British Way in Warfare 1688–2000* (London: Unwin Hyman, 1990), esp. chap. 7, "Deterrence and Dependence," 175–201.

74. Liddell Hart diary note, 9 November 1932, Liddell Hart Papers, LHCMA.

75. Liddell Hart to Hankey, 2 December 1932, Liddell Hart Papers, LHCMA.

76. Michael Howard, *The Continental Commitment: The Dilemma of British Defence Policy in the Era of the Two World Wars* (London: Maurice Temple Smith, 1972), 79.

77. Remainder of paragraph based on Howard, *Continental Commitment*, and Bond, *British Military Policy*, 214–311.

78. Albrecht-Carrié, *European Diplomacy*, 461–532.

79. Wright, *France in Modern Times*, 483–509.

80. Mowat, *Britain between Wars*, 555–56.

81. Mowat, *Britain between Wars*, 433–34.

82. A. A. Milne, *Peace with Honour* (New York: E. P. Dutton, 1934) and David Lukowitz, "British Pacifism and Appeasement: The Peace Pledge Union," *Journal of Contemporary History* 9 (January 1974): 115–27.

83. Howard, *Continental Commitment*, 107.

84. *Cmd. 5107, Statement Relating to Defence* [1936].

85. Origins and conduct of the mobile force exercise are based largely on material in Lindsay's papers, LHCMA, and author's 27 September 1972 interview with Viscount Bridgeman, Lindsay's brigade major before and during the exercise.

86. For commentary on the mobile force exercise see A. G. Cunningham, "The Training of the Army, 1934," JRUSI 79 (November 1934): 729, and Liddell Hart, *The Tanks*, 1:332–33.

87. Montgomery-Massingberd remarks following a RUSI lecture by G. N. MacReady, "The Trend of Organization in the Army," JRUSI 80 (February 1935): 20.

88. Liddell Hart, *The Tanks*, 1:339–40.

89. CIGS to Secretary of State, 9 September 1935, "Future Organization of the British Army," W.O. 32/4612.

90. Liddell Hart, diary note, 14 December 1935, Liddell Hart Papers, LHCMA.

91. Secretary of State minutes, 24 November 1936, W.O. 32/4614, Committee on the Cardwell System: Report.

92. Cabinet meeting, 5 May 1937, Cab., 23/88.

93. Duff Cooper felt sure he would be dropped from the cabinet when Chamberlain came to power. Alfred Duff Cooper, *Old Men Forget* (London: Rupert Hart-Davis, 1953), 206.

94. Chamberlain to Hore-Belisha, n.d., quoted from Keith Feiling, *The Life of Neville Chamberlain* (London: Macmillan, 1946), 317.

95. Liddell Hart, *Memoirs*, 2:2–3.

96. This paragraph based on Liddell Hart, *Memoirs*, 2:55–59.

97. Liddell Hart, *Memoirs*, 2:42.

98. Liddell Hart, *Memoirs*, 2:50.

99. The depth of feeling at the War Office is indicated in a 2 February 1938 diary entry by then-Maj. Gen. Henry Pownall, who alluded to "some creature like Pile" becoming CIGS. See Brian Bond, ed., *Chief of Staff: The Diaries of Lieut.-Gen. Sir Henry Pownall*, 2 vols. (London: Leo Cooper, 1972–75), 1:131.

100. "Defence Expenditure in Future Years," C.P 316(37), Cab. 24/273, and cabinet meeting of 22 December 1937, Cab. 23/90.

101. Liddell Hart, *Memoirs*, 2:97.

102. J. R. Colville, *Man of Valour: Field Marshal Lord Gort, V.C.* (London: Collins, 1972), 86.

103. Liddell Hart, *Memoirs*, 2:109–13.

104. Liddell Hart, *Memoirs*, 2:116.

105. Liddell Hart, *Memoirs*, 2:121–24.

106. Albrecht-Carrié refers to this enlightenment as "tearing off the veil of British illusions." *Diplomatic History of Europe*, 531.

107. Bond, *British Military Policy*, 304–11.

108. Brian Bond, *Britain, France, and Belgium 1939–1940* (London: Brassey's, 1990), 15.

109. E. K. G. Sixsmith, review of Jay Luvaas's *The Education of an Army*, AQ 90 (April 1965): 245–47.

110. Michael Howard's recollection of a remark made to him by Raymond Aron, in Robert Pocock, "Liddell Hart: The Captain Who Taught Generals," *The Listener* 88 (28 December 1972): 895.

111. Particularly galling was Liddell Hart's entry in the 1940 *Who's Who*, which stated that he had "collaborated with the War Minister, Mr. Hore-Belisha, in the reorganization of the Army, 1937–1938, suggesting a programme of reforms, of which sixty-two were achieved by 1939." See *Who's Who*, 1940, p. 1890.

112. Anthony Trythall, *"Boney" Fuller: The Intellectual General* (London: Cassell, 1977), 180–212, and Brian Holden Reid, *J. F. C. Fuller: Military Thinker* (New York: St. Martin's Press, 1987), 175–94.

113. In this regard Mearsheimer's critique of Liddell Hart for leading British policy down the primrose path of limited liability makes the mistake of accepting too much at face value Liddell Hart's estimates of his influence on government policy. See John Mearsheimer, *Liddell Hart and the Weight of History* (Ithaca NY: Cornell University Press, 1988), 127–31. Mearsheimer's assertion that Liddell Hart made little contribution to the concept of strategic penetration of enemy lines by armored formations has also been convincingly rebutted. See Azar Gat, "Liddell Hart's Theory of Armoured Warfare: Revising the Revisionists," *Journal of Strategic Studies* 19 (March 1996): 1–30. Gat does not, however, entirely discredit the larger Mearsheimer criticism, for he fails to deal with Liddell Hart's *volte-face* on the subject of offense versus defense as expressed in articles in the *Times* in October 1937 and also that same year in *Europe in Arms*. Instead, Gat approvingly cites the May–June 1940 campaign in France and Flanders as vindication of Liddell Hart's earlier ideas on armored warfare. Any balanced evaluation of Liddell Hart's career must deal with both.

114. The two most notable exceptions to this critique were Burnett-Stuart, who advocated a mobile division designed for imperial warfare in conjunction with a blue water strategy, and Hobart, who pushed for an armored division designed for continental warfare in conjunction with an interventionist strategy.

4. MILITARY REFORM AND THE RED ARMY, 1918–1941

Bolsheviks, *Voyenspetsy*, and the Young Red Commanders

Jacob W. Kipp

An examination of Soviet military reform in the interwar years is very much a matter of perspective. And in the history of Russia perspective is everything, for it defines the historical subject under study.[1] Seen from the context of the two world wars as the key points of reference, the military historian's task seems simple: assess the performance of the tsarist army in World War I against the performance of the Soviet army in World War II. The former lost while the latter won. Therefore reform in the interwar period must have been a success. The creation of a mass industrialized army possessing the economic and technological base to fight a total war laid the foundation for victory against the Wehrmacht on the eastern front in the decisive theater of military action and against the opponent's strategic center of gravity.[2] This interpretation fit Soviet military historiography very well and provided one of the key sources for regime legitimacy in the postwar period: the Communist Party led the army and people to victory. This approach minimized the significance of the disasters of the initial period of war and ignored the staggering human costs of the final victory. As the Russian military historian N. G. Pavlenko has pointed out, "Stalinism always looked on the social sciences as supporting adjuncts to propaganda and therefore they forced historical science and all other sciences to respond to all the nuances of the Communist Party's propaganda campaigns."[3] This usable past changed often in the postwar period. Nonpersons reappeared; the cult of Stalinism was condemned; wartime heroes were reduced to minor players; and new heroes, such as Leonid Brezhnev of Malaya Zemlya fame, were suddenly discovered.

Another view would look at interwar military reform from the perspective of past Russian military reform efforts. This view emphasizes the larger historical context and the relationship among the state, the army, and the society.[4] The Soviet state in this case is the de facto heir of tsarist Russia. From this perspective the interwar military reforms are seen as the continuation of the evolution of Russian military institutions. This process of reform has usually been divided into two parts. The first began with the military reforms of Ivan the Terrible, including the creation of the *pomestnaya* (gentry estate) system for raising troops, and continued with the birth of the Imperial Russian Army and Navy under Peter the Great at the end of the seventeenth century. That system continued to function until the middle of the nineteenth century. In this period westernization of the state apparatus and the gentry elite went hand in hand with the creation of a regular standing army and the birth of the navy. The military system rested on twenty-five-year conscription of the peasantry, be they serfs on the gentry's estates or state peasants who made up the vast majority of the population. For a century and a half this marriage, while adapting to tactical changes, provided a stable foundation for Russian military power. The coming of mass armies in the wake of the French Revolution and the early industrialization of warfare in the mid-nineteenth century severely challenged not only the Russian military system but also the entire political, social, and economic fabric of the imperial culture.

Thus the period after the Crimean War of 1853 to 1856 brought profound changes in both Russian society and the army. The era of the great reforms during the reign of Alexander II saw the abolition of serfdom, the creation of the Zemstvo system of local government, establishment of a new court system and trial by jury, the creation of a state bank, reforms in education, and the state's promotion of economic development and railroad construction. In military affairs Count D. A. Milyutin reformed the system of military administration; introduced the military districts as the basis for administration and mobilization; created a mass army based upon universal conscription; began the process of peacetime war planning; and embarked upon meeting the challenge of change produced by rapid technological innovations (including rifled weapons, breechloaders, smokeless powder, magazine rifles, quick-firing artillery, field telegraphs, and railroads). For a backward Russia such technological innovations imposed additional financial burdens upon state and society. The reformed army met its first challenge in the Russo-Turkish War of 1877–78 with final victory in the field. Military victory did not, however, deliver political success; an economically weak and politically isolated Russia had to accept a settlement imposed by the other European powers at the Congress of Berlin. A second period of reform followed defeat in the Russo-Japanese War of 1904 to 1905.[5]

Once again military reform went hand in hand with political, social, and economic changes brought about by a general systemic crisis, in this case the revolution of 1905. Military reformers believed the cause of defeat in the Far East was linked to the inability of the army to meet the demands of modern war. In addition to tactical changes to an expanded battlefield, Russian military reformers began to address the conduct of operations and to propose the creation of a military doctrine that would enhance combined arms actions in modern combat. The Imperial Russian Army that fought World War I was a product of these reforms but the reforms had hardly been implemented when that war began. The interwar reforms in this context were a further step in this ongoing process of adapting to modern warfare, a process that has continued through the Cold War to today when the challenge is adapting the Russian armed forces to the information age and the revolution in military affairs.[6] This approach invites comparative study of the Russian experience against a larger backdrop of European military history. It does not, however, highlight the peculiarities of the interwar Soviet experience, especially the revolutionary origins of the new regime.

The revolutionary origins of the Soviet regime, the impact of the civil war and war communism on the regime, the militarization-mobilization of Soviet society by Stalin's revolution from above, and the distinct linkage of war and revolution in the Bolshevik world-view gave a distinct character to Soviet military reform in the interwar years and had a profound influence on Soviet state and society. Together they not only explain the final success of the Soviet Union in the Great Patriotic War and reveal the sources of the Red Army's initial disasters but also provide key clues to the ossification of the Soviet state, society, and military that came to exist by the last decade of the Cold War and the dismal failure of military reform during *perestroyka* and in post–Soviet Russia.[7] In this approach to military reform the interwar period falls into five distinct periods: war and revolution, 1917–18; the civil war and war communism, 1918–20; the New Economic Policy (NEP) and the Frunze reforms, 1921–29; the Stalin revolution from above and mechanization, 1929–36; and the Stalinist terror and military decline, 1937–41.

War and Revolution: The Origins of the Red Army

The Red Army of Workers and Peasants (Raboche-Krest'yanskaya Krasnaya Armiya or RKKA) drew upon four distinct and contradictory sources in its approach to military reform during the two decades that separated its founding in the aftermath of the Bolshevik revolution and the onset of Operation Barbarossa in June 1941. The first source for the "reform" of the Red Army ironically was the revolutionary movement of the Bolshevik party that seized power in October 1917 (Julian calendar); that dismantled the last vestiges of the tsarist army; and in early 1918 that began the process of constituting a new, revolutionary army. This process gave the Red Army its class, revolutionary, and international character and served as the basis for its claim to being the unique instrument of the world proletarian revolution. The revolutionaries who created the Red Army saw it as a product of the revolution and an institution that was distinct from the Russian army of World War I. This was to be a workers' and peasants' army. The Bolsheviks compared it with earlier revolutionary armies: Cromwell's New Model Army, the army of the French Jacobins, and the militia of the Paris Communards. The very idea that this army could be reformed was an ideological contradiction because reform was a bourgeois term implying orderly change and continuity. As D. Fedotoff-White has pointed out in his history of the Red Army, "The process of change from the old army to the new was not that of evolution. It was decidedly a revolutionary one, and a clear break is easily seen between the agony of the first and the birth of the second."[8] This new army was the product of war and revolution. The very titles of its military periodicals proclaimed that linkage: *Voyna i revolyutsiya* (War and revolution), *Revolyutsiya i voyna* (Revolution and war), *Armiya i revolyutsiya* (Army and revolution), *Voyennaya nauka i revolyutsiya* (Military science and revolution), and *Voyennaya mysl– i revolyutsiya* (Military thought and revolution). In dramatic contradistinction it was the various white armies, defeated by the Red Army in the Russian civil war, that claimed to be the heirs of the tsarist army.

The Red Guards and the Red Army

When the Bolsheviks came to power their only military units were radicalized formations from the tsarist army and navy and workers' militia, that is, the Red Guards, formed in the revolutionary upheaval of 1917. The Red Guards, as Rex Wade has pointed out, were voluntary formations formed spontaneously within factories and enterprises by workers wanting to protect themselves and the revolution. Though only a small portion of the empire's population, workers exercised a leading role in the revolution of 1917 because of their level of organization, cohesion, and dynamism.[9] These formations were the very antithesis of regular formations and were noteworthy for their radical democratization as embodied in the concept of *komitetshchina* (the cult of decision making by committee), in their egalitarianism (that is, the popular election of officers and the abolition of ranks), and in their politicization (that is, their commitment to giving all power to the soviets, to the popular class-oriented councils of workers, and to soldiers' deputies who exercised both executive and legislative authority). Their conscious model was the army of the Paris commune.[10] The very existence of the Red Guards was a confirmation of what Lenin described as "dual power," the unstable struggle for power between the provisional government and the soviets of workers' and soldiers' deputies. Another manifestation of this situation was the widespread political agitation within the Russian army between February and October 1917 in which the Bolsheviks played a prominent and subversive role.

In the face of this agitation the provisional government under Alexander Kerensky had already carried the process of politicization within the army forward by creating the position of political officer to oversee the loyalty and political education of officers and men, although it did not save that government from a massive political disaffection during and after the Kornilov affair (an attempt by Gen. Lavr Kornilov to advance on Petrograd in order to impose order and continue the war). By October 1917 the Bolsheviks could count upon the Red Guards as well as army and navy units in Petrograd for support in overthrowing the provisional government under the slogans "All Power to the Soviets!" and "Bread, Land, and Peace!"

Soviet power thus had a markedly democratic and decentralized character. In military terms it relied upon volunteerism to raise troops that were initially needed to carry out the consolidation of power and strangle the challenge to Soviet legitimacy that came from the democratically elected constituent assembly, which was sent packing after only one day in session. Red Guards were asked to volunteer to serve when and where the revolution needed them and they responded, providing a cohort of ideologically committed troops for far-off fronts as the revolutionary government sought to consolidate its authority throughout the country. Once in power Lenin and the Bolsheviks also sought to turn the world war into a world revolution. However, this effort failed and, faced with the prospect of renewed war they set out to create a revolutionary army for the new state.

Here they confronted a number of contradictions within their own ideology. On the one hand European social democrats, of which the Bolsheviks formed the most radical, internationalist element, had spent decades struggling against the evil of militarism (by which they meant professional military establishments created to defend and protect the internal status quo and the external interests of the ruling classes). The common assumptions of such social democrats prior to World War I had been that a citizens' militia (as opposed to a mass, conscript army) and the general strike were the preferred instruments for preventing the use of the army for either external or internal functions against the interests of the working class. When the guns of August roared and Europe plunged into a general, protracted war, however, Europe's social democrats split into three camps: nationalists who supported or at least accepted their nation's cause, pacifists who opposed the war in general, and internationalists who sought to turn the "imperialist war" into the world revolution. Lenin and the Bolsheviks were consistent supporters of the last position and so brought into play a number of key assumptions: a distrust of the military establishment as the embodiment of militarism; a strong sentiment in favor of a militia system as both democratic and revolutionary; a clear requirement that the new military draw its strength from among the working class, that is, industrial workers and poor peasants, in order to sustain its class character and loyalty to the regime; and an internationalism that accepted the notion of national, class-based formations to spread the revolution. Finally, on the basis of their analysis of the fate of revolutionary movements in power, especially the commune, they were committed to the use of Red terror to preempt the inevitable White terror and to sustain their hold on power. For this reason one of the first acts of the new regime was to create the All-Russian Extraordinary Commission for the Struggle with the Counter-Revolution and Sabotage (Chrezvychaynaya Komissiya po bor'be s Kontrrevolyutsiey i Sabotazhem or *cheka*) under Felix Dzerzhinski. Taken as a whole the regime's values negated those of the old regular army as well as the political ideas that had informed the army's training as a regular, conscript force officered by men drawn from the old elites who were loyal to the tsar and mother Russia. The RKKA was a class army drawn from the proletariat and peasantry. It was also internationalist, accepting the creation of national formations that were often based on partisan detachments willing to fight for national liberation and Soviet power.

These assumptions guided the disbandment of the old army in late 1917 and early 1918. The new groups floundered, however, when the Bolsheviks found that they could not radicalize the Central Powers but instead would have to make peace with them. When the negotiations at Brest-Litovsk collapsed after Trotsky unilaterally declared the war over and the German army renewed its advance, the regime called for an end to demobilization and demanded the formation of a new army. The call for volunteers and a scorched-earth policy went hand in hand with intensified class warfare against the possessing classes, which were deemed to be the natural allies of the external enemy. Any sign of resistance was to be met with immediate violent measures. Throughout the civil war the Soviet state would rely on worker and communist volunteers to provide the backbone of their units in times of crisis and during major operations. On 23 February 1918 *Pravda*, the newspaper of the central committee of the Bolshevik party, called upon all workers, peasants, and soldiers to defend the socialist republic from the German White guards.[11] Five days later, as the German advance continued and the Red Army screening forces proved ineffective, various units began to call upon "comrade soldiers and former officers" to defend the revolution and freedom.[12] Desperation forced a radical shift in Bolshevik military policy.

Military Specialists and the Red Army

The second influence on reform was the legacy the Red Army inherited from the tsarist army, especially the imperial general staff that it absorbed via the military specialists (*voyenspetsy*). These specialists were former tsarist officers whom the Bolsheviks had incorporated into their military structure to meet the threat of the German advance in the winter of 1918; to lead Red Army units in the first battles of the civil war; later to oversee the creation of a mass army based upon general conscription; and, finally, to staff this army's central institutions and high command. Distrustful of class enemies overseeing the direction of its army, the Bolsheviks created a system of dual command by regular officers and political commissars to maintain an effective and loyal force. Fearing that their revolution would follow the path of France after 1789, the Bolsheviks worried about a Bonapartist threat from within their own military and sought to overcome it by creating a politically indoctrinated and ideologically loyal military elite. This elite would be drawn from the ranks of junior officers who joined the party. One of the tasks of the military specialists, in addition to providing professional leadership to win the civil war, was to train this cadre of young, politically conscious Red commanders to replace the military specialists themselves. The Red commanders, having fought the civil war in the field and been politically indoctrinated by the party, were supposed to be immune to any Bonapartist sentiments.

Although in some respects they could be considered heirs of the military specialists, the Red commanders sought to create a military theory based upon their own experience during the civil war that would be informed by communist political and ideological assumptions. This desire had a profound influence on their vision of future war and the military instrument necessary to fight such a conflict. With the end of the civil war and the associated crisis of war communism, the regime entered into an unstable transition period marked by a consolidation of party control, military demobilization, a retreat from the immediate construction of a communist society, and an experiment with a mixed market system to bring about economic recovery and stability that Lenin called the NEP. This coincided with the political struggle for leadership following Lenin's incapacitation and death. The debate between military specialists and young Red commanders during this period involved significant contributions to military theory and art that had long-term implications for the reform of the Red Army even after many of its participants had become nonpersons, dead at the hand of the regime they served.

In order to stem the immediate military crisis facing the regime Lenin badgered his colleagues into accepting the bitter terms imposed by the Central Powers. Lenin denounced the calls for revolutionary war as "so much phrase making." Brest-Litovsk was, according to Lenin, a "Tilsit peace," designed to buy time while the new state gained the strength to defend itself, consolidate its hold on power, and challenge the agreement by the export of its revolution. Germany and its allies were imposing a harsh peace on the Soviet regime just as Napoleon had imposed one upon Russia in 1807. While Lenin believed the international socialist proletariat would come to the aid of the Soviet regime, he also stressed the need to consolidate Soviet power and to build up the new army for the tests that were sure to come.[13]

When analyzing their own situation, that is, coming to power in the least advanced capitalist country or the most advanced underdeveloped country, the Bolsheviks looked to two processes for their salvation: the world revolutionary process (which was to disappoint them bitterly) and the radical transformation of the Russian state along the lines of a socialist democracy of decentralized power and authority. In military terms this meant an army of volunteers drawn from class-conscious elements among industrial workers and poor peasants. The training of a manpower pool for the new army was a top priority. In the spring of 1918 the All-Russian Central Executive Committee, or Vsesoyuznyy Tsentrail'nyy Ispolnitel'nyy Komitet (VTSIK), decreed obligatory military training but not service for all workers and peasants "who did not exploit others' labor." To direct this training program the VTSIK created the Universal Military Administration (Vsevobuch). The training was put into the hands of Red Guards as well as former tsarist soldiers, noncommissioned officers, and officers loyal to the new regime.[14] Given the sizeable manpower pool that had been trained and had gained combat experience during World War I, the Bolsheviks assumed that a large army could be quickly trained and fielded. Sergei Gusev, who would later become a strong advocate of a regular army, wrote of the ease with which a Soviet army might be created.[15]

The task proved anything but easy. As the threat to the regime in 1918 evolved from that of the Central Powers to the various white forces sponsored by the Entente on Russia's periphery, the challenge to the regime's survival became more and more serious. Early white successes in the fall of 1918 brought their armies into the Urals only to be stopped by the newly raised Red Army. Another round of revolutionary enthusiasm associated with the collapse of imperial Germany and the Habsburg Monarchy in the fall and winter of 1918 failed once again to deliver the world revolution and end the isolation of the Soviet regime. Now forced to rely upon its own resources the regime mobilized for a total struggle.

When the civil war became serious and significant military challenges emerged on the Russian periphery, the regime shifted its economic policy toward a variant of state capitalism that had been practiced by the major belligerents of World War I. In the face of civil war, famine, and industrial chaos, the regime sought to establish centralized control over production, distribution, and utilization of all the state's resources. The model was one of a large industrial enterprise in which all aspects of production were subject to centralized discipline. This revolutionary policy took apart the existing remnants of the national economy, nationalized many of them, and mobilized for the war effort. The Communist Party, the new name taken by the Bolsheviks to reflect their revolutionary program, became the bridge between front and rear. War communism rested upon forced extraction of resources and sustained production to support a total war effort. Because the forced requisition of grain continued, middle peasants continued to feel alienated. Furthermore, because this policy also sought to replace volunteers with conscripts that included the independence-minded peasantry, it brought the question of the peasantry into the very heart of the Red Army. It also made for tense relations between the Red Army and the peasantry in many theaters, tensions that would turn into peasant revolts in the aftermath of the civil war.

Lacking in tactical sophistication, adequate command and control, reliable logistics, and stable troops, the Red Army found itself limited in both tactical effectiveness and operational endurance. Early failures highlighted the need for urgent reforms. Successes often depended upon the use of "ram tactics" to break a White Army position and subsequent actions by partisans (*partizanshchina*) to disrupt its reconstitution. This combination of ram and partisan tactics became the dominant form of warfare in early stage of the civil war but it had serious disadvantages. The partisans proved to be politically and militarily unreliable. Additionally, the regime sought to use the poor peasants against the rich peasants (*kulaks*) to effect the forced requisitioning of grain. This policy, however, alienated the vast majority of the rural population who, with the transfer of gentry, church, and state lands to their control, were now self-sufficient smallholders. Thus the middle peasants who made up the partisan detachments had not been neutralized as the party had hoped. They refused to accept central authority, fought for local interests, and were prone to anarchist sympathies. Red Army units that fought in the line with partisan units often were infected with these same values, thus threatening discipline and control. By the end of the civil war, most Red commanders viewed *partizanshchina* as a threat to order in the army and society. As a rural population based on family and communal ties, the peasantry was hostile to the organizing tendencies of the Communist Party as it sought to build a regular, conscript army. Mikhail Frunze, an old Bolshevik with both theoretical and practical military expertise, noted this problem when he commanded on the eastern front.[16]

The new national army, while retaining its class nature, came to reject both *komitetshchina* and *partizanshchina* in favor of a regular, conscript army led by professional officers, reinforced by levies of communists, overseen by political commissars, and penetrated by the Special

Sections (Osobye Otdely) of the CHEKA. Lenin, the most professional of revolutionaries, made Leon Trotsky the first people's commissar of military (and later naval) affairs. Trotsky agreed with Lenin about the need to enlist tsarist officers, that is, military specialists (*voyenspetsy*) to provide professional leadership for the new army. As chairman of the Revolutionary-Military Council (Revvoyensovet), Trotsky recognized his own lack of military expertise; as a political figure, however, he understood the importance of competent professional leadership to guide the creation, deployment, and utilization of the Red Army.[17] When left-wing communists objected to the recruitment of military specialists, arguing that no references to such a policy could be found in the works of Marx or Engels, Lenin replied that this problem had not existed for the fathers of communism because it only arose when a revolutionary socialist regime came to power and embarked upon the building of the Red Army.[18]

The military specialists' leadership began at the level of tactical command and extended to the field staffs, special services, and national command authorities. Ironically, as the Revolutionary Military Council of the Republic noted in 1919, "the higher the command category, the fewer the number of communists we can find for it."[19] Thus the two commanders in chief of the Red Army during the civil war were military specialists: I. I. Vatsetis and S. S. Kamenev, both of whom had been colonels in the tsarist army. Indeed, military specialists dominated the senior positions at the center, at the fronts, and in the armies and divisions.[20] This kind of leadership also encompassed military training, education, and publications, and extended to the study of the lessons to be drawn from World War I. Enlisting "class enemies" was a calculated risk that the regime proved willing to take so long as it could count on political oversight, blackmail, and terror to keep the specialists in line. As Ya. M. Sverdlov, a leading old Bolshevik, wrote, the military specialists were a necessary evil for the Red Army: "[I]n order to be armed for modern war we need the specialists, but we have no specialists of our own and therefore we decided to take specialists from the other camp. But in order to protect ourselves from these specialists in case of the organization of a counter-revolution, we have placed them under such strict control, it would be difficult for them to do anything. If even under this watchful eye they should try to do something, then as we have told them they will be immediately shot."[21] The system of dual command exercised by the military specialist in his area of professional competence and by the military commissar in the political arena was supposed to provide effective oversight. It could not, however, completely prevent disaffections, desertions, and even betrayals to the enemy by some specialists.

While the Red Army was born to meet the immediate threat of a German advance in the west, it took its initial form during the civil war and intervention that began in the spring of 1918 with the revolt of the Czech Legion in Siberia then assumed a massive scale to combat the White armies and interventionist forces arrayed around the periphery of the Soviet state. Because troops were desperately needed at the various fronts the state moved to achieve greater control over the army and to regularize military service. By late 1918 Trotsky had rejected both the Red Guard model that had failed against the German advance and the partisan model that had not stopped the Whites' advances in the fall. Trotsky handed to the military specialists the task of writing new service and garrison regulations as well as disciplinary codes. He also introduced other elements of a regular army including a standard uniform and insignia of rank.[22] These initiatives pushed leftist communists in the Red Army to attack the entire program of using military specialists. Their criticisms were directed at Trotsky on two grounds: his sponsorship of the military specialists and his efforts to establish centralized control of the entire military establishment. Both issues came to a head at the eighth party congress in the spring of 1919.

Furthermore, during the civil war some Red commanders and party figures blamed military specialists for their own failures, as in the case of Stalin and his deputy, K. E. Voroshilov, in Tsaritsyn. Thus the debate over the legitimacy of military specialists marked the beginning of a political quarrel between Trotsky and Stalin that ultimately turned into the struggle for control of the communist movement after Lenin's death. At the eighth congress, while facing of a powerful military opposition, the party approved the policy of retaining the military specialists provided they were kept under the watchful eye of political commissars. It also accepted mass conscription as the manpower basis for the Red Army. Additionally, the party shifted its policy toward the middle peasantry in order bring them into an alliance with the urban proletariat and the poor peasantry and thereby broaden the regime's base of support.

To find officers for the new army the Bolsheviks drew upon the *voyenspetsy*, who made up the great majority of its senior leaders. Military schools and academies were re-established and given the task of creating Red commanders, that is, a new cohort of officers who by social background, political orientation, and party membership would be loyal to the new regime. But their teachers were former tsarist officers. There consequently developed a fundamental tension between the professional officers of the old army and the new Red commanders who were politicized and saw the Red Army as both the organizational and ideological expression of Soviet power. While a very few military specialists eventually joined the Communist Party, most did not. Instead the vast majority, as A. G. Kavtaradze has pointed out, adopted the position of apolitical professional service to the Soviet Russian Republic.[23] Their ideology might best be described as supporting a powerful Russian state. In the training of the new officers the military specialists relied upon the techniques and methods developed by the tsarist army, thereby creating an unacknowledged bond between the old army and the new.

Thus the Red Army had access to the imperial army's approach to training. This legacy can be seen in the institutional continuities in higher military schools and academies, in military publications, and in training traditions. The Frunze Military Academy founded in 1918 and the Academy of the General Staff (spun off the Frunze in the 1930s) were both heirs of the Nikolaevsk Academy of the general staff of the imperial army. *Voyennaya mysl'* (Military thought), which can trace its roots back to *Voyennoye delo* (Military affairs, founded in 1918), has its roots in *Voyennyy sbornik* (Military digest), the imperial army's theoretical journal. In the navy's case a single title covers the entire period from 1849 to the present: *Morskoy sbornik* (Naval digest). What was distinctive in the Soviet publications was the imposition of Communist Party control, which made the military press ideologically conditioned to and immersed in the political struggles of the party leadership. In the area of troop training the traditions of the imperial army survived. Thus training for combat situations continued to have top priority with the specialists training the Red Army, just as Marsh. Alexander Suvorov had recommended in his *The Art of Victory* (published in the late eighteenth century) and Gen. Mikhail Dragomirov had taught (in the late nineteenth century). Likewise, in an army drawn from the Russian peasantry instruction in basic literacy remained a prominent ingredient of military training.

Until the Russo-Japanese War the training of individual units had been left in the hands of the commanders of the various military districts, who adapted the training program to fit their own particular styles and approaches. After Milyutin's reforms the Ministry of War decreed that the training year should be divided into two parts: winter and summer. The first period after induction was devoted to drill, adaptation to unit life, and small unit training. The summers were devoted to unit and formation training and exercises. Maneuvers and exercises were conducted by troops within a military district, between two military districts, or among several military districts. The exercises could be one-sided, two-sided with free play, or one-sided with a designated opposing force. Although a very expensive activity, the War Ministry viewed such maneuvers with troops as both a necessary training device and a way of developing and testing new concepts and approaches in military art. Command-staff exercises and staff rides were also used to train officers.[24] Under this system the center of gravity for training was the military district and the regiment. This approach built an army of good battalions and regiments but had severe weaknesses at the division, corps, army, and front command levels, a point recognized by reformers after the Russo-Japanese War but not successfully resolved. Carried over into the Soviet period this approach to training led to an emphasis upon competent junior officers and noncommissioned officers, both trained within their regiments. The model officer was a knowledgeable, professional small-unit commander. As one instructor observed, the goal was not to train young Napoleons but rather to train "Captain Tushins," an allusion to the battery commander in Tolstoy's *War and Peace* whose precise execution of battle drills had kept his guns covering the Russian withdrawal after the battle of Austerlitz. Professional competence in small-unit leaders was to have first priority. Indeed, most of the newly trained young Red officers served under military specialists who commanded the regiments of the Red Army. The new Captain Tushins, however, also received political indoctrination in keeping with Marxist ideology and the class spirit of the Red Army.[25]

The tsarist army had also conducted large-scale maneuvers involving the forces of one, two, or several military districts. Assessments of the value of such exercises differ among contemporary officers and historians. Gen. Aleksei Kuropatkin, the war minister and future commander in chief in Manchuria, categorized such maneuvers as costly but vital. P. A. Zaionchkovsky, a leading historian of the Russian army, raised serious doubts about their value in his study of that institution in the late nineteenth and early twentieth centuries. M. A. Gareev, an experienced soldier and military theorist, while noting the weaknesses of these maneuvers and exercises evaluated them as having had a positive influence on the imperial army and a foundation upon which the Red Army could build.[26]

Another of the legacies of the tsarist army that profoundly influenced the Red Army was the debate surrounding military reform and new field regulations following the Russo-Japanese War. A. A. Neznamov had provided the intellectual leadership for the reform movement under the banner of understanding the nature of "modern war." Experience in Manchuria pointed to a number of deficiencies in tactics, especially combined arms combat, which reformers pointed out in the postwar period. Actual combat experience in Manchuria drew attention to serious problems in fire and maneuver capabilities and led reformers to call for tactics in offense and defense that took into account the impact of modern arms. This experience also led to recommendations for more effective use of terrain in the attack and defense. Effective use of all arms in tactical combat required a common understanding of the dynamics of combat. Neznamov focused on three interrelated problems that had reduced Russian combat effectiveness in Manchuria: the lack of initiative among junior commanders in tactics, the ineffective troop control of large units in operations, and the lack of an agreed-upon approach to combined arms combat at all levels. On the last point Neznamov had suggested that the solution was to develop a military doctrine that would provide a common understanding of terms, techniques, and procedures. The field service regulation of 1912, which served the tsarist army throughout World War I, set off a debate over the need for and dangers of a military doctrine. The debate over military doctrine in the Russian military press continued until Nicholas II ended it by stating that Russia's military doctrine was what its sovereign said it was. The Tsar's decree did not, however, end agitation by reformers for a military doctrine. Thus the debate over a unified military doctrine, which Mikhail Frunze and Sergei Gusev initiated after the civil war, can be looked upon as a continuation of the tsarist army's debate but with the venue changed to the military circles of the Communist Party.[27]

At the same time the education of selected Red Army officers for senior command and staff assignments also went forward. While it is true that some of these officers, such as the legendary Vasiliy Ivanovich Chapayev (1887–1919), did not take to such professional training, others did. These officers were particularly fortunate that the seasonal pace of campaigning during the civil war permitted them to combine formal academic study at the military academy with active operations and thus test against their own practical experience the theories of military art they received in the classroom. Unlike the military amateurs, such as the former worker Klimenty Voroshilov and the former NCO Semen Budenny, both of whom surrounded Stalin, these officers combined their ideology and experience with serious study of the military art.

A cohort of young Red commanders who emerged from this process began to speak of a proletarian military art and revolutionary warfare, which they saw as having unique features and being the model for future revolutionary struggles. The most prominent of these commanders, Mikhail Tukhachevsky, was a junior guards officer who had served in World War I, been captured, escaped after repeated attempts, and joined the Red Army in 1918 as "one of the few military specialists of the Communist Party."[28] Tukhachevsky went on to command various armies during the civil war and in 1920 led the western front in its unsuccessful attempt to capture Warsaw.

The peculiar conditions surrounding the civil war—the low density of forces, a weak and often interrupted logistical system, underdeveloped command and control mechanisms, and chronic combat instability— made it distinctly different from World War I. In World War I the tsarist army was never able to translate its occasional tactical and operational successes into strategic victory. In the civil war, however, the use of the ram and partisan method under optimal conditions, such as those experienced in Siberia against Adm. Alexander Kolchak, did lead to strategic success. Later in the civil war the idea of using mobile forces to disrupt a defense and bring about an enemy collapse through deep raids became part of Red Army doctrine. The Whites had achieved excellent results using a cavalry corps during Gen. Konstantin Mamontov's cavalry raid; the Reds subsequently developed this organizational form for deep penetrations into cavalry armies, eventually using them against Gen. Anton Denikin during the ill-fated Polish campaign of 1920 and during Frunze's final assault on Gen. Peter Wrangel's positions. Red commanders thus came to believe that such mobile operations and the use of partisans were manifestations of a new revolutionary style of warfare not connected to specific theater conditions. They began to link such mobile warfare with the export of the revolution, reasoning that a combination of shock and deep penetration would not only disorganize a defense and create panic but also set off a class struggle in the enemy's rear. The First Cavalry Army, created in late 1919 and commanded by the former tsarist noncommissioned officer Semen Budenny, played a critical role in the final campaign against General Denikin, led the Red advance into the Ukraine against the Poles in the spring of 1920, and was employed with the Second Cavalry Army by Frunze against Baron Wrangel's forces in the conquest of the Crimea.

By the end of the Civil War, in late 1920, the Red Army had 5.5 million men under arms, but most of these were in rear and support services. It was, as Sheila Fitzpatrick has pointed out, the preeminent bureaucratic institution of the Soviet state.[29] In the summer of 1920 the party and state sought to use this instrument to spread the revolution and ignite the world on its bayonets. The Red Army's most ambitious campaign, that of the Polish-Soviet War, ended in the defeat of Mikhail Tukhachevsky's forces on the outskirts of Warsaw in August 1920, which significantly dampened the prospects of using the Red Army as the instrument of world revolution. The causes of the Warsaw defeat became one of the most hotly debated topics among Soviet military reformers in the 1920s. This argument also became entangled with high politics because the First Cavalry Army, for which Stalin had acted as Budenny's political commissar, had attacked toward Lvov rather than Lublin and thereby failed to support Tukhachevsky at a critical moment in the campaign. Military specialists who rejected revolutionary warfare pointed to Warsaw as a clear sign that revolutionary élan was no substitute for a proper understanding of military science or the effective application of military art.[30] Tukhachevsky complained about the lack of support from First Cavalry Army. In truth the Red Army had tried to do too much with too little. After this debacle the national economy was in ruins and significant opposition to the regime in the countryside and within the military itself still existed. Having defeated the White forces in the civil war the Red Army next did battle against its own sailors at Kronstadt and the peasant "greens" who fought against communist power for retention of their own village rights, particularly in areas such as Tambov in 1921. Here Tukhachevsky implacably rooted out counterrevolutionary forces by using the so-called special sections to seize hostages in villages that supported the "bandits" and employing poison gas against rebel bands that had fled into the woods.[31]

The New Economic Policy (NEP) and the Red Army

The emergence of a debate over military doctrine, the nature of military art, and the role of operational art as a specific topic of study within the Red Army coincided with the end of the civil war, the introduction of the NEP at home, and the recognition of a temporary restabilization of the world capitalist system. The party's leadership and the military had to deal with the pressing problem of postwar demobilization and the creation of a military system that would provide standing cadre forces and mobilization potential. This included the establishment or maintenance of national formations on a territorial or cadre basis to provide extended mobilization potential in all areas of the union. The party and state tied military policy to the demands of its overall nationality policy.[32] By the mid-1920s, and simultaneously with Lenin's death and Trotsky's removal from the post of commissar of war, these reforms were enacted under the party's new collective leadership. The military reforms of this period were thus closely tied to the political struggle over the succession to party leadership.

Specifically, Soviet military reforms begun by Frunze in the 1920s became embroiled in the struggle between Stalin and Trotsky for political power. The result, when the former ultimately triumphed over the latter, was a military system that rejected Trotsky's concept of "permanent revolution" in favor of Stalin's "socialism in one country." Before his untimely and mysterious death under a surgeon's knife in 1925, Frunze oversaw a series of measures that created a mixed cadre and territorial system and a smaller standing force of about a half-million men. These so-called Frunze reforms introduced the concept of unity of command to the RKKA, abolished the political commissars, and provided the basis for a mass-mobilization army and the militarization of Soviet society to support this force. The war scare of 1927, which highlighted the regime's isolation, reinforced calls for militarization. The Soviet state was, however, still a predominantly rural society in which peasantry and agriculture dominated. This was a Russia with no illusions about fighting short wars of annihilation, and its preferred strategy was to use time and space to mobilize for a war of attrition.

There was, however, an inherent tension between a system dominated by a party elite and a limited base of industrial workers and a society that was predominantly rural and peasant. This was particularly true by the late stages of the NEP when urban unemployment began to mount and the regime became increasingly concerned with placing economic power in the hands of the peasantry, especially the *kulaks*. The communists continued to view the peasantry as an unstable social class which could, under the threat of external attack, become an internal ally of counterrevolution. Thus one of the key areas of militarization after the reforms of 1925 was the use of the Red Army as a school to create the military manifestation of a workers-peasants alliance (*smychka*).[33]

By the late 1920s Red commanders were openly calling for massive industrialization to support the creation of a large mechanized army. But the regime had another immediate use for military cadres: employing them in carrying out the forced collectivization of the countryside upon which the party embarked in late 1927. The nature of these duties and the decline of professionalism within the Red Army alarmed senior military commanders. By 1930 warning signs from the units deployed to support collectivization indicated that if the regime persisted in the use of the army to impose the regime's will on a stubborn and hostile peasantry under the slogan "eliminate the *kulak* as a class," the army would crack.[34] In the midst of this crisis Stalin announced the regime's retreat and blamed the excesses that were taken on lower officials who were "dizzy with the heights of success." Stalin's decision allowed the young Red commanders to devote their attention to their favorite topic: the conduct of large-scale operations with industrialized mass armies.

Red Army Reform and the Birth of Operational Art

In January 1924 a plenum of the party's central committee created a special commission under the chairmanship of Sergei Ivanovich Gusev to study the condition of the Red Army. In March Frunze was appointed deputy commissar for military and naval affairs. On 6 April he was named chief of the RKKA staff and less than two weeks later was named chief of the military academy of the RKKA. In May the thirteenth party congress approved the commission's reform program to strengthen combat readiness and combat capabilities and to carry out a purge of Trotsky's supporters within the commissariat. The program called for a mixed cadre-and-territorial militia system for raising the force and introduced other measures to improve military education and strengthen party control over the armed forces.[35] In the anti-Trotsky battle over succession, Stalin and his supporters could use the substantive differences over military doctrine between Trotsky and Frunze to recruit the latter in the political struggle with the former. Within this context Frunze was entrusted with the task of putting these reform measures into practice. For him, as for the party leadership, the nature of the threat confronting the Soviet state was quite clear. As opposed to Trotsky, who had told the Red Army's leadership that it should use the postwar period to master mundane matters of troop leadership and leave strategy to the party, Frunze had explicitly defined the threat posed by capitalist encirclement as one demanding constant vigilance and military preparations:

Between our proletarian state and the rest of the bourgeois world there can only be one condition—that of a long, persistent, desperate war to the death: a war which demands colossal tenacity, steadfastness, inflexibility, and a unity of will. . . . The state of open warfare may give way to some sort of contractual relationship that permits, up to a certain level, the peaceful coexistence of the warring sides. These contractual forms do not change the fundamental character of these relations. . . . The common, parallel existence of our proletarian Soviet state with the states of the bourgeois world for a protracted period is impossible.[36]

This threat created the need to study future war (*budushchaya voyna*) not as an abstract proposition but as a foreseeable contingency that would guide war planning in peacetime. In the 1920s the study of past campaigns, military theory, current trends in weapons development, and force structure requirements coalesced around the concept of operational art (*operativnoye iskusstvo*).

The foremost personalities in this development were A. A. Svechin, Frunze, and Tukhachevsky, each of whom wrote widely, promoted the development of military scientific societies, and identified a group of talented officers, some of whom were destined to become the first members of the Red general staff (*genshtabisty*). Many of these officers entered the military academy during Tukhachevsky's short tenure as its commandant in 1921–22. Others came later when Frunze took over as commissar of war. Two of the most prominent Red *genshtabisty* were N. E. Varfolomeev and V. K. Triandafillov.

During the academy's first few postwar years the problem of developing a new paradigm with which to articulate the realities of modern warfare remained unresolved. The academy's academic program reflected the conventional categories of strategy and tactics, but new terms were being used to describe the more complex combat of World War I and the civil war. "Grand tactics" and "lower strategy" were employed but without rigor or definition. Given the scale and scope of the campaigns of the civil war, especially regarding their area and decisiveness, some proponents of a unified military doctrine began to speak of these campaigns as "strategic" events.

The development of the "operational art" concept was closely connected with the evolution of higher military education in the post–civil war period. In this area Svechin played a prominent role by promoting the study of military classics and interpreting the core of military strategy for the academy's students. His goal was to provide for them a context in which to study the evolution of military art and thereby grasp the salient features of World War I and the civil war that would shape its further evolution. This process included a major translation effort of foreign military works such as Carl von Clausewitz's *On War*; memoirs of senior commanders from World War I that included Erich Ludendorff, Franz Conrad von Hötzendorf, and Erich von Falkenhayn; and recent theoretical works such as Alfred von Schlieffen's *Cannae*. Svechin's broad and profound contributions to this endeavor included editing and providing commentary on selected essays on strategy written by military theorists from the eighteenth to the twentieth century.[37]

Svechin did not tackle the problem of redefining the content of military art until the period of 1923 to 1924. At this point he proposed adding an intermediary category between strategy and tactics which he referred to as "operational art." He defined this term as the "totality of maneuvers and battles in a given part of a theater of military action directed toward the achievement of the common goal, set as final in the given period of the campaign."[38] Svechin's rationale for the three-fold structure of military art was that the former two-fold division had been based on the concept of "the general engagement" (the decisive, single battle), which had disappeared in practice.[39] Svechin's lectures on this subject served as the basis for his work *Strategiya* (*Strategy*), which appeared in 1926. In it he elaborated on the nature of operational art and its relationship to strategy and tactics.[40] Svechin formulated the relation thusly: "Then, battle is the means of the operation. Tactics are the material of operational art. The operation is the means of strategy, and operational art is the material of strategy. This is the essence of the three-part formula given above."[41]

Svechin's conceptualization of operational art coincided with Frunze's appointment as chief of staff of the RKKA and chief of the military academy. At Frunze's initiative a chair of army operations was established at the academy in 1924, but it did not survive for long.[42] Originally the operational portion of the academy's curriculum emphasized general commentary more than practical preparation. Typical of this literature was M. Bonch-Bruevich's essay on principles of operational leadership in modern war, which described the content of an operational plan: mission statement, intelligence on enemy forces and their probable courses of action, information on the status of one's own forces, the specific missions of subordinate units, the structure of rear services, the organization of supply, and the support of the operation. Bonch-Bruevich emphasized the role of the organs of troop control in turning the commander's intent into an operational plan and outlined the various areas where the staff had to conduct its estimates of the situation. His extensive list of such activities encompassed all aspects of operational planning. Bonch-Bruevich emphasized that the art of troop control was critical to operational leadership and pointed out the role of the struggle for time in "all preparatory actions and during execution."[43]

Frunze invigorated the academy's higher military-academic course for senior Red Army commanders and focused it on the further education of brigade and higher-level commanders.[44] Frunze's commitment to this program brought more attention to the strategy chair and led to its further development. Frunze also shifted the focus of operational instruction from general observations about the nature of operations to the practical details and techniques for their conduct.[45] Over the next several years Frunze's efforts led to the development of a program of operational war gaming in which students were expected to make the calculations and produce the estimates necessary to prepare for an army-level operation. Frunze's approach of unifying theory and practice in the education and training of future commanders and staff officers constituted a major break with past Russian tradition, which had tended to keep the conceptual and the practical in separate compartments. Triandafillov, Varfolomeev, and K. Berends were the academy's leading spirits in the actual development of operational war gaming as a pedagogic technique.[46] Because it embraced action along a major operational axis in a war against one of the most probable future opponents of the Soviet state, the Polish campaign of 1920 served as both a model and a case study for such operational gaming.

Tukhachevsky, who served as deputy chief of staff to Frunze from 1924 to 1925, took over the strategy chair. He worked closely and effectively with Svechin though their strategic concepts were radically different. Each man had his own set of supporters within the academy. It seemed that as long as Frunze lived their differences were argued out in a spirited but collegial fashion. Shortly after Frunze's death, however, this situation changed dramatically. In early 1926 at a special conference held to debate the merits of strategies of attrition (*izmor*) and annihilation (*sokrushenie*), faculty members from the military academy and officers of the main staff of the RKKA took opposing sides.[47]

Svechin's views on the advantages of a strategy of attrition were significantly influenced by his assumptions about the protracted nature of a future war and the relative inability of Soviet Russia to mount a decisive initial blow against a major opponent. This led him to turn his attention to the problem of linking national strategy to prewar preparation for war. Here he emphasized the need to address both political and economic preparation of the nation for war. Svechin argued that Russian statesmen in the nineteenth century had surmised that after Napoleon's defeat Russia was as invulnerable as England. Its great distances, they assumed, played the same role as the Channel did for England, making invasion and strategic defeat impossible. Svechin labeled such ideas "dangerous illusions."[48] In his formulation of the alternative strategic concepts of annihilation and attrition, a host of issues regarding the relationship between operational art and the paradigm of future war quickly emerged as topics for debate. Drawing upon the work of Hans Delbrück, Svechin also criticized the German general staff's misguided attempt to conduct decisive operations in the initial period of World War I.[49] Svechin saw the seeds of disaster in such short-war illusions. Given the geostrategic and political situation confronting the USSR, he stressed the need to prepare for a long war.

Here Svechin emphasized the political and economic objectives of strategy rather than an immediate attempt to annihilate the enemy's armed forces. He defended the Russian general staff's 1912–14 assessment of the problems of deploying its forces in the initial period of a war against Germany and Austria-Hungary. Where it had gone wrong, Svechin argued, was tying Russian war plans to French requirements for immediate offensive operations particularly when the mobilization, concentration, and deployment of forces could not be completed in a timely manner. Svechin noted that the Russian reforms of 1908–09 had been designed to move the weight of the army away from the frontier in order to provide greater depth for deployment. For him the most central and conspicuous problem was the commitment to the initial forward deployment of Russian forces in Poland. The proper Russian answer to the Schlieffen plan was not plans "A" and "G" with their immediate offensive objectives in East Prussia or Galicia. A "Russian Schlieffen Plan" was an invitation to disaster: "Plans of deployment are two-sided affairs, affecting each side. This the author seems to forget. The Russian General Staff was not running away from an 'apparition' but provoked the transformation of German power along the Russian border into an apparition. By doing that did it betray Russian interests?"[50]

For Svechin the answer to Russia's strategic situation was to pull the forward armies' points of concentration back from the border, trading time for space in order to complete deployments. In the end the very nature of the Russian state made it suited for a strategy of protracted war and attrition:

> The development of the Russian state, as of other states, moved in the direction of preparing it for a protracted war, for attrition, and not annihilation. This process took place unnoticed even by the very leaders of reform in the army. . . . But a cruel evolution led change of preparation of Russian deployment toward attrition. Russia's force for annihilation had not increased during those 14 years [1900–14]. In this direction, which the evolution of Russian military power took, the single correct decision would be not an immediate campaign against Berlin, but a struggle for a further stage of deployment on the front Danzig-Peremyshl'.[51]

This focus led Svechin and others to a consideration of the problem of the relationship between the civilian and military leadership in the conduct of and preparation for war. Svechin argued that one of the legacies of Russia's heritage of frontier warfare was the tendency of military commanders to turn their own rear areas into satrapies in which the immediate supply requirements of front commands took precedence over a rational mobilization of the entire state economy. He criticized such a narrow perception of military logistics and called for a unification of front and rear through the planned mobilization of the entire national economy, which he referred to as the "state rear."[52]

Svechin was not a dogmatist. He understood that his views had been shaped by the experiences of his own generation of general staff officers. He was a professional who appreciated the need for a rigorous and structured approach to the study of combat experience. The key to that method was military history joined with the examination of current military problems. Such military history was "not a lifeless monument but a weapon for struggle in the present, the key to its understanding. Each generation must itself forge a new historical weapon no matter how difficult that might be and master it in order to have the possibility of freely setting off on its own road and not be stuck at the tail of the column behind others."[53]

For his promotion of the general staff and its central role in preparing for war and planning operations, Svechin was attacked by a host of politically minded opponents who accused him of promoting a "narrow-caste group" the class essence of which was hostile to socialism. V. Levichev saw a distinct challenge to the young Red commanders' authority in Svechin's calls for operational art: the knowledge of "the general staff" invested it with a special privileged trust in operational art and insight to the secrets of victories. This special position of officers of the general staff in the army created much internal hatred and open hostility from rank and file commanders, who, because they lacked family connections and the landed titles of officers of the general staff, had no advantages in promotion."[54] According to Levichev the Soviet state had the party to guide its preparations for war. Thus it needed commander-generalists trained to lead regiments and larger formations, not a "narrow group of red military specialists" calling themselves the general staff.[55]

The issue was not simply one of an old caste institution being hostile to a workers' state or even party guidance. The general staff was critical to the development of operational art in practice because it possessed the skills necessary to answer the most pressing military-technical questions associated with planning and preparing for war. Using Conrad von Hötzendorf's memoirs as a vehicle to explore the role of the general staff in modern war and preparations for it, the *voyenspets-genshtabist* Boris Mikhailovich Shaposhnikov characterized that role as "the brain of the army."[56] As Svechin warned in his introduction to *Strategy*, the brain itself had to be educated to grasp the connections between the theory and practice of strategy; no amount of tactical experience would prepare commanders to conduct the operations of large formations in keeping with strategic requirements.[57]

In *Mozg armii* Shaposhnikov stressed the linkage between the political and military sides of doctrine in the process of war planning. Central to this point were Shaposhnikov's invocation of Clausewitz to stress the concept of "war as a continuation of politics by other means" and his assertion of the necessity to fit war and mobilization plans to political requirements rather than the reverse (as had happened in 1914). Indeed, the conception of politics in this case embraced both the international class struggle and that found within each of the belligerents. Whereas Svechin clung to the idea of the general staff as the apolitical agents of a supra-class state, Shaposhnikov, himself a *voyenspets* and yet not a member of the Communist Party, embraced the idea of a politically literate general staff operating under the party's guidance.[58]

Several years ago General of the Army V. N. Lobov brought to light a previously unpublished essay by Svechin entitled "Future War" (*budushchaya voyna*) along with Shaposhnikov's commentary upon it. Lobov noted Svechin's complaint that the Red Army undervalued the importance of strategic defense while Shaposhnikov responded that the roots of that undervaluation were deeply connected to the revolutionary origins of the Red Army. In the same commentary Shaposhnikov introduced a political subtext to the debate: the conflict over annihilation versus attrition. Svechin had assumed that a future war would be a coalition war of east European successor states, sponsored by one or more of the leading capitalist powers, against the Soviet Union. Shaposhnikov accepted this assumption but saw offensive action as the only way in which such a war could be won. Where Svechin had emphasized an indirect approach during the initial period of war (an effort to husband forces and create opportunities to pit stronger Soviet forces against weaker attacking forces away from main axis), Shaposhnikov emphasized the struggle against the main enemy concentration in the field. His rationale was political: "One must not forget that for decision in war it is important to get not just military successes but also political successes, that is, to achieve victory over the politically important enemy. . . . In the other case, only over a protracted period of time, even with accompanying military successes, we will find it necessary to join battle with the main enemy, against whom we only defended initially." Immediate and decisive victories raised the possibility of breaking the enemy coalition and changing the correlation of forces in favor of the Soviet Union.[59] Shaposhnikov argued that by its very nature as a revolutionary force the Red Army was required to use its offensive élan.

Svechin's argument for a national strategy based upon attrition had its roots in his particular vision of Russian society and the historical experience of the world war. His fellow professor and colleague, A. Verkhovsky, enraged the offensive-minded young Red commanders when, in an effort to defend an attrition strategy, he asserted that it might be better in the initial period of a future Polish-Soviet war "to give up Minsk and Kiev than to take Bialystok and Brest." To those who identified Marxism-Leninism with a strictly offensive style of war such retreats were simply unthinkable.[60]

A. Verkhovsky, the Red Army's leading author on tactics, championed the idea of preparing for battle with a concrete enemy in specific circumstances. This "new school" of tactics was distinguished from the old by a comprehensive analytical framework. Verkhovsky's tactical paradigm included consideration of the following issues: a) the characteristics of one's own weapons; b) the influence of class and national conflict within which a future war would be fought; c) the quantity of troops available to the enemy and the Red Army, the size of the theater, density of forces, and depth of deployments; d) the action of opponents "not with our weapons but with his and according to his own regulations which are in keeping with his weapons and his troops"; e) the decisive influence of locality in both the theater of war and the confines of the battlefield; and, finally, f) the influence of time on the forms of struggle of both sides.[61] Although primarily tactical in focus, these points addressed strategic and operational issues as well. Density and depth of forces, as expressed in number of troops and guns in a given sector, could be reduced to calculations of density of forces per kilometer of front. "Without calculations all these forms lack content. Furthermore, it is very important to know the density of forces in a given front at which the saturation point is reached in those cases when we wish to set the form of a march-maneuver in a future war."[62]

A much narrower critique of attrition strategy was built on Svechin's own observation that in the initial period of war the attacker, that is, the side adapted to decisive initial operations, could impose its style of warfare upon the defender. Viktor Novitsky noted that a strategy based upon attrition stood on totally different principles than one based upon annihilation. Annihilation required the ability to conduct large-scale, immediate, decisive, lightning-fast operations. In place of mobilizing the civilian economy for war, an annihilation strategy required an extant war industry that even in peacetime would provide the weapons and materiel necessary to conduct decisive operations. Svechin had assumed that the side adopting a strategy of annihilation would initially be able to impose its style of war on the other side by seizing the initiative and mounting early offensive operations. Counting upon victory in a short war, the side adopting a strategy of annihilation could avoid a host of difficult peacetime sacrifices necessary to create a unity of front and rear in a protracted war. However, failure in those initial operations would expose the adventurism at the heart of such a policy by underscoring the lack of coherence between military strategy and political-economic preparations. Victor Novitsky reformulated Svechin's assumption that the initiative would always go to the side following a strategy of annihilation by focusing on the problem of the struggle for mobilization and deployment. In an age of airpower he advocated employment of a covering force army to conduct initial operations that would disrupt enemy mobilization and deployment, and thereby win the "struggle for the nature of future war."[63] Novitsky's work on this aspect of future war contributed to the development of a specific line of Soviet military writings devoted to the nature, form, content, and law-governed patterns (*zakonomernosti*) of the development of the "initial period of war."[64]

The problem of studying the details of operational art was left to a chair at the military academy established in 1924 that was dedicated to the "conduct of the operation." This chair immediately took on the problem of studying the conduct of operations during World War I and the civil war. Special attention was devoted to the 1920 summer campaign against Poland. Leadership of the new chair went to N. E. Varfolomeev, who had graduated with the final class from the old general staff academy, had volunteered for service with the Red Army in 1918, and had served as chief of intelligence for one of the first Red Army divisions raised in the Moscow military district. Varfolomeev had also fought on the western front during the Vistula operation and served as chief reporter on the large-scale maneuvers that Tukhachevsky conducted on that front in 1922.[65] The scenario was a Soviet-Polish struggle for the "Gates of Moscow" along the Minsk-Smolensk axis on lands between the Dvina and the Dnieper Rivers.

Following the civil war Varfolomeev turned his attention to the difficult problem of conducting a deep pursuit so as to bring about the conditions for the annihilation of the enemy. The focus of his attention was the advance on Warsaw and the failure of the western front to achieve a decisive victory. Varfolomeev emphasized the need to organize a relentless pursuit by the advance guards, the use of army cavalry to turn the enemy's flanks and preclude the organization of a defense on a favorable line of terrain, the sustaining of close contact between the advance guard and main forces to allow for the timely commitment of fresh forces to the attack, and the maintenance of a viable logistical system in support of the advance. Varfolomeev still spoke in terms of pursuit to "the field of the decisive engagement," but his attention was focused on the utilization of reserves to maintain the pace of the pursuit without risking pauses in the advance, which would permit the enemy to recover.[66]

Varfolomeev's arrival at the military academy in 1924 coincided with Tukhachevsky's return to Moscow as deputy chief of staff of the RKKA. Over the next three years, from 1924 to 1927, the chair addressed the problem of how to conduct operations of annihilation that would bring about the total destruction of enemy forces in the field. Varfolomeev summed up this problem in two propositions. First was the need to combine breakthrough and deep pursuit so as to destroy the enemy forces throughout their entire depth. Under conditions of modern warfare this could not be achieved in a single operation but required successive deep operations, "the zigzags of a whole series of operations successively developed one upon the other, logically connected, and linked together by the common final objective." Second, success in such successive, deep operations depended fundamentally on the "successful struggle against the consequences of the attendant operational exhaustion." Logistics, that is, the unity of front and rear as an organizational problem, thus assumed critical importance as an aspect of operational art. In both teaching and research the faculty at the academy sought the means of defining operational norms or parameters for such deep operations.[67]

Varfolomeev found the roots of the theory of deep, successive operations in Tukhachevsky's attempt to use the techniques of class war and civil war in an "external war" against a much more well-prepared adversary. He believed the failure of the Vistula operation was rooted in Tukhachevsky's overly optimistic evaluation of the potential for "intensification of the revolution" within Poland by means of "a revolution from without [*revoliutsiia izvne*]" as well as the progressive exhaustion of the Red Army brought on by attrition and the disorganization of the rear services during the advance.[68] Prudent operational plans that took into account the need to break through and penetrate the enemy's defenses along their entire line sobered revolutionary élan. In the 1930s Varfolomeev turned his attention to the employment of shock armies in the offensive, as well as the problem of overcoming enemy operational reserves as they joined the engagement. In these studies he focused upon the German and Allied offensives of 1918, especially the Anglo-French offensive at Amiens in August. The Amiens operation was noteworthy both for the achievement of surprise and for the mass employment of armor and aviation to achieve a breakthrough.[69]

The logistical parameters demanded by such deep, successive operations to a great extent depended upon the vision of the Soviet Union as a political economy and the nature of the external threat. In the hands of Svechin and those like him who emphasized the need to prepare for a long war, maintaining the worker-peasant alliance became the central reality of the Soviet Union's domestic mobilization base. Such a view assumed that Lenin's NEP, which emphasized agricultural recovery, would be the long-term policy of the USSR. At the same time these authors cast the nature of the external threat posed by the states immediately bordering the USSR. These writers could not ignore postwar developments in military technology; they concluded that Europe was, in fact, divided into two military-technical systems. The industrialized West had the clear potential for mechanized warfare. Conversely, eastern Europe, which included the USSR, was dominated by a peasant economy and a "peasant rear" (*krest'ianskii tyl*) and therefore lacked such potential.[70]

One of the most important advocates of creating an operational art that was adapted to the realities of a future war, a war that would be fought on the basis of a peasant rear, was V. K. Triandafillov. Triandafillov had served in the tsarist army during World War I; he had taken an active part in the revolutionary politics within the army in 1917; and he had joined the Red Army in 1918 where he commanded a battalion, a regiment, and a brigade. He fought on the Ural front against Dutov and on the south and southwest fronts against Denikin and Wrangel. After joining the party in 1919 he was a natural choice for education as a Red *genshtabist* and was posted to the academy in the same year. During his four years at the academy he divided his time between theory and praxis. As a brigade commander with the Fifty-first Rifle Division, one of the best divisions in the Red Army, he took an active part in Frunze's successful offensive at the Perekop Isthmus against Wrangel. At the same time Triandafillov began writing military analyses of operations that occurred during the civil war as his part in the activities of the academy's military scientific society. These studies included essays on the southern front's offensive against Denikin and the Perekop offensive against Wrangel.[71] He also took part in the suppression of the Tambov insurrection in 1921, where he served under Tukhachevsky. Like Varfolomeev, Triandafillov also wrote on the Polish-Soviet war. However, whereas Varfolomeev had concentrated on the problem of pursuit during a general offensive, Triandafillov used a small-scale action from the final phase of the war—the Twenty-seventh Omsk Rifle Division against the Polish Fifteenth Poznan Division near Volkovysk in mid-September 1920—to address the problem of troop control at the tactical level as it contributed to a force's achievement of surprise and its vulnerability to unexpected combat developments.[72] Following Triandafillov's graduation from the military academy in 1923, Frunze chose his former subordinate to join the main staff of the RKKA where he became chief of the operations section in 1924. From there he moved on to command a rifle corps and then returned to Moscow as deputy chief of staff of the RKKA in 1928.

Charged with putting operational art into practice, Triandafillov wrote *The Nature of Operations of Modern Armies*, which became the Red Army's chief work on this subject. The book described in detail the military context of the theory of successive deep operations. Triandafillov called attention to the rapid technological development that was making possible the "machinization" of warfare but noted its limited impact upon the economically backward regions of eastern Europe with their peasant rear areas. Triandafillov argued that new automatic weapons, armor, aviation, and gas would affect a machine-age war but would not become decisive. He also treated the problem of manpower mobilization and the reality that mass war could quickly become a war of conscripts and reservists. This brought him to the problem of the means of achieving breakthrough and sustaining pursuit in successive deep operations. Here he drew upon Frunze's use of shock armies against Wrangel for the breakthrough, and the employment of echeloned strategic cavalry forces to facilitate exploitation and pursuit. Much of the success in these operations turned on two related problems: the organization of an effective command and control system to coordinate the operations of several fronts and the establishment of realistic logistical norms in keeping with the geographic-economic realities of the theater of military action.[73]

As deputy chief of staff of the RKKA, Triandafillov's views reflected several basic assumptions regarding the sort of war the Red Army planned to fight in the future. The field regulations of 1929 touched on many of the same themes of offensive operations that had been previously developed by Triandafillov in greater depth.[74] They also provided the framework for successive deep operations based upon a combined-arms offensive. The armies described both by Triandafillov and the 1929 regulations were in reality modernized versions of the Red Army as it had existed during the civil war. This vision was in keeping with what Shaposhnikov had described as the political-military context of Soviet strategy.

Stalin, the Red Army, and Mechanization

The final source of Red Army reform during the interwar years was the emergence of the Stalinist system with its commitment to the revolutionary transformation from above to force the industrialization and collectivization of the Soviet state. Having defeated Trotsky and confronted a crisis in the NEP, Stalin in 1929 made his own sharp turn to the left and embarked upon a radical transformation of Soviet society. To accomplish this revolution the regime relied upon totalitarian controls inspired by those employed during the civil war but directed against its own population. The professional military elite sided with the regime in its struggle against *kulaks* and specialists—including their own mentors—as class enemies, and endorsed large-scale industrialization as the path to create a mass, mechanized army. For their support of collectivization the Red Army was rewarded with a return to professional training and a program of force modernization that gave it a worldwide lead in mechanization and modernization in the early to mid-1930s. The high point of success of this program came in 1936 with large-scale maneuvers that demonstrated the Red Army's mechanized power and the publication of new field regulations that incorporated deep operations as the vision of future combat.[75] The party leadership could then claim that Soviet Russia had the means to carry the war to its enemies.

Triandafillov died in an airplane crash in 1931 before he had a chance to complete a revised edition of his book. The outline for this revision (published in the posthumous editions) contains several clues as to the major changes that he envisioned. First, in keeping with the new party line on the external threat Triandafillov addressed both the crisis of capitalism and the increased risk of direct attack upon the USSR by one or more major capitalist powers. Second, he began to contemplate the problem of employing massed armor in the offensive. The first five-year plan had promised to industrialize the USSR, and by 1931 it was possible to put the USSR within the ranks of the modern western European states and the United States. Third, Triandafillov specifically turned his attention to the problem of mechanized combined arms in the conduct of deep operations. Although Triandafillov's outline is at best a broad sketch, some Soviet officers have been willing to interpret his prognostications as an anticipation of the mechanization of successive deep operations presented in the 1936 field regulations.[76]

Other advocates of operational art argued that technological developments and the nature of the external threat made it absolutely essential to carry out a total mechanization of the Red Army and the Soviet rear. M. V. Tukhachevsky, Triandafillov's immediate superior as chief of the RKKA staff from 1925 to 1928, was one of the leading proponents of such a view. Tukhachevsky argued that nothing less than "complete militarization" of the national economy was required to provide the new instruments of mechanized warfare. Committed to creating the capability to execute operational art on a vast scale that would end in the total destruction of the enemy, Tukhachevsky crossed pens with Svechin whom he accused of being an advocate of attrition.[77] According to G. S. Isserson, one of Tukhachevsky's closest collaborators in the 1930s, during the war scare of 1927 when the party leadership feared conflict with Great Britain, Tukhachevsky came forward with a master plan for the mechanization of the Red Army only to have it turned down by the party leadership under Stalin.[78]

This limited edition study, prepared by a group of researchers from the intelligence directorate of the RKKA staff under Tukhachevsky's guidance, was circulated in 1928 to central administrative organs and to the military districts. Its purpose was to forecast the conditions of a future conflict involving the USSR. The report encompassed the general political situation and political factors; the human resources available to the USSR and its probable adversaries; economic factors affecting supply and logistics, to include the economic bases of war potential; technological factors; the influence that weapons modernization and innovation would have on the nature of a future war; an assessment of class, agrarian, and national conflicts within probable opponents; and operational and organizational problems affecting the conduct of war.[79]

As Jan Berzin, head of the intelligence directorate, pointed out in his introduction, the task of adapting a state's military system to the needs of and preparations demanded by a "future war" was common to all states. Berzin noted the mistakes made by the European powers in their preparations prior to World War I and identified the underestimation of the changed conditions brought about by the development and hegemony of imperialism as their basic error. By this Berzin meant those characteristics associated with total war, the "monstrous material scale of the war, the unprecedented intensity of the struggle, the colossal shocks in the areas of economic and political life."[80] The armies and states of Europe, including their general staffs, were not prepared for the war that they faced. Berzin discussed the origins of this project and called attention to the fact that in 1926 Tukhachevsky, as chief of the RKKA staff, had ordered the study of future war in keeping with the party's directives on the industrialization of the country.[81] In explaining the methodology applied to the study of future war, Tukhachevsky observed: "The most important basis for determining the nature of war is the character of the condition of productive forces of the opposing sides, the assessment of possible coalitions etc. *From the time of the Civil War many had the impression of future war as our revolutionary war, that is, lightning warfare, based on revolutionary elan etc.* Of course, only a few suffer from such sins now."[82] Tukhachevsky described such sentiments as "revolutionary idealism" that had nothing in common with Marxism.

Much of the importance of Tukhachevsky's study derives from its identification of the threat as Poland, Romania, and the other successor states along the USSR's western border. The study addressed their existing military systems, mobilization potential, and industrial bases and examined the possibility of these potential adversaries' external military assistance from the leading imperial powers. It made a very powerful case for the militarization of the Soviet economy to meet these threats and examined a wide range of operational issues. The final chapter of the study was a ringing endorsement of the industrialization of the national economy to meet the needs of the military.[83] In the end Tukhachevsky's study came down on the side of preparing for a future war on the basis of "total war." In operational terms it advocated the improvement of the Red Army's ability to conduct deep battle, that is, increasing the "far-battle nature (*dal'noboinost'*) of contemporary operations."[84] The study went on to highlight the logistical constraints on such operations, noting that limited rail capacity available to the support of large-scale offensive operations reduced the distance forces might advance before exhaustion set in. Motorization might ameliorate but could not eliminate this problem. Thus operational pauses and the regrouping of forces had become a necessity.[85]

The development of deep battle capabilities went hand in hand with the planning for successive operations. Regarding this issue Tukhachevsky's study ran into a distinct problem. On the one hand the Red Army had to prepare for the conduct of decisive operations in the initial period of war while recognizing that it lacked the means to achieve a rapid and decisive victory. Civil war operational lessons, including those gleaned from the "Campaign beyond the Vistula," were irrelevant and could not be compared with those of World War I: "Thus, just as the experience of the World War so also the experience of 1920 shows that: a) one should not build on horse transport the logistical base of modern troops, even if very few in number, at a great distance; b) a sufficiently rapid re-establishment of RR behind advancing troops and the structure of their rear remains an unresolved task for contemporary technology. Therefore, the operational capabilities of contemporary armies still remain limited."[86]

The point became one of conducting each operation so that it would be decisive within its own depth, that is, bring about the destruction of the opposing enemy forces throughout the depth of their deployments by means of breakthroughs and encirclements. On this point the study cited no less an authority than J. F. C. Fuller, Britain's leading proponent of mechanized warfare. The architect of "Plan 1919" and the primary promoter of the mechanization of the British army had written in 1926 of the possibility of using new technology in deep battle: "At present aviation can attack the enemy rear; tanks can break through the front and attack the rear; armored cars can turn his flank and once again attack his rear, that is, mount attacks against the most sensitive part of the force, in his stomach. The attack of the rear at the present time is quite possible and in my opinion has become one of the most important tactical operations in war."[87]

These partial destructions could not prevent a large economically developed state from redeploying forces to meet the threat or from mobilizing additional resources. However, the combination of such operations was the most likely road to decisive victory.[88] At the same time the study admitted that the threat of exhaustion and positional warfare could not be precluded. In that case the Soviet Union had to prepare for protracted war and mobilize its entire economy and society.[89] The key to overcoming the threat of positional warfare was the mechanization of the armed forces to assist in breakthrough and exploitation: "The density of the front in our theater of military actions has approached the density of the Russo-Austro-German front of the beginning of the 1914–1917 war. Therefore for the best operational preparation of the Red Army for future war *the center of gravity of the study of the experience of past wars must be concentrated on the maneuver period of the 1914–1917 war and not on the operations of the Civil War. In the study of the Civil War for the future it is necessary to take, primarily, the political factors of the war.*"[90]

Thus just as Stalin was consolidating his power and setting out upon the revolution from above, the debate about two views of Warsaw, that is, the "revolution from without" versus "modern war and successive operations" was resolved. Operational art had become an accepted category within military art. It remained to be seen how the relationship between operational art and strategy developed, and in that regard the civil war still loomed large in defining the threat and formulating the political objectives to which military power would be applied. On that issue Stalin had a decisive influence.

In 1930 Tukhachevsky's views won favor after Stalin had parted from Bukharin's thesis on the stabilization of capitalism and began to associate the west's economic depression with a rising threat of war to the Soviet Union. The party leadership openly used this threat to justify the brutal processes of industrialization and forced collectivization, which by then linked them with an improvement in the level of national defense. In 1931 Stalin employed a basic calculus to justify the drive for modernization in which he linked backwardness and defeat: "Those who fall behind, get beaten. . . . Such is jungle law of capitalism. You are backward, you are weak—therefore, you are wrong. Hence you can be beaten and enslaved. You are mighty; therefore, you are right. Hence, we must be wary of you. . . . We are 50 to 100 years behind the leading countries. We must make up this distance in ten years. Either we do that or they will suppress us."[91]

During the intervening two years Tukhachevsky had left the RKKA staff to assume command of the Leningrad military district where he conducted a number of experiments relating to mechanization. These experiments came at a time when motorization versus mechanization had emerged in western Europe as alternative solutions to the problem of integrating the internal combustion engine into the armed forces. Motorization implied grafting automobile transport on to existing combat arms, while mechanization called for the creation of "self-propelled combat means" with an emphasis upon armor, especially tanks, armored cars, and self-propelled artillery.[92] Soviet officers who followed developments in France, England, and the United States noted that all armies were exploring both paths but that, owing to strategic, operational, tactical, political, and financial circumstances, the French army was more sympathetic toward motorization and the British more toward mechanization.[93] In his comments on the training exercises of the troops of the Leningrad military district Tukhachevsky emphasized the need to increase their mobility as a combined-arms force that could engage in a multi-echeloned offensive. His interest in the development of tank, aviation, and airborne forces during this period marked him as an advocate of mechanization.[94]

At the sixteenth party congress and the ninth congress of the Komsomol in 1930-31, K. E. Voroshilov, the commissar of war and one of Stalin's closest collaborators, spoke of the mechanization of warfare as bringing about a qualitative change in the nature of future wars. But in Voroshilov's case mechanization would in the future bring about the possibility of a short bloodless war carried quickly on to the territory of the attacking enemy.[95] Such views emerged at a time when it appeared that world capitalism had gone back into a profound political-economic crisis that was creating greater instability and increased risks of war. This economic turmoil, it was feared, had created the basis for the formation of a broad anti-Soviet alliance that threatened war on every frontier. At home the strains of the first five-year plan were also underscoring the possibility of an alliance between the external threat and the so-called internal enemy, that is, the forces of counterrevolution.

Stalin had already put that interpretation on the so-called Shakhty Affair at the April plenum of the party central committee in 1928. His "facts" argued that an "economic counterrevolution" was being led by "*spetsy*" and being funded by capitalist organizations in the west, in order to sabotage the Soviet coal industry. Stalin linked this "economic intervention of west European, anti-Soviet capitalist organizations" with the earlier military-political intervention of the civil war. In both cases the appropriate answer was to liquidate the threat and in both cases the threat came from class enemies, that is, bourgeois specialists who put their talents in the service of the encircling capitalist powers. Stalin warned: "We have internal enemies. We have external enemies. Comrades, we can not forget about this for even one minute." From *spetsy* to *kulaks* to wreckers within the very highest reaches of the party itself, that was the terrible logic of Stalin's campaign against wreckers and enemies of the people.[96]

In 1930 Tukhachevsky presented his own powerful arguments that a mass, mechanized army was the means with which to implement the concept of operational art. In June 1930, three months after Stalin announced a retreat from forced collectivization, Tukhachevsky wrote directly to Stalin outlining his concept for the reconstruction of the Red Army. The Red Army staff had given Stalin its own interpretation of Tukhachevsky's "sums" which they had categorized as insane. In the essay he defended his proposals to those critics within the Red Army staff who had altered his figures and increased them to the point where they indeed seemed "crazy." Tukhachevsky called for an artillery park of twenty thousand guns of all calibers with a stockpile of shells for the first year of war equal to 180 million rounds. He proposed a mobilization strength for the Red Army of 260 divisions. On the central issue of tank and aviation production Tukhachevsky called for a tank force of fifty thousand vehicles. "According to my calculation for the organization of the new type of deep battle, it is necessary during mobilization to deploy 8–12 thousand tanks."[97] In addition he proposed acquiring an air force of eight thousand planes. Tukhachevsky also used many public forums to present this argument. One was the foreword to the Russian translation of Hans Delbrück's *History of the Art of War in the Framework of Political History* in which he attacked Svechin's concept of attrition as the appropriate strategy for the USSR.[98] This work was conspicuous for the tenor of the political-ideological assault Tukhachevsky mounted against the old *genshtabist*. In a time of heightened suspicions toward all specialists as wreckers Tukhachevsky called his colleagues "idealists" in Marxist dress.

Worse attacks followed within the confines of the section for the study of the problems of war in the communist academy, which was organized in 1929 as part of an effort to infuse Marxism-Leninism into military science. Within this section, as within the communist academy as a whole, the notion of a struggle between an old bourgeois past and a young, dynamic communist future was given free reign. The debates over "unified military doctrine" of 1921–22 were recalled, but now within the context of a struggle over the issue of where the center for the study of military problems in the USSR was going to be. The leaders of the section were promoting the communist academy as a rival to the military academy and looked to enhance their position through party ties and by building "strong ties with the Institute of Red Professorship and those young Marxist-Leninist forces which now move our Bolshevik science."[99]

Tukhachevsky, armed with the appropriate citations from Lenin, Stalin, and Voroshilov, attacked professors Svechin and Verkhovsky. He described their writings as infested with bourgeois ideology. Svechin was blamed for not believing in the possibility of decisive operations but rather defending the idea of limited war. Verkhovsky was charged with favoring a professional army at the expense of mass. At the time of Tukhachevsky's attacks, Svechin and Verkhovsky had been sent to labor camps as enemies of the people.[100] Tukhachevsky spoke positively of Triandafillov's book, which had critiqued Verkhovsky's concept of cadre-mechanized forces but also noted several shortcomings.[101] His line of criticism paralleled arguments made in a spring 1930 review of Triandafillov's book in which the reviewer took the author to task for talking of a peasant rear without noting the possibility of transforming that rear through industrialization. Industrialization, the reviewer pointed out, would make it possible to speed up the massing of forces and their maneuver creating opportunities for decisive operations if the political, that is, revolutionary, possibilities were exploited.[102] As noted above, Triandafillov was already responding to those new possibilities when he died in 1931.

That same year Tukhachevsky became deputy commissar of military and naval affairs, a member of the Revvoyensovet, and director of armaments for the RKKA. Over the next six years he directed the mechanization of the Red Army, laying the foundations for the creation of a mass mechanized force designed to conduct successive deep operations in a war of annihilation. The Stalinist industrialization transformed the USSR into a major industrial power with the capacity to mechanize its armed forces to an extent undreamed of by Triandafillov. During that same period the nature of the military threat confronting the USSR became more complex and serious. To his credit Tukhachevsky never fell into the trap of assuming that mechanization would negate mass war. He was an informed critic of "blitzkrieg theory," and his criticism of the works of Fuller, Liddell Hart, and others deserves serious attention. These writings contain useful insights into the emerging Soviet way of war. In 1931 he wrote regarding the professional mechanized army:

> Let's imagine a war between Great Britain and the USA, a war, for example, which breaks out along the Canadian border. Both armies are mechanized, but the English have, let's say, Fuller's cadres of 18 divisions, and the US Army has 180 divisions. The first has 5,000 tanks and 3,000 aircraft, but the second has 50,000 tanks and 30,000 planes. The small English Army would be simply crushed. Is it not already clear that talk about small, but mobile, mechanized armies in major wars is a cock-and-bull story? Only frivolous people can take them seriously.[103]

Thus in Tukhachevsky's work Soviet military theory, while building upon the work of the tsarist general staff and the combat experience of four industrial wars—the Russo-Turkish war, Russo-Japanese war, World War I, and the civil war—focused on the mechanization of the mass army as the means of conducting decisive operations in a total war. For Tukhachevsky, independent tank and mechanized formations formed the keystone to such deep operations. The "long-range tanks," which would make up such mobile groups, had to be fast, rugged, reliable, and most of all armed with a heavy cannon to fight and defeat enemy tanks.[104] Tukhachevsky's concept for employing tank, air, and airborne forces in "deep battle" did not meet with universal acceptance or praise. In 1933 Tukhachevsky wrote People's Commissar of Defense Voroshilov about the latter's contribution to the confusion. At the plenum of senior military leadership Voroshilov had said that "deep battle" was only one type of battle. Tukhachevsky disagreed: "This deep battle is not a synonym for breakthrough, but new forms of battle, arising from new armaments, about which you yourself have often spoken."[105] Tukhachevsky went on to describe the application of the new forms of deep battle to the envelopment of a flank, a meeting engagement, and a frontal assault. He warned: "These forms of new battle, it seems to me, will be very mutable and complex when our en[emie]s will, to some degree, be equipped with aviation and tanks like the RKKA. But for now that is a question for further study."[106] That problem was, in fact, quite close at hand.

Paying the Price: The Red Army in Stalin's Hands

In exchange for mechanization, the creation of mobile forces, and the ability to conduct deep operations Tukhachevsky and other Red commanders had become Stalin's political allies. But that alliance foundered on Stalin's basic assumption regarding the nature of the class struggle as the process of building socialism went forward. Thus ended the fruitful debate of the 1920s, eventually replaced by political terror and intimidation. For their support the Red Army got promises of materiel, modern equipment, and an industrial mobilization base of great extent and modernity. In the first five-year plan tank production had been set at 6,695 units, including 1,100 tankettes, with production rising from 340 in 1929–30 to 2,830 in 1932–33. In 1932 the Revvoyensovet approved a plan to produce ten thousand that year as a test of the state's production mobilization capabilities and as a means for accelerating the development of the tank-building industry. This ambitious project collapsed, however, in a chaos of unfinished tanks; only some 2,585 tanks were delivered to the Red Army—at once a far cry from its original goal but also evidence of the progress achieved since 1929 and the scale of the Soviet regime's commitment to mechanization.[107]

The emergence of Nazi Germany and Japan as ideological and political threats in the mid-1930s challenged Stalin's assumptions concerning the nature of the class struggle and became entangled with his efforts to consolidate his personal power within the party and the state. This new situation played a role in his purge of party leaders, including former political allies. The rise of Hitler created a serious dilemma for Stalin's foreign policy, which was trapped between ideological assumptions on promoting the proletarian revolution and the dictates of Machtpolitik.

As has been well-documented in the history of the Comintern, during Hitler's rise to power Stalin had followed a line supporting greater desta-bilization in Germany by identifying German social democrats (natural allies in the struggle against Hitler and the revanchist right) as "social fascists." Only after Hitler's consolidation of power and the beginning of German remilitarization did Stalin's foreign policy begin to shift toward collective security. In early 1933 Hitler's government put an end to the close, covert, technical cooperation between the Reichswehr and the RKKA in the areas of aviation, chemical warfare, and armor development, which had been going on since 1922. One of the cardinal subthemes of that cooperation had been the mutual hostility of both armed forces toward Poland.[108]

In February 1935, just over a year after Nazi Germany and Poland had signed a nonaggression pact, Tukhachevsky informed People's Com-missar Voroshilov that the rise of Germany and its possible alliance with Poland against the USSR had called into question the basic assumptions of the existing Soviet war plan for the west, which still called for the destruction of the Polish state as its main goal. He argued that the existing force levels of the RKKA were unequal to the successful execution of the mission and outlined the additional forces necessary to meet the challenge of German-Polish War.[109] In March 1935 Tukhachevsky outlined Nazi Germany's growing military potential and assessed the threat this buildup posed to the Soviet Union. On the basis of recently published materials it is clear that Tukhachevsky sent his article to Stalin for comment and correction before its publication in *Pravda* on 31 March 1935. Stalin's chief changes were in the title, which he altered from "Hitler's Military Plans" to "The Military Plans of Today's Germany," as well as in the emphasis placed upon the threat which Nazi Germany posed not only to the USSR but also to western and central Europe. Speaking of the anti-Soviet tenor of German policy, Stalin wrote:

This [anti-Soviet] point is useful screen for concealing the revanchist plans in the west [Belgium, France] and in the south [Poznan, Czechoslovakia, Anschluss]. Apart from all this one can not deny that Germany needs French ore. It needs to broaden its naval basing. The experience of the war, 1914–1918, has shown with complete clarity that without secure control of the ports of Belgium and the northern ports of France, Germany's naval power can not be built. Thus, for the achievement of its revanchist and expansionist plans, Germany will have by the summer of this year an army with a minimum of

849,000 men, that is, an army more than 40% larger than France and almost as large a force in number as the USSR [The USSR had 940,000 troops]. And this is so in spite of the fact that the USSR has 2 1/2 times more population and ten times more territory than Germany. So one sees in this matter the so-called, equal right in armaments.[110]

In response to this turn of events Soviet foreign policy began to shift toward collective security under the nominal leadership of Maxim Litvinov, people's commissar of international affairs. In May 1935 the USSR concluded a treaty with France, pledging to protect Czechoslovakia in case of attack. Regarding the primary objectives of Hitler's foreign policy, Litvinov wrote to Stalin in late 1935, were: "Hostility to the USSR, the Jewish Question and Anschluss."[111] Yet Litvinov pointed out that Hitler's anti-Soviet campaign was one way of making German revisionism acceptable to anti-communists in the capitals of western Europe. Litvinov proposed that the Soviet Union answer Nazi Germany's anti-Soviet propaganda with its own "counter-campaign" against German fascism and fascists.[112] Thus the case for collective security rested upon shared fears of German revisionism.

Nevertheless, Stalin's views were also a clear manifestation of the Soviet desire for room to maneuver should collective security fail. In the summer of 1936 the Soviet ambassador in Berlin, Ia. Z. Surits, discussed Hitler's foreign policy and his anti-Soviet line. While recognizing the ideological element in German foreign policy, he pictured it as a tactical manifestation of a search for larger support but argued that no solid foundation for a German bloc in Europe existed. German-Italian relations provided for instrumental cooperation on individual issues, but no long-term alliance. In the case of Poland, long-range cooperation was quite unlikely. If Germany turned east Poland would be the first target of that aggression. But Germany's military capabilities were still insufficient to fight and win a general European war.[113] Collective security, given the resolve shown by the Soviet Union in its policy toward the Spanish Civil War and the existing possibility of Soviet-Anglo-French cooperation, still remained a viable instrument for dealing with German revanchism.

It was at this juncture that internal Soviet developments had their most decisive and profound impact on Soviet military reform. The domestic crisis associated with Stalin's extension of the terror to the deepest ranks of the party in 1936 had already led to charges in Moscow's show trials that some military commanders were involved in the various rightist and leftist plots in connection with foreign intelligence services to overthrow Stalin, the party, and the state. In the summer of 1937 this process reached to the very foundation of Soviet national security.[114]

In May 1937 Tukhachevsky and his closest associates were arrested as German agents. The arrest resulted from a plot engineered by the NKVD under N. I. Ezhov and provoked by the Nazi SS security service under Richard Heydrich. Heydrich used the White émigré general N. V. Skoblin (as a double agent) and diplomatic channels to create the impression that Tukhachevsky was conspiring with senior German officers to overthrow Stalin. The plot's many authors counted on Stalin's own paranoia to make their conspiracy work.[115] In June Tukhachevsky and his associates were shot. The purge did not stop with a few senior commanders but swept away much of the Red Army's senior leadership with disastrous consequences. Once the terror machine was let loose within the army it reached into every level of command and every unit until tens of thousands of officers and men had been purged. Some were shot, others were sent to camps, and still others were arrested and released. From 1937 to 1938, 1,230 persons were shot in the Kiev, Kharkov, and Trans-Baikal military districts alone.[116] Writing on this period, N. G. Pavlenko, the former editor of *The Military-Historical Journal*, observed recently:

> After the repression of a large part of the scholar-teacher cadre in military science a vacuum appeared. It was filled in part by individual military researchers, including M. N. Tukhachevsky, N. E. Varfolomeev, S. M. Belitsky, A. M. Vol'pe, G. S. Isserson, V. A. Melikov, and several other scholars, but the previous scale and variety in scientific research was not sustained. And these cadres worked only a short time. In the second half of the 1930s and beginning of the 1940s almost all of them were either killed or found themselves behind bars and in camps—in logging camps. The extermination of the most prepared scientific cadres brought on a weakening of scientific-research in the army, and in the final analysis major errors in working out the means of military action.[117]

The purge also decimated Red Army intelligence, including its chief, Jan Berzin, following his return from command in Spain.

The record of the Red Army in the immediate prewar period is one of rapid expansion; constant and disjointed reorganization, first abolishing and then reconstituting its mechanized formations; hurried rearmament as the masses of equipment produced in the early 1930s became obsolete;

strategic redeployment into areas seized after the Nazi-Soviet pact of 1939; and a very mixed combat experience that included operational success by G. K. Zhukov's mobile forces against Japan's Kwantung Army at Khalkhin Gol in August 1939 and initial disasters against Finland in the winter war of 1939–40, as a result of which Voroshilov lost his position as people's commissar of defense.[118] The report on the change of command contained a litany of weaknesses ranging from a weak and disorganized high command, poor operational preparation, incomplete plans for mobilization, a critical shortage of junior and mid-level officer cadres, ineffective combat training, poor combined arms performance among all arms and branches, to a total failure of intelligence analysis. In early 1941, after a major staff conference of RKKA leadership in December 1940 and a war game for senior commanders, Stalin changed the chief of the general staff once again, replacing K. A. Meretskov (who had broken the Mannerheim Line in the final offensive of the winter war) with the victor at Khalkhin-Gol, G. K. Zhukov. Zhukov, commanding the "blue" in the war game, had achieved the sort of deep operational successes in the same theater—northwest Belorussia—where German forces would strike six months later. In the months before the blow Stalin seems to have been aware of the weakness of the Red Army and the opportunity that its eviscerated state offered to Hitler to launch a preemptive war, but he continued to hope war could be delayed until 1942.

Stalin did appreciate the difference in combat capabilities between a deploying Wehrmacht, combat-tested and fresh from decisive victories in Poland, France, the Low Countries, and the Balkans, and the Red Army carrying out covert mobilization and deployment in a peacetime environment. But Stalin seems to have believed that Hitler would have to "creep up to war" with the Soviet Union, that is, mount provocations that would seem to place responsibility for war on the Soviet Union and its leadership. Someone in the general staff did propose a preemptive offensive in the face of German troop concentrations along the Soviet border on 15 May 1941. This would have involved overt mobilization and deployment of Soviet forces for an offensive operation designed to destroy German forces deployed south of Brest. Apparently the proposal was written by Zhukov's Deputy General A. M. Vasilevsky, but it was never signed by General Zhukov or countersigned by Marshal S. K. Timoshenko, the people's commissar of defense.[119] According to Zhukov nothing could shake Stalin from his resolve to not provoke Germany.[120] Only in early June did Stalin authorize the covert mobilization of an additional eight hundred thousand troops under the cover of summer exercises.[121] Dmitriy Volkogonov's masterful biography of Stalin leaves no doubt about Stalin's responsibility for the disasters of the initial period of war. Citing A. M. Vasilevsky, Volkogonov observed: "[T]he cause of delaying as long as possible the entry of the USSR into the war had a real basis. Stalin's strict line to prevent anything that could be used by Germany as an excuse to unleash war was justified by the historical interests of the Socialist Motherland. But his error (or, more precisely, guilt) was that he did not see and did not grasp that point beyond which such a policy would become not only unnecessary but also dangerous."[122] Vasilevsky suggests that at such a point a prudent leader would have declared mobilization and turned the nation into an armed camp.

In his analysis of the terror in the late 1930s and early 1940s Volkogonov suggests why such a course was not open to Stalin. According to his study, Stalin was aware of the terrible costs that this mad process of destruction had inflicted upon the nation. "But Stalin did not stop the insanity. This senseless terror went beyond the limits, threatening the functioning of the system itself. Threatened on the eve of the most difficult trials, such was the fate of the Soviet people: to suffer and overcome, to struggle and hope, to sacrifice and to win."[123] To delay the war as long as possible became his only hope, so he rejected all moves that might provoke the war he was seeking to avoid. In the face of the mounting evidence of German capabilities along the German-Soviet border Stalin waited for Hitler's signal of his intent, but none came until after the crash of shell and the roar of motors announced the Wehrmacht's advance. Hitler saw no need for a protracted propaganda campaign leading up to war against communist Russia. According to his ideology anticommunism, anti-Semitism, and Lebensraum were sufficient justifications for a war of annihilation.

Thus the central legacy of Stalinism on the eve of the German assault was distinctly contradictory. On the one hand the regime had created a modern industrial plant, militarized the society, and created powerful instruments of mobilization and control. On the other hand it had decapitated its own elite, including the officer corps of the Red Army, leaving insufficient numbers of middle and senior grade officers to oversee its expansion from 900,000 men in 1935 to 5.5 million on the eve of the war. In addition, by introducing systemic terror into the command echelons of the Red Army the regime undermined the professional autonomy of its officer corps, including the general staff. Moreover, having pushed rearmament in the early 1930s, the Red Army found itself equipped with massive quantities of obsolete or obsolescent equipment for which it could not provide adequate spare parts and because of which the process of introducing new equipment was slowed. Having lost the authors of the very concepts of mechanized warfare in the late 1930s, the Red Army underwent a process of radical restructuring on the basis of the wrong lessons learned in Spain and had to begin another restructuring after its own failure in Finland and the Wehrmacht's blitzkrieg in France and the Low Countries. In 1940 the Red Army undertook the creation of eight mechanized corps. In 1941 the creation of another twenty began. None was combat-ready when war came in June. Finally the impact of terror on the Red Army and its intelligence service proved profound in the immediate prewar period when intelligence suggested an impending German attack and called for countermeasures to lessen the impact of tactical and operational surprise on Soviet covering forces. The terror created a mindset among senior officers that made Stalin's call for no provocative actions overwhelm their professional judgment in the face of solid intelligence that an attack was imminent.[124] As David Glantz has noted, the excesses of Stalinism had turned the Red Army on the eve of the Great Patriotic War into a "stumbling colossus."[125]

This terror, which had its roots in Stalin's recasting of the regime's revolutionary nature, did much to nullify the successful military reforms of the early interwar period and set the stage for the disasters of 1941.[126] It was in spite of the totalitarian excesses and terror that the peoples of the Soviet Union, especially the Russian nation, endured disasters and defeats and found the will and courage to fight on. The Red Army that fought on after the initial disasters was not Tukhachevsky's massive mechanized force—destroyed in the frontier battles—but Svechin's national army. It traded men and space for time, stopped the Wehrmacht from reaching Moscow in December 1941, mounted Zhukov's counteroffensive, and set the stage for the creation of the tank armies that would put into practice deep operations at Stalingrad and after.

Notes

This essay draws upon earlier work done by the author. See: Jacob W. Kipp, "Lenin and Clausewitz: The Militarization of Marxism," *Military Affairs* 49 (December 1985): 184–91; "Mass and Maneuver and the Origins of Soviet Operational Art" in *Transformation in Russian and Soviet Military History: Proceedings of the Twelfth Military History Symposium*, USAF *Academy, 1986*, ed. Karl Reddel (Washington DC: United States Air Force Office of Air Force History, 1990), 87–116; and "Soviet Military Doctrine and the Origins of Operational Art, 1917–1936," in *Soviet Military Doctrine from Lenin to Gorbachev, 1915–1991*, ed. Philip S. Gillette and Willard C. Frank Jr. (Westport CT: Greenwood Press, 1992), 85–133.

1. Makhmut Gareev, "Aktual'nye problemy voyennoy istorii," *Muzhestvo*, no. 5 (1992): 176–77.

2. *Istoriya Velikoy Otechestvennoy voyny Sovetskogo Soyuza, 1941–1945*, 6 vols. (Moscow: Voyenizdat, 1960–65).

3. N. G. Pavlenko, *Byla voyna* . . . . (Moscow: Rodnik, 1994), 5.

4. V. N. Lobov, *Voyennaya reforma: Svyaz-vremen* (Moscow: Aviar, 1991).

5. Bruce W. Menning, *Bayonets before Bullets: The Imperial Russian Army, 1861–1914* (Bloomington: Indiana University Press, 1992).

6. Kipp, "Mass and Maneuver and the Origins of Soviet Operational Art."

7. James J. Schneider, *The Structure of Strategic Revolution: Total War and the Roots of the Soviet Warfare State* (Novato CA: Presidio Press, 1994), 267–79.

8. D. Fedotoff-White, *The Growth of the Red Army* (Princeton: Princeton University Press, 1944), 4.

9. Rex A. Wade, *Red Guards and Workers' Militias in the Russian Revolution* (Stanford: Stanford University Press, 1984), 1ff.

10. Gerhard Ritter, *Das Kommunemodell und die Begruendung der Roten Armee in Jahre 1918* (Berlin: Osteuropa-Institut, 1965).

11. *Pravda*, 23 February 1918.

12. L. S. Gaponenko, ed., *Oktyabr'skaya revolyutsiya i russkaya armiya* (Moscow: Nauka, 1973), 405ff.

13. For Lenin's speech advocating ratification of the treaty see John W. Wheeler-Bennett, *Brest-Litovsk: The Forgotten Peace, March 1918* (New York: W. W. Norton & Company, 1938), 409–26.

14. Mark von Hagen, *Soldiers in the Proletarian Dictatorship: The Red Army and the Soviet Socialist State, 1917–1930* (Ithaca NY: Cornell University Press, 1990), 28–29.

15. S. I. Gusev, "Kak stroit- sovetskuyu armiyu," in *Grazhdanskaya voyna i Krasnaya Armiya*, ed. S. I. Gusev (Moscow: Voyenizdat, 1958), 27–37.

16. M. V. Frunze, *Izbrannye proizvedeniya* (Moscow: Voyenizdat, 1940), 45.

17. Dmitriy Volkogonov, *Trotskiy* (Moscow: Novosti, 1992), 1:211–14.

18. V. I. Lenin, *Polnoe sobraniye sochinenii Lenina* (Moscow: Progress, 1966–70), 38:139–40.

19. A. G. Kavtaradze, *Voyennye spetsialisty na sluzhbe Respubliki Sovetov, 1917–1920 gg.* (Moscow: Nauka, 1988), 211.

20. Kavtaradze, *Voyennye spetsialisty*, 201–12.

21. S. A. Fedyukin, *Sovetskaya vlast- i burzhuaznye spetsialisty* (Moscow: Mysl', 1965), 55.

22. Von Hagen, *Soldiers in Proletarian Dictatorship*, 53–54.

23. Kavtaradze, *Voyennye spetsialisty*, 211.

24. M. A. Gareev, *Obshchevoyskovye manevry i ucheniya* (Moscow: Voyenizdat, 1970).

25. A. Neznamov, "Prepodavanie taktiki," *Voyennoye znanie*, no. 15 (1921): 4–5.

26. M. A. Gareev, *Obshchevoyskovye ucheniya*, 2nd ed. (Moscow: Voyenizdat, 1990), 66–82.

27. On the Gusev-Frunze position at the tenth party congress see Gusev, *Grazhdanskaya voyna i Krasnaya armiya*, 120–27. On the relationship of the drive for a unified military doctrine for the Red army and the reformers' advocacy of a military doctrine for the tsarist army before World War I see D. Petrovskiy, "Edinaya voyna doktrina v A. G. Sh.," *Voyennoye znanie*, nos. 14–15 (August 1921): 13.

28. "Udostoverenie voyennogo komissara Moskovskogo rayona M. N. Tukhachevskogo, 19 iyunya 1918 g.," in *Rossiyskiy Gosudarstvennyy Voyennyy Arkhiv, Marshal M. N. Tukhachevskiy (1893–1937 gg.): Komplekt dokumentov iz fondov RGVA*, ed. N. E. Eliseeva, comp. P. A. Aptekar' and I. V. Uspenskiy, delo 1, /1.

29. Sheila Fitzpatrick, "The Civil War as a Formative Experience," in *Bolshevik Culture: Experiment and Order in the Russian Revolution*, ed. Abbott Gleason, Peter Kenez, and Richard Stites (Bloomington: Indiana University Press, 1985), 64–65.

30. For more on the influence of the Vistula campaign on Soviet military thought in the 1920s see Jacob W. Kipp, "Two Views of Warsaw: The Russian Civil War and Soviet Operational Art, 1920–1932," in *The Operational Art*, ed. B. J. C. McKercher and Michael A. Hennessey (Westport CT: Praeger, 1996), 51–85.

31. "Prikaz komanduyushchego voyskami Tambovskoy gubernii M. N. Tukhachevskogo o poryadke iz'yatiya zalozhnikov i konfiskatsii imushshestva u uchastnikov Tambovskogo vosstaniya, 15 maya 1921 g." in *Rossiyskiy Gosudarstvennyy Voyennyy Arkhiv, Marshal M. N. Tukhachevskiy (1893–1937 gg.): Komplekt dokumentov iz fondov RGVA*, delo 8/1, and "Prikaz komanduyushchego voyskami Tambovskoy gubernii M. N. Tukhachevskogo o primenenii protiv povstantsev otravlyayushchikh veshchstv, 12 iyunya 1921 g." in *Rossiyskiy Gosudarstvennyy Voyennyy Arkhiv, Marshal M. N. Tukhachevskiy (1893–1937 gg.): Komplekt dokumentov iz fondov RGVA*, delo 9/1.

32. Scott R. McMichael, "National Formations of the Red Army, 1918–1938," *The Journal of Soviet Military Studies* 3 (December 1990): 628–40.

33. Von Hagen, *Soldiers in Proletarian Dictatorship*, 295–305.

34. Von Hagen, *Soldiers in Proletarian Dictatorship*, 317–20.

35. I. B. Berkhin, *Voyennaya reforma v* SSSR *(1924–1925 gg.)* (Moscow: Voyenizdat, 1958), 77ff.

36. M. Frunze, "Edinaya voyennaya doktrina i Krasnaya armiya," *Voyennaya nauka i revolyutsiya*, no. 2 (1921): 39.

37. I. Marievskiy, "Stanovlenie i razvitie teorii operativnogo iskusstva," *Voyenno-istoricheskiy zhurnal*, no. 3 (March 1962): 27–28.

38. N. E. Varfolomeev, "Strategiya v akademicheskoy postanovke," *Voyna i revolyutsiya*, no. 11 (1929): 83–84.

39. *Krasnye zori*, no. 11 (22) (November 1924): 23.

40. A. Svechin, *Strategiya*, 2d ed. (Moscow: Voennyy Vestnik, 1927), 14ff.

41. Varfolomeev, "Strategiya v akademicheskoy postanovke," 84.

42. *Akademiya im. M. V. Frunze* (Moscow: Voyenizdat, 1973), 98.

43. M. Bonch-Bruevich, "Nekotorye osnovy operativnogo rukovodstva v sovremennoy voyne," *Voyna i revolyutsiya*, no. 12 (1927): 46–63.

44. *Akademiya General'nogo Shtaba: Istoriya Voyennoy ordenov Lenina i Suvorova I stepeni akademii General'nogo Shtaba Vooruzhennykh Sil* SSSR *imeni K. E. Voroshilova*, 2nd ed. (Moscow: Voyenizdat, 1987), 22–24.

45. Frunze, *Izbrannye proizvedenniya* (Moscow: Voyenizdat, 1957), 2:35.

46. Varfolomeev, "Strategiya v akademicheskoy postanovke," 92–93; N. E. Varfolomeev, "Operativnaya voyennaya igra," *Voyna i revolyutsiya*, no. 6 (1928): 18–35; K. Berends, "Shtabnye voyennyye igry," *Voyna i revolyutsiya*, no. 6 (1928): 36–55; and V. Triandafillov, "Materialy dlya zadachi na shtabnuyu voyennuyu igru," *Voyna i revolyutsiya*, no. 12 (December 1927): 31–45.

47. I. A. Korotkov, *Istoriya sovetskoy voyennoy mysli: Kratkiy ocherk 1917-iyun' 1941* (Moscow: Nauka, 1980), 121.

48. A. Svechin, "Opasnye Illyuzii," *Voyennaya mysl- i revolyutsiya*, no. 2 (February 1923): 90–97.

49. Svechin, *Strategiya*, 6–26.

50. A. Svechin, "Evolyutsiya operativnogo razvertyvaniya," *Voyna i revolyutsiya*, no. 5 (1926): 20.

51. Svechin, "Evolyutsiya operativnogo razvertyvaniya," 24.

52. A. Svechin, "Gosudarstvennyy i frontovoy tyl," *Voyna i revolyutsiya*, no. 11 (1930): 94–108.

53. A. Svechin, "Izuchenie voyennoy istorii," *Voyna i revolyutsiya*, no. 4 (April 1927): 66.

54. V. Levichev, "Genshtab i voyennaya akademiya RKKA," *Voyna i revolyutsyia*, no. 7 (1928): 75.

55. Levichev, "Genshtab i voyennaya," 77.

56. B. M. Shaposhnikov, *Mozg armii* (Moscow: Voyennyy Vestnik, 1927–29), 1:112ff.

57. Svechin, *Strategiya*, 21–23.

58. B. M. Shaposhnikov, *Mozg armii*, in *Vospominaniya: Voyenno-nauchnye trudy*, 425–29.

59. V. N. Lobov, "Aktual'nyye voprosy razvitiya teorii sovetskoy voyennoy strategii 20-kh—serediny 30-kh godov," *Voyenno-istoricheskiy zhurnal*, no. 2 (February 1989): 44.

60. A. Svechin, *Klauzevits* (Moscow: Zhurnal'no-Gazetnoe Ob'edinenie, 1934), 19. This introduction was written to make certain that no one missed the ideologically subversive tendencies in Svechin's writings.

61. A. Verkhovsky, "Novaya i staraya shkola," *Voyna i revolyutsiya*, no. 4 (April 1928): 100–101.

62. Verkhovsky, "Novaya i staraya shkola," 109.

63. Viktor Novitsky, "Bor'ba za kharakter budushchey voyny," *Voyna i revolyutsiya*, no. 5 (May 1929): 1–13.

64. A. Lapchinskiy, "Deistvie aviatsii v nachal'nom periode voyny," *Voyna i revolyutsiya*, no. 6 (June 1929): 55–66; Ia. Alksnis, "Nachal'nyy period voyny," *Voyna i revolyutsiya*, no. 9 (September 1929): 3–22, and no. 10 (October 1929): 3–15; V. Novitsky, "Deistviya aviatsii v nachal'nom periode voiny," *Voyna i revolyutsiya*, no. 9 (1929): 23–31; R. P. Eideman, "K voprosu o kharaktere nachal'nogo perioda voyny," *Voyna i revolyutsiya*, no. 8 (August 1931): 3–12; E. Shilovskiy, "Nachal'nyy period voyny," *Voyna i revolyutsiya*, no. 9–10 (September–October 1933): 3–11; M. N. Tukhachevsky, "Kharakter pogranichnykh operatsii," in *Izbrannye proizvedeniya* (Moscow: Voyenizdat, 1964), 2:212–21; S. N. Krasil'nikov, "Nachal'nyy period budushchei voiny," *Pravda*, 20 May 1936, 2; G. Isserson, *Novye formy bor'by* (Moscow: Voyenizdat, 1940); and A. I. Starunin, "Operativnaya vnezapnost'," *Voennaya mysl'*, no. 3 (March 1941): 27–35.

65. N. Varfolomeev, "Manevry na zapfronte," *Revolyutsiya i voyna*, no. 19 (1923): 5–26 and no. 20 (1923): 77–104. On the influence of Frunze and Tukhachevsky on the academy see A. I. Radzievsky, ed., *Akademiya imeni M. V. Frunze: Istoriya voyennoy ordena Lenina Krasnoznamennoy ordena Suvorova Akademii* (Moscow: Voyenizdat, 1972): 71–77.

66. N. Varfolomeev, "Dvizhenie presleduyushchei armii k polyu reshitel'nogo srazheniya," *Revolyutsiya i voyna*, no. 13 (1921): 69–96.

67. Varfolomeev, "Strategiya v akademicheskoy postanovke," 87–88.

68. N. Varfolomeev, "Strategicheskoye narastanie i istoshchenie v grazhdanskoy voyne" in *Grazhdanskaya voyna 1918–1921: Voyennoe iskusstvo Krasnoy armii*, ed. A. S. Bubnov et al. (Moscow: Voyennyy vestnik, 1928), 260–81. What Varfolomeev called "strategic intensification" was termed "intensification of the revolution" (*narostanie [sic.] revoliutsii*) by Tukhachevsky. See M. Tukhachevsky, "Revolyutsiya izvne," *Revolyutsiya i voyna*, no. 3 (1920): 47–54.

69. N. E. Varfolomeev, *Udarnaya armiya* (Moscow: Gosvoyenizdat, 1933), 169–89, and *Nastupatel'naya operatsiya (po opytu Am'enskogo srazheniya 8 avgusta 1918 g.)* (Moscow: Gosvoyenizdat, 1937), 169–76.

70. V. K. Triandafillov, "Vozmozhnaya chislennost- budushchikh armii," *Voyna i revolyutsiya*, no. 3 (1927): 14–43. Triandafillov's assumptions about the prospect of war were those of the party's right, the advocates of the continuation of the NEP. He even cited Bukharin on the stabilization of the world capitalist economy (p. 17).

71. V. K. Triandafillov, *Kharakter operatsii sovremennykh armii*, 3rd ed. (Moscow: Gosvoyenizdat, 1936), 7–9, 255. Triandafillov's study of the Perekop operation was later revised and published as part of the three-volume history of the civil war. His essay is noteworthy for its attention to the problem of combined arms (especially the coordination of infantry and artillery in the attack) and the analysis of the role of the high density of machine guns in this breakthrough operation. See N. Triandafillov, "Perekopskaya operatsiya Krasnoy armii (takticheskiy etyud)" in Bubnov et. al., *Grazhdanskaya voyna 1918–1921: Boyevaya zhizn- Krasnoy armii*, 1:339–57.

72. V. Triandafillov, "O Volkovysskoi operatisii," *Krasnaya Armiya: Vestnik Voenno-nauchnogo obshchestva pri Voyennoy Akademii*, no. 10–11 (January–February 1922): 34–43.

73. Triandafillov, *Kharakter operatsii sovremennykh armii*, lst ed. (Moscow: Gosizdat, Otdel Voyenlit, 1929), 1ff.

74. *Field Regulations of the Red Army 1929* (Washington DC: Foreign Broadcast Information Service, 1985), 63–93. The connection between future war (*budushchaya voyna*) and operational art (*operativnoye iskusstvo*) was elucidated by I. Ivanov in a bibliography he published in 1934. There the posthumous second (1933) edition of Triandafillov's book was listed as the basic work in four out of twelve major categories, that is, contemporary operational means, conduct of operations, meeting operations, and offensive operations. Under the subtopics listed for conduct of operations, *Kharakter operatsii sovremennykh armii* was listed as the basic work for studying general questions, control of operations, and transport and rear. See I. Ivanov, "Voyenno-tekhnicheskaya literatura po voprosam kharaktera budushchey voyny i operativnogo iskusstva," *Voyna i revolyutsiya*, no. 2 (March–April 1934): 13–30.

75. USSR, *Narodnyy Komissariat Oborony, Vremennyy polevoy ustav RKKA 1936 (PU 36)* (Moscow: Gosvoyenizdat, 1937), 1ff.

76. V. K. Triandafillov, *Kharakter operatsii sovremennykh armii*, 4th ed. (Moscow: Voyenizdat, 1937), 235–54.

77. M. N. Tukhachevsky, "K voprosu o sovremennoy strategii," in *Voyna i voyennoe isskustvo v svete istoricheskogo materializma* (Moscow: Gosizdat, 1927), 127–33.

78. G. S. Isserson, "Zapiski sovremennika o M. N. Tukhachevskom," *Voyenno-istoricheskiy zhurnal*, no. 4 (April 1964): 65–67.

79. USSR, RKKA, *IV Upravlenie Shtaba, Budushchaya voyna* (Moscow, 1928), i–iv.

80. USSR, RKKA, *IV Upravlenie Shtaba*, vii.

81. USSR, RKKA, *IV Upravlenie Shtaba*, xi.

82. USSR, RKKA, *IV Upravlenie Shtaba*, xii.

83. USSR, RKKA, *IV Upravlenie Shtaba*, 724–35.

84. USSR, RKKA, *IV Upravlenie Shtaba*, 638.

85. USSR, RKKA, *IV Upravlenie Shtaba*, 645–46.

86. USSR, RKKA, *IV Upravlenie Shtaba*, 650.

87. USSR, RKKA, *IV Upravlenie Shtaba*, 653.

88. USSR, RKKA, *IV Upravlenie Shtaba*, 653–54.

89. USSR, RKKA, *IV Upravlenie Shtaba*, 656–57.

90. USSR, RKKA, *IV Upravlenie Shtaba*, 690.

91. I. V. Stalin, "O zadachakh khoziaistvennikov," in *Sochineniya* (Moscow: Gosizdat politicheskoy literatury, 1951) 13:39.

92. The terminology used for various approaches to the modernization of land warfare was even more confusing across cultures than it was within cultures. The Soviet usages have been retained in this essay in accordance with the author's explanation provided in the text. However, the Soviet term "motorization" equates roughly to the English term "mechanization," while the Soviet term "mechanization" equates roughly to the English term "armored warfare." *Ed.*

93. See "Motorizatsiya i mekhanizatsiya inostrannykh armii (k nachalu 1929 g.)," *Informatsionnyy sbornik*, no. 12 (December 1928): 145–57. Actually, as noted in the previous chapter, the British attitude was more ambivalent than the Soviet analysts detected.

94. M. N. Tukhachevsky, "Na baze dostignutogo—k novym zadacham," *Izbrannye proizvedeniya*. 2:67–68, and D. N. Nikishev, "Chelovek dela," in *Marshal Tukhachevskiy: Vospominaniya druzei i soratnikov*, ed. N. I. Koritsky, et al. (Moscow: Voyenizdat, 1965): 199–202.

95. *Sovetskaya voyennaya entsiklopediya* (Moscow: Sovetskaya entsiklopediya, 1933), 2:842–43.

96. I. Stalin, "O rabotakh aprel'skogo ob'edinennogo plenuma TsK i TsKK," in *Sochineniia*, 11:53–63.

97. "Dokladnaya zapiska komanduyushchego voyskami Leningradskogo voyennogo okruga M. N. Tukhachevskogo v Politbyuro TsK VPK(b) o rekonstruktsii RKKA, 19 iyunya 1930 g." in *Rossiyskiy Gosudarstvennyy Voyennyy Arkhiv, Marshal M. N. Tukhachevskiy (1893–1937 gg.): Komplekt dokumentov iz fondov RGVA*, delo 11/2–7.

98. M. Tukhachevsky, "Predislovie k knige G. Del'bryuka Istoriya voyennogo iskusstva v ramkakh politicheskoy istorii," in *Izbrannye proizvedeniya*, 2:116–46.

99. A. S. Bubnov, "Voyennaya sektsiya i ee blizhaishie zadachi," in *Kommunisticheskaya Akademiya, Sektsiya po izucheniyu problem voyny, Zapiski*, 1 (1930): 5.

100. Pavlenko, *Byla voyna . . . .*, 89–90.

101. M. N. Tukhachevsky, "O kharaktere sovremennykh voyn v svete resheniy VI kongressa Kominterna," in *Kommunisticheskaya Akademiya: Sektsiya po izucheniyu problem voyny, Zapiski* 1 (1930): 21–29.

102. *Voyna i revolyutsiya*, no. 3 (1930): 140–47.

103. Tukhachevsky, "Predislovie k knige Dzh. Fullera Reformatsiya voyny," *Izbrannye proizvedeniya*, 2:152.

104. Tukhachevky, "Novye voprosy voyny," in *Izbrannye proizvedenniya*, 2: 184–87.

105. "Pis'mo M. N. Tukhachevskogo K. E. Voroshilovu o raznoglasiyakh v srede kommandnogo sostava RKKA po voprosu o primenenii novykh form vedeniya boevykh operatsiy, 20 noyabrya 1933 g." in *Rossiyskiy Gosudarstvennyy Voyennyy Arkhiv, Marshal M. N. Tukhachevsky (1893–1937 gg.): Komplekt dokumentov iz fondov* RGVA, delo 16/1.

106. RGVA, delo 16/3.

107. Lennart Samuelson, *Soviet Defence Industry Planning: Tukhachevskii and Military-Industrial Mobilization, 1926–1937* (Stockholm: Institute of East European Economies, 1996), 168–73.

108. Olaf Groehler, *Selbstmoerderische Allianz: Deutsch-russishce Militaerbeziehungen, 1920–1941* (Berlin: Vision Verlag, 1992), 70–71.

109. "Doklad zamestetilya narkoma Oborony SSSR M. N. Tukhachevskogo Narkomu Oborony SSSR K. E. Voroshilovu o neobkhodimosti izmeneniya strategicheskogo plana vedeniya voyny na Zapade, 25 fevralya 1935 g." in *Rossiyskiy Gosudarstvennyy Voyennyy Arkhiv, Marshal M. N. Tukhachevskiy (1893–1937 gg.): Komplekt dokumentov iz fondov* RGVA, delo 18/1–11.

110. M. N. Tukhachevsky, "Rukopis' stat'i M. N. Tukhachevskogo 'Voyennye plany Gitlera' s pravkoy I. V. Stalina, 29 marta 1935 g." in "Iz arkhivov partii," *Izvestiya TsK* KPSS, no. 1 (January 1990): 169.

111. "O podogotovke germanii k voine: Zapiska M. M. Litvinova I. V. Stalinu, 3 dekabrya 1935 g." in "Iz arkhivov partii," *Izvestiia TsK* KPSS, no. 2 (February 1990): 211.

112. "O podogotovke germanii," 212.

113. "Pis'mo Ya Z. Suritsa N. N. Krestinskomu, 28 avgusta 1936 g." in "Iz arkhivov partii," *Izvestiya TsK* KPSS, no. 2 (February 1990): 212–15.

114. Robert Conquest, *The Great Terror*, 2nd ed. (New York: Oxford University Press, 1990), 167–81.

115. John Erickson, *The Soviet High Command, 1918–1941* (New York: St. Martin's, 1962), 433–76; Conquest, *The Great Terror*, 182–213; Pavlenko, *Byla voyna . . . .*, 94–137; and Donald Cameron Watt, "Who Plotted against Whom? Stalin's Purge of the Soviet High Command Revisited," *The Journal of Soviet Military Studies* 3 (March 1990): 46–65. There is little doubt that the NKVD started a black operation about conspiracy among senior German and Soviet military commanders and that Heydrich found it a useful vehicle to turn back

on the Soviet leadership. What is not as clear is the actual target of the initial NKVD black operation: was it seeking to undermine Hitler's confidence in the German officer corps or simply to discredit the Soviet officers as part of an NKVD action or at Stalin's personal direction? Stalin's biographer, Gen. Dmitriy Volkogonov, saw Stalin as responding to two fabricated conspiracies: Heydrich's operation linking Tukhachevsky to the German generals and Yezhov's operation that linked Tukhachevsky to Trotsky. See Dmitriy Volkogonov, *Triumf i tragediya: I. V. Stalin, politicheskiy portret* (Moscow: Izdatel'stvo Agentstva pechati Novosti, 1989), bk. 1, pt. 2, 254–59.

116. A. S. Stepanov, "O Masshtabakh repressiy v krasnoy armii v predvoyennye gody," *Voyenno-istoricheskiy zhurnal,* no. 5 (1993): 59–65.

117. Pavlenko, *Byla voyna* . . . . , 93.

118. "Akt o prieme narkomata oborony soyuza SSR tov. Timoshenko S. K. ot tov. Voroshilova K. E.," *Izvestiya TsK* KPSS, no. 1 (1990): 193–209, and M. Moiseev, "Smena rukovodstva Narkomata oborony SSSR v svyazi s urokami sovetsko-finlyandskoy voyny 1939–1940 gg.," *Izvestiya TsK KPSS,* no. 1 (1990): 210–15.

119. On Zhukov's proposal and its significance see E. I. Zyuzin, "Upryamye fakty nachala voyny," *Voyenno-istoricheskiy zhurnal,* no. 2 (February 1992): 14–22.

120. G. K. Zhukov, *Vospominaniya i razmyshleniya,* 3 vols. (Moscow: Izdatel'stvo Agenstva pechati "Novosti," 1984), 1:287.

121. V. B. Makovsky, "Prikrytie gosgranitsy nakanune voyny," *Voyenno-istoricheskiy zhurnal,* no. 5 (1993): 51–58.

122. Volkogonov, *Triumf i tragediya: I. V. Stalin, politicheskiy portret,* bk. 2, pt. 1, 142.

123. Volkogonov, *Triumf i tragediya,* bk. 1, pt. 2, 308.

124. Robert Savushkin, "In the Tracks of a Tragedy: On the 50th Anniversary of the Start of the Great Patriotic War," *The Journal of Soviet Military Studies* 4 (June 1991): 213–51.

125. David M. Glantz, *Stumbling Colossus: The Red Army on the Eve of World War* (Lawrence: University Press of Kansas, 1998).

126. Jacob W. Kipp, "Barbarossa, Soviet Covering Forces and the Initial Period of War: Military History and AirLand Battle," *The Journal of Soviet Military Studies,* 1 (June 1988): 188–212. For the best single-volume treatment of the operations of the Great Patriotic War see David M. Glantz and Jonathan House, *When Titans Clashed: How the Red Army Stopped Hitler* (Lawrence: University Press of Kansas, 1995).

5. FROM FRONTIER CONSTABULARY TO MODERN ARMY

The U.S. Army between the World Wars

David E. Johnson

The English historian C. V. Wedgwood perceptively noted that "history is lived forward, but it is written in retrospect. We know the end before we consider the beginning and we can never wholly recapture what it was like to know the beginning only."[1] This intellectual constraint is particularly compelling in a study of the American army between the two world wars. Conditioned by the reality of World War II it is easy to approach the interwar period from a teleological perspective that has assumed virtually mythological dimensions.

The most familiar version of the "fate" of the army during the interwar era is one that argues that although it endeavored to maintain its readiness, the army was unprepared for the enormous demands of World War II mainly because a miserly Congress supported by a "peace-minded" and isolationist American public denied it the funds and manpower needed to maintain an adequate military establishment.[2] This view was eloquently expressed by John S. Wood, an officer who served in the interwar army: "Back to normalcy was the postwar slogan, and back to normalcy the postwar Army went, struggling to keep alive a flickering flame and faltering spirit of national preparedness, struggling to maintain and modernize its arms and equipment, and struggling for its very life to obtain the funds necessary for its meager existence. Back it went to promotions few and far between, to small posts and small units, and to the apathy that follows periods of high endeavor."[3]

This public and official malaise had dire consequences because the army "became tragically insufficient and . . . incapable of restoration save after the loss of many lives and the expenditure of other resources beyond man's comprehension."[4] In short, "Although many dedicated individual professional soldiers had during the 1920s and 1930s conscientiously studied to be ready for the next war, decline, neglect, and stagnation marked America's military forces."[5]

This essay presents a different perspective, arguing that in addition to the external challenges the army faced during the interwar period, the War Department had internal problems that contributed significantly to its unpreparedness for World War II. Even though the army faced severe resource constraints, it also had intellectual and institutional defects that exacerbated fiscal and manpower shortfalls. Ironically, the army faced these same weaknesses before World War I. Maj. Gen. Johnson Hagood, a member of the War Department general staff before World War I, argued in 1927: "Our unpreparedness did not come from lack of money, lack of soldiers, or lack of supplies. It came from lack of brains, or perhaps it would be fairer to say, lack of genius."[6] Hagood, echoing Wedgwood's insight, noted the difficulty in addressing the army's deficiencies: "Why, seeing these things did I not do something to correct them? The answer is that I did not see them, or seeing them did not understand. Hindsight is better than foresight."[7]

Hagood was unable to gauge events accurately because of the culture in which he had spent his career. He faced a challenge before World War I similar to the one his successors faced during the interwar period: immersion in the day-to-day realities of an army making the difficult cultural and institutional transition from frontier constabulary to modern army, from absolute faith in man and animal to reliance on machines and science. These transitions began after the Spanish American War and received added impetus during and after World War I.

The Origins of the Modern American Army

The army's abysmal performance in the Spanish American War, when "the absence of any planning and preparation, the lack of co-ordination and co-operation among the bureaus, and the delay caused by red tape had become a public scandal," led to significant reform efforts.[8] That war and the subsequent Philippine insurrection clearly demonstrated that existing institutional arrangements were woefully inadequate. No longer could the army rely on poorly trained volunteers to man its ranks or on an inefficient bureau system to plan and support operations in the field.

The army also faced significantly expanded responsibilities. For the first time in its history the United States was an imperial power. Permanent garrisons in the Caribbean and the Pacific required manning and support. In short, the U.S. Army was being forced to adapt to a new reality far beyond its prewar capabilities.

By the eve of World War I, the foundations for fundamental change in the army, laid by Elihu Root, secretary of war in the aftermath of the Spanish American War, were beginning to take hold. Root's most difficult challenge was the creation of a general staff with a chief of staff at its head. Inherent in this new arrangement was the abolition of the position of commanding general and the curtailing of the powerful bureaus. Still, although a general staff act was passed in February 1903, it took a decade of infighting—culminating in the Wood-Ainsworth controversy—to establish the ascendancy of the chief of staff's position.[9]

Root also made significant strides in military education. The haphazard army school system was rationalized; a tiered system was established where, based on their ability, officers progressed through a system that began with post schools with prescribed courses of instruction and concluded with special service schools for the technical branches. The ablest graduates attended the General Service and Staff College at Fort Leavenworth, Kansas, and the best from Leavenworth eventually studied at the Army War College in Washington DC.[10] Additionally, the students at the War College complemented their studies with staff work, providing needed assistance to the small general staff.[11] The establishment of a Joint Army and Navy Board in 1903 enhanced interservice cooperation and planning.[12]

Root also took on the thorny problem of manpower mobilization. The passage of the Dick Act in January 1903 was the first in a series of bills that attempted to increase the efficiency of the reserve forces using federal funding and standards. The National Defense Act of 1916 was the last such measure before the American participation in World War I. It authorized a regular army of 175,000 and a national guard of more than 457,000.[13]

Thus the army had begun to reform itself from a frontier constabulary, augmented in time of crisis by an infusion of amateur volunteers, to a modern army. Nevertheless these efforts were clearly inadequate in the face of the test posed by the entry of America into World War I. When the United States entered the war on 6 April 1917, the regular army numbered 127,588 officers and men and was bolstered by 181,620 national guard soldiers in federal and state service. That same month 800,000 French forces, under the command of Gen. Robert Nivelle, attacked along the Aisne River. When the offensive ended in mid-May, the combined French and German casualties numbered over 290,000 men—a total twice the size of the American regular army.[14]

After three years of slaughter in the trenches, French Marsh. Joseph Joffre stated succinctly what the Allies needed from the United States: "men, men, men."[15] The Allies would have to wait—in part because the American army insisted that it remain a separate entity rather than have its manpower amalgamated into existing formations as the Allies wanted, and in part because the entire American Expeditionary Force (AEF) had to be built from the ground up.

The AEF as a whole needed to be armed, trained, equipped, and organized to fight a European war. Furthermore, division and higher level staffs required reorganization along the lines of French and British models.[16] To train these staffs the AEF created an Army General Staff College at Langres, France, since the prewar army school system had not produced sufficient graduates "trained for staff duty . . . and there were many phases of modern warfare staff requirements with which even they were not familiar."[17] Consequently, the AEF was not ready for even limited offensive operations until May 1918.[18]

The war the American army entered not only required mass armies but also mass firepower and mountains of materiel. Again, the United States was ill-prepared. The artillery, machine guns, airplanes, poison gas, tanks, and munitions that were the staples of modern war were beyond the production capacity of American industry. In the past the army had relied upon its limited technical services and bureaus for its modest needs; for the war in Europe the Allies had to supply virtually all of the AEF's requirements. Brig. Gen. Fox Conner, AEF G-3, noted the pervasiveness of this dependence: "Not one American-made gun of the most essential calibers appeared upon the battle front in the 18 months from our declaration of war to the Armistice."[19]

Finally, World War I showed that the largely autonomous bureaus and a constrained general staff could not meet the demands of mobilizing, deploying, or supplying the AEF. When the United States entered the war, a mere nineteen general staff officers were assigned to Washington; they had been censured in 1916 by President, Woodrow Wilson for making plans for a war with Germany.[20] The deficiencies of the system soon became apparent; and the War Department was reorganized under a new chief of staff, Gen. Peyton C. March, who returned from the AEF to assume the post. The general staff rapidly grew to 1,072 personnel to cope with the immense requirements posed by the war. Using the powers of the May 1918 Overman Act, which gave the president the authority to reorganize government agencies for the duration of the war, March ruthlessly streamlined, centralized, and restructured the War Department.[21] Temporarily, at least, the chief of staff and the general staff gained control of the bureaus, making it possible to man and support the growing AEF.

Despite its deficiencies the American army tipped the scales in the war. The failure of the final German offensives and the immense casualties they produced devastated the morale and discipline of Germany's military forces and civilian populace at precisely the time the Americans were coming into their own: "It was the Americans—not the handful of divisions in the line, but the huge and growing reserve of well-fed, unwearied and unshaken men they supplied. Whereas in August the average field strength of a German battalion had sunk to 660–665 men, and the only fresh reserves were 300,000 men of the 1900 class called up in June, the American army in France had risen to 1,473,190. It was not the present that was impossible; it was the future. The British and French had won the battles of 1918, but it was the Americans who won the war."[22]

The Lessons of the Great War

When the Great War ended on 11 November 1918, the American army faced two major challenges: demobilization and the determination of its postwar military policy. Demobilization, although not without problems, proceeded rapidly: within ten months 3,280,000 soldiers returned to civilian life.[23] The framing of a new military policy in light of the experiences of the war was a more difficult issue.

The army's leadership understood that its nation and its service had been unprepared for a major war. Gen. Fox Conner stated the case quite clearly in his "Final Report" to the AEF G-3: "The unprepared nation is helpless in a great war unless it can depend upon other nations to shield it while it prepares." Conner also pointed out that unpreparedness had a price: "The necessity of saving a defeat and, next, the possibility of winning the war in 1918 . . . required putting the American soldier into battle without the training, discipline, and leadership which he deserved."[24]

Even though there was a broad consensus that the lessons of the war had to be institutionalized, there were differing ideas about the means of doing so. Understandably the key players were Gen. John J. Pershing, the commander of the AEF, and General March, the chief of staff. The efforts of these two officers were not coordinated, probably because of the enmity that had developed between them during the war.

In the aftermath of the war the AEF examined its experiences. Each of its staff sections and services prepared reports, and a number of boards convened. General Pershing convened the most authoritative of these boards, the "Superior Board," which met from 27 April to 1 July 1919.[25] The wartime experience of the AEF framed the context within which the Superior Board deliberated—a frustrating year of organization, mobilization, and deployment followed by a brief period of spectacularly successful offensive operations (at least by World War I standards). Consequently, the board's recommendations addressed the army's structural and administrative deficiencies but affirmed the correctness of American doctrine.

The board acknowledged the complexity of modern war and logistics, the need for functional staffs, and the importance of sufficient training before combat.[26] Echoing Conner's views, the board recognized that the hasty American mobilization and a national "policy of unpreparedness" had made it necessary to send insufficiently trained men and leaders into combat, jeopardizing operations and causing needless casualties.[27] To remedy this situation the board urged that "Every man that we expect to utilize in war should have the benefit of training in peace for the role he is expected to play."[28]

The members of the Superior Board, in a rather astounding misreading of the realities of the brutal trench warfare that had characterized the war before American involvement, extolled offensive operations as the only decisive course in war and conceded the expectation of heavy infantry casualties.[29] The board also somewhat arrogantly maintained that the AEF's brief experience validated the American doctrine of "open warfare" that hinged on two long-established tenets of war: "decisive results are obtained only by the offensive" and "aggressiveness wins battles."[30] Indeed, the board claimed: "The stabilized trench warfare which prevailed in France in 1917 was due in a great measure to the lack of aggressiveness of both sides. Infantry must be self-reliant. Too much reliance was placed by the infantry on the auxiliary arms and not enough on the means within the infantry itself. This tended to destroy the initiative."[31] This dismissive statement likely was the result of the American army's having been spared the years of slaughter in the trenches and the murderous "big pushes" before it became involved in operations late in the war against a German army that was largely exhausted and demoralized. Additionally, the American army suffered relatively light casualties when compared to the other combatants. According to U.S.

Army official figures, of the 4,057,101 men who served in the American army during the war and in northern Russia and Siberia immediately after the war, only 50,510 died in battle while another 193,663 were wounded. Indeed, the army's 55,868 losses to disease and injury exceeded its combat deaths.[32] These figures pale in comparison to the losses suffered by the other major combatants: Germany, over 2 million dead; Russia over 1.8 million dead; France over 1.3 million dead; and Great Britain, over 700,000 dead.

The board clung to a belief in the ascendancy of man on the battlefield even in the face of the increasing technological sophistication evidenced in airplanes, tanks, modern artillery, machine guns, and poison gas. Thus the board concluded: "The infantry of an army must be recognized as the basic arm and all other arms must be organized and made subordinate to its needs, functions and methods."[33] The board also concluded that there was still a need for horse cavalry because "it is improbable that the conditions of Northern France will ever be reproduced on American soil" and "on other fields and under different conditions our cavalry will find useful employment as in the past."[34] Therefore the board accommodated some of the realities of modern war but it did so with one foot firmly planted in its past.

The assumptions that guided General March differed little from those of the members of the Superior Board. March confidently proclaimed: "The war has taught many lessons; the principles of warfare, however, remain unchanged. It was not won, as some had predicted it would be, by some new and terrible development of modern science; it was won, as has every other war in history, by men, munitions, and morale."[35] March, like his contemporaries on the Superior Board, was convinced "it is now, as always heretofore, the Infantry with rifle and bayonet that, in the final analysis, must bear the brunt of the assault and carry it on to victory."[36]

As the AEF demobilized and returned to the United States, General March and Secretary of War Newton Baker framed a bill to correct the deficiencies encountered by the army during its mobilization and prosecution of the war. Key provisions included strengthening the general staff, enhancing officer education, rationalizing industrial mobilization capabilities and procedures, and institutionalizing many of the organizational changes made under the aegis of the Overman Act. The real heart of the Baker-March bill was, however, its proposal for a five hundred thousand–man regular army, augmented in wartime by reservists prepared through a compulsory system of universal military training.[37]

The regulars were to be the "half-strength skeleton of a field army of five corps" augmented in an emergency by the mobilization of reserves prepared through universal military training.[38] It was, in essence, a return to Emory Upton's vision of a large, expansible regular army.[39]

Passage of the bill as envisioned by March would have been difficult even for a chief of staff on excellent terms with Congress. For March, who was deeply resented by many in Congress for his "highhandedness" during the war, failure was virtually inevitable. Some even attributed less-than-selfless motives to the drive for a large regular army. A *New York Times* article charged: "The truth is that a force of 500,000 is looked upon with favor by every officer who has been demoted and would like to resume his war grade."[40] There was some basis for suspicion since the authorizations for officers and general officers, even after Congress trimmed March's request, almost tripled as compared to prewar figures.[41] Regardless of the reasons behind his proposal for a large regular army, March was completely out of step with two fundamental American traditions: distrust of standing armies and unswerving belief in the preeminence of the citizen soldier. To Congress the war record of the AEF, rather than being a cause for dramatic change, was proof that these cherished traditions served the nation well.[42]

March's arguments for an unprecedentedly large army also lacked a compelling rationale because they were not based on any present or future threats to the nation. Clearly March never satisfactorily answered the crucial question posed by Representative John F. Miller of Washington during hearings on the bill: "What world conditions would make it necessary to have a force of such size?"[43] Had not the country just won the "war to end all wars?" Were not the physical isolation of the United States and the shield provided by the navy still sufficient to avoid having to invest in a large regular army? Instead, March seemed to conclude that because the army had new training camps, large numbers of veterans, and stockpiles of equipment and munitions that would support a system of universal training it would be a shame to waste these resources.[44] These arguments backfired on the chief of staff. For an economy-minded Congress the army's surpluses would save money by curtailing appropriations for weapons procurement and development.[45] General Pershing, the returned hero of the AEF, likely did the most harm to the five hundred thousand–man army concept when he testified: "I am of the opinion that we can place the outside figure at from 275,000 to 300,000, officers and men."[46]

In June 1920 Congress passed a watered-down national defense act that authorized a regular army of 17,717 officers and 280,000 men, with no requirement for universal military training. The War Department had dropped the training measure when it threatened passage of the bill. Without mandatory training the regular army had to rely on the voluntary national guard and organized reserves for augmentation during an emergency.[47]

The National Defense Act of 1920 also changed the army's structure, with a goal of instituting a peacetime establishment "capable of effecting a complete and rapid mobilization in time of war."[48] The old territorial departments in the continental United States, Alaska, and Puerto Rico were replaced by nine corps areas, each, according to the act, having one regular army, two national guards, and three organized reserve divisions. Together these divisions were to form the army's mobilization base in the event of an emergency. The corps were then grouped into three field armies for the prosecution of any war. Overseas forces were allotted to the territorial departments in the Panama Canal Zone, Hawaii, and the Philippine Islands.[49]

The 1920 National Defense Act also modified the structure of the War Department general staff. The change was along lines similar to those created by March during the war. Initially the functional staff agencies consisted of an operations division, a military intelligence division, a war plans division, and a supply division.[50] The responsibility for procurement and mobilization planning shifted to the assistant secretary for war.[51] The central assumption undergirding this organization was that the general staff would limit itself to mobilization and support of "autonomous theater commanders" who would retain responsibility for combat operations. Such had been the case during the war, when March and the general staff had supported Pershing and the AEF.[52]

When Pershing became chief of staff in 1921 he again reorganized the War Department general staff. These changes, along the lines of the structure of the AEF general staff, were based on recommendations by a board headed by Maj. Gen. James G. Harbord. The new structure consisted of a G-1, personnel division; a G-2, military intelligence division; a G-3, operations and training division; a G-4, supply division; and a war plans division. More important, the War Department general staff took on a new role: the coordination of combat operations and the responsibility for strategic planning. From his new perspective as the chief of staff Pershing was apparently comfortable with the increased authority of those in Washington over commanders in the field—a possibility he had vigorously resisted at every opportunity when he himself commanded the AEF.[53]

The National Defense Act of 1920 had many positive attributes. The army school system was strengthened, with service on the general staff restricted to officers qualified through higher military education. The promotion system was changed to a single army list (less chaplains and medical officers) instead of the previous system in which each branch of the line and each bureau maintained its own list. This improvement had the potential to lessen branch parochialism among officers. Nevertheless, this new system, like the old one, was based on seniority rather than on merit; promotions during the interwar period slowed to a glacial pace. The act better defined the roles of the National Guard and the organized reserves and established a structure for manpower mobilization. Additionally, the responsibility for procurement and industrial mobilization planning shifted to the assistant secretary for war in order to avoid the chaos experienced during World War I.[54] Despite these improvements the 1920 National Defense Act and the resulting reorganization of the War Department also had several significant deficiencies that created institutional barriers to innovation.

For example, the act limited the control that March and the general staff had established over the bureaus during the war; the War Department "returned generally to the prewar traditional pattern of fragmented, diffused authority and responsibility with effective control again at the bureau level, subject as before to detailed Congressional supervision."[55] In essence the general staff was relegated to the functions of planning and coordinating the activities of the branches, services, and bureaus, instead of the operating and directing roles it had had during General March's tenure.[56] The situation actually worsened because the number of bureau equivalent structures increased with the addition of the Finance Department, the Chemical Warfare Service, the Air Service, the Chief of Chaplains, and branch chiefs for the infantry, cavalry, and field artillery. There was, however, one deletion. The Tank Corps, established during the war, was abolished; its functions were transferred to the infantry.[57] Its demise was quite logical because the prevailing view among the army's leadership was essentially that of the Superior Board: "The tanks should be recognized as an infantry supporting and accompanying weapon incapable of independent decisive action."[58]

The National Defense Act of 1920 produced seventeen branches, bureaus, and services as well as an Adjutant General's Department within the War Department.[59] Meanwhile the role of the War Department general staff was circumscribed because "It was not to 'assume or engage in work of an administrative nature that pertains to established bureaus or offices of the War Department' which might 'imperil [their] responsibility or initiative,' impair their efficiency, or unnecessarily duplicate their work."[60] Indeed, the bureau chiefs had direct access to Congress and sometimes undercut the chief of staff and secretary of war.[61] The general staff would have had difficulty accomplishing more than its mandate because its authorized strength was only ninety-three officers, including the chief of staff. This small body had responsibility for war planning, manpower mobilization, preparing for military operations, and keeping tabs on "all questions affecting the efficiency of the Army."[62]

The 1920 National Defense Act created a highly decentralized system. To the already powerful bureaus and services, chiefs of the combat arms were added. This was a structural change that Maj. Gen. Hugh L. Scott, chief of staff from November 1914 to September 1917, had recommended as early as 1915. Testimony by army officers during congressional hearings on the National Defense Act strongly supported the addition of branch chiefs.[63] Although created for the laudable purpose of strengthening the voice of the "line" within the War Department hierarchy, these new offices added to the fragmentation of the prewar system. The chiefs of the combat arms, each a major general, reported directly to the chief of staff and had responsibility for supervising their branch service schools, formulating tactical doctrine for their arms, developing organization plans, preparing instructional and training publications, cooperating with the supply branches in the development of arms and equipment, assigning and classifying personnel within their branches, and preparing mobilization and war plans.[64] In short, the chiefs of arms had broad authority over virtually everything that affected their branches. What was missing in the new War Department structure was a method for coordinating these largely autonomous branches.

The reorganization of the War Department under the National Defense Act of 1920 reflected the recognition that the army's raison d'être was to prepare for modern, total war. In the minds of the majority of the army's leaders the act established a system that would correct the two principal deficiencies encountered during World War I: mobilization of a mass army and supply of the resulting force.

One particularly contentious issue, however, confronted the War

Department as it tried to forge a new postwar organization—the role of military aviation. This issue in many ways defined the line between the old army and the new throughout the interwar era—between those who saw technology as a way to revolutionize warfare and those who clung to the past and saw machines merely as a means to improve existing concepts.

At the poles of the argument were those who believed that military aviation was merely an adjunct to ground operations and those who were convinced that it could be an independent and decisive combat force. Secretary of War Baker had attempted to defuse the issue by sending his assistant secretary of war, Benedict C. Crowell, to Europe in early 1919 to study British, French, and Italian aviation experiences. Baker also told Crowell that an independent American air organization was not an option. When Crowell returned he exceeded his instructions and recommended a cabinet-level national air service.[65] Baker was incensed almost to the point of asking for Crowell's resignation, and denounced Crowell's findings.[66]

The aviation debate soon spilled over into Congress. Shortly after Crowell submitted his report to Baker in July 1919, Representative Charles F. Curry of California and Senator Harry S. New of Indiana introduced bills to establish a separate department of aeronautics.[67] Baker then appointed a board under Maj. Gen. Charles T. Menoher, the War Department's director of air service, to review proposals for a separate air organization. Not surprisingly, the Menoher Board recommended that the air service should remain within the War Department.[68]

In their testimony before Congress traditionalists such as Baker, March, and Pershing supported the conclusions of the Menoher Board and stressed the subordinate role of aviation to ground commanders. To these officers, aviation—like artillery and armor—was an auxiliary of the infantry.[69] The essence of their views was perhaps best captured by the Superior Board:

Nothing so far brought out in the war shows that Aerial activities can be carried on, independently of ground troops, to such an extent as to materially affect the conduct of the war as a whole. It is possible, perhaps, that future wars may develop aerial forces of far greater extent than those provided in this war. It is safe to assume that Air forces will not be developed for war purposes to such an extent as to largely supplant ground and water forces, until such a proportion of the people become air-faring people as now are known as sea-faring people. In other words, aerial activity must bear much the same relation to the commercial life of the nation as at present sea-faring activities bear to public trade and commerce.[70]

Others, however, had different perspectives. Joining the already vocal Crowell were officers such as Brig. Gen. William (Billy) Mitchell and Maj. Benjamin D. Foulois. In their testimony before Congress the two presented arguments that resounded throughout the interwar era: the importance of establishing a strong commercial aviation industry; the belief that the air weapon was decisive; and the conviction that the main impediment to the development of military aviation was the conservatism of ground officers. Mitchell claimed that the air weapon was not only decisive but that it also had the potential to make navies useless.[71]

The immediate postwar status of the air service was specified in the National Defense Act of 1920. Even though no separate aviation department was established, army aviators made some gains. The air service became a combatant arm, more or less equivalent to the infantry, cavalry, and field artillery, but with an important difference: the air service had the authority to develop and supply its own technical equipment. Unlike the other combat arms it was not dependent on the services and bureaus for materiel. Additionally, officers would in the future be assigned to the air service rather than detailed from other branches, as had been the practice until that time. Finally, the act placed the operational control of flying units firmly in the hands of pilots by specifying that only flying officers could command flying units.[72]

The National Defense Act of 1920 was "the axis about which all army activities . . . revolved during the interwar years."[73] The act reflected the recognition by both Congress and the War Department that the army's fundamental reason for being was to prepare for modern, total war. In the minds of the majority of the army's leadership this meant establishing a system that would correct the two principal deficiencies it had encountered during World War I: providing for the manpower mobilization of a mass army and supplying its materiel needs. Although the act did not address all of the army's concerns (required universal military training being the most obvious loss), it had incorporated most of the measures the War Department had requested. In the wake of the act's passage the army set about reorganizing itself, basing its plans on a force of 17,700 officers and 280,000 soldiers. The American domestic situation soon forced a reassessment of these plans.

America between the Wars

In the aftermath of the Great War, President Wilson attempted to change the traditional course of American foreign policy by embracing an internationalist role. The linchpin of Wilson's agenda was the entry of the United States into the League of Nations. Wilson failed in this effort despite a two-year campaign to get the United States into the league. The "irreconcilables" in the Republican-dominated Senate, led by majority leader Henry Cabot Lodge, refused to ratify the Treaty of Versailles or the League of Nations Covenant and ended the war by joint resolution of Congress on 2 July 1921.[74]

From a post–World War II perspective the rejection of Wilsonian internationalism is often cited as a shortsighted abrogation of responsibility by the United States and a key to the failure of the League of Nations. Thus the world was irrevocably placed upon the path to another international conflict.[75] From the perspective of the times, however, the Senate had good reason for concern.

When the Armistice ended World War I, the United States had troops on occupation duty in Germany and others fighting in Russia. Additionally, Wilson wanted to establish a mandate over the state of Armenia. A military commission to Armenia reported the expected high costs of the mandate to the United States: 59,000 soldiers and a five-year cost of more than $750 million.[76] To take the further step of joining the League of Nations implied even greater military commitment because the treaty required signatories "to respect and preserve as against external aggression the territorial integrity and existing political independence of all Members of the League."[77]

Aside from the arguments that internationalism had obvious costs and that it conflicted with the American tradition of avoiding entangling alliances, Wilson faced growing popular disillusionment with a greater American role in world affairs. The January 1919 publication of the "secret treaties" negotiated among the Allies during the war that seemingly divided up the spoils of victory gave lie to Wilson's idealistic Fourteen Points.[78] The reprinting in the United States of John Maynard Keynes's *The Economic Consequences of the Peace* in 1920 fueled further disenchantment. This blistering polemic paraded the failures of the Versailles peace process and harshly criticized its architects, particularly Wilson.[79]

The American people ended the discussion of Wilsonian internationalism when they elected Republican Warren G. Harding to the presidency in 1920. Promising a policy of "Back to Normalcy," Harding made rejection of the League of Nations Covenant a key plank in his campaign platform.[80] In the domestic sector, normalcy signaled a return to laissez-faire economics and a reduction in government expenditures. On the international scene, normalcy meant the avoidance of entangling alliances and reliance on the rule of law, rather than force.[81]

At the time the prudence of this course seemed obvious. After a brief recession in 1920, the American economy boomed for nearly a decade. Several diplomatic initiatives seemed to portend a world less likely to resort to war. Treaties, resulting from conferences in Washington in 1922 and London in 1930, limited naval armaments. More significant, the very concept of war was challenged when fifteen nations signed a treaty negotiated between American Secretary of State Frank B. Kellogg and French Foreign Minister Aristide Briand. Sixty-two nations eventually subscribed to the Kellogg-Briand Pact, which outlawed war.[82]

Quite simply, the prospects for an enduring peace never seemed more promising than in the 1920s. The absence of any military threat and the physical isolation of the United States only heightened this optimism and made the army an attractive source for budget cuts in the congressional drive for government economy. In February 1921 Congress passed a joint resolution that capped the number of enlisted men in the regular army at 175,000, even though President Wilson attempted to stop the measure because "such a reduction would cut down our armed forces below the margin of safety to the Nation."[83] Wilson's successor was less concerned with the size of the army and formulated a military budget that capitalized on the opportunity offered by the peaceful environment. President Harding based his military program on economy, a small expandable regular army, voluntary reserve training, and disarmament.[84] Harding's policy became the interwar standard, and army strength soon dropped below 140,000 officers and men—where it would remain until the late 1930s. Indeed, the 280,000-man limit stipulated in the National Defense Act of 1920 was not approached until 1940.[85]

Not surprisingly, army officers opposed the reductions in defense spending. General Pershing spoke for most, warning against "drifting into a pacifist state of mind" and arguing for the continuation of army and navy programs to ensure against the possibility of being "caught unprepared as we were at the beginning of the World War."[86]

Other officers wrote in service journals and made public and official statements that cautioned against reducing the War Department budget. Their actions soon brought official sanction that sharply limited their ability to have a voice. In June 1922 Secretary of War John W. Weeks issued a public statement that he would not allow serving officers "to go around the country attacking the organization of which he is a part."[87] Weeks made the rules clear: if an officer felt compelled to criticize policy he should resign first or face disciplinary action.[88]

In August 1923 Calvin Coolidge succeeded Harding and quickly made it clear that he wanted to reduce government spending and reduce taxes. Once again the army was an obvious target for cuts, and officers expressed their concerns. Coolidge viewed the public pleas by officers for an end to army reductions as "propaganda" and made it clear that he found their arguments "annoying."[89] Coolidge expanded on his views in an October 1925 speech, expressing what was a widely held national perception: "I can see no merit in any unnecessary expenditure of money to hire men to build fleets and carry muskets when international relations and agreements permit the turning of such resources into the making of good roads, the building of better homes, the promotion of education and all the others [sic] arts of peace which minister to the advancement of human welfare."[90]

Coolidge also warned that he believed it inappropriate for military officers to attempt to bring pressure on government policies by appealing to public opinion.[91] Coolidge backed his words with action, personally bringing charges against Col. Billy Mitchell when the latter alleged that the crash of the navy airship *Shenandoah* was the "direct result of incompetency, criminal negligence and almost treasonable administration of the national defense by the Navy and War Departments."[92] In the aftermath of the sensational Mitchell trial, the *New York Times* reported that Secretary of War Dwight F. Davis "is preparing to read the riot act to certain elements in the army if the Mitchell court-martial conviction fails to make a sufficient impression on officers involved as a disciplinary object lesson."[93]

Still, some officers persisted in their public arguments for preparedness until President Coolidge made the rules perfectly clear. In October 1927, army Chief of Staff Maj. Gen. Charles P. Summerall castigated the administration's military program during a speech in San Diego, California.[94] President Coolidge recalled Summerall to Washington, ostensibly to confer on the budget.[95] In reality, it was widely accepted that the president had summoned Summerall to discipline him.[96]

The lessons of the Mitchell and Summerall incidents changed the parameters of acceptable discourse: open criticism of public policy was clearly no longer an option available to serving officers.[97] Henceforth debates would center on purely military issues and take place largely within the army itself.

The prosperity of the 1920s abruptly halted with the onset of the Great Depression, and the army budget came under even heavier assault. On the eve of the depression President Herbert Hoover ordered a review of the military establishment, with the purpose of "making extensive reductions in the cost of the Army."[98] Following the stock market crash in 1929 the American economy spiraled downward; by 1933 there were fifteen million unemployed Americans.[99] In his autobiography, General of the Army Omar N. Bradley recalled the tenor of the times: "In those dark days, when almost every family in America was struggling to survive, and the possibility of war seemed as remote as the moon, money for a standing army seemed an absurd luxury."[100] Consequently, as the depression deepened Congress slashed the War Department's budget even further. Army appropriations plummeted from $346,979,179 in fiscal year 1931 to $277,066,381 in fiscal year 1934.[101]

Throughout the depression the national focus turned increasingly inward, a fact certainly driven by economic hardship, but also fueled by American disenchantment with international affairs and increased clamoring for isolation. In 1931 Japan, a signatory of the Kellogg-Briand Pact, invaded Manchuria, dashing hopes that the rule of law and moral sanctions could prevent aggression.[102] American antimilitarist sentiment grew with the highly publicized claims of the Senate Munitions Investigating Committee, chaired by Gerald P. Nye, that American armament makers had pulled the United States into World War I because of their lust for profits. Works such as the Book-of-the-Month-Club selection *Merchants of Death* contributed to public disillusionment by arguing that "the arms maker has risen and grown powerful, until he is one of the most dangerous factors in world affairs—a hindrance to peace, a promoter of war."[103] The American peace movement grew to twelve million members in the 1930s and had an audience of between forty-five and sixty million people. Finally, the regular army's widely publicized 1932 repression of the "bonus army" of veterans encamped in Washington DC did not enhance its reputation.[104]

Antagonism toward Europe also grew in the 1930s. As the depression gripped Europe, former allies failed to make payments on their World War I debts to the United States. An angry Congress passed the Johnson Default Act in 1934, which prohibited future loans to any foreign government in default. When fascist armies marched in Ethiopia and Spain, the United States passed a series of neutrality acts between 1935 and 1937 that tightened controls over American assistance to belligerents. An indication of the level that isolationist sentiment had reached is apparent in the constitutional amendment proposed by Representative Louis Ludlow of Indiana. The Ludlow resolution required a national referendum on any American declaration of war short of an invasion of the nation or its possessions. The measure failed in the House by the narrow margin of 209-188.[105]

The German invasion of Poland in September 1939 began to turn the tide of American isolationist and antimilitary sentiment. Domestically, a limited state of emergency declared by President Franklin D. Roosevelt started the nation rearming in earnest.[106] On the international scene the November 1939 Neutrality Act allowed "cash and carry" arms sales to belligerents.[107] By the December 1941 Japanese attack on Pearl Harbor, the United States was actively supporting potential allies through Lend-Lease aid, Anglo-American staff conferences, and secret talks between President Roosevelt and British Prime Minister Winston Churchill.[108] For the army this new threat to the nation meant vastly increased funding and rapid expansion. Indeed, the budget for 1942 totaled $29.5 billion, compared to $7.3 billion in 1941.[109] Active duty strength in 1942 surged to 206,422 officers and 2,869,186 soldiers, up from 99,536 officers and 1,362,779 soldiers in 1941.[110] What the army's leadership did with these vast resources was largely predetermined by decisions it had made before Pearl Harbor.

The Army between the Wars

The domestic and international forces at play in the United States between the world wars served mainly to constrain, rather than shape, army policies. The army believed that it had the basis for the institutional structures and organizations necessary to ensure preparedness. The national mood, which dictated "that the United States should not enter into military alliances or maintain military forces capable of offensive operations," did not find many army detractors; army strategic planning reflected this reality.[111] Throughout most of the interwar era, War Department planning remained theoretical, and planning was mainly for the sake of the exercise itself since there was no imminent threat to the United States.[112] The resulting "color" plans had as their aim "the classic General Staff ideal of being prepared with detailed military plans for action in any conceivable emergency."[113] These plans all focused on the unilateral defense of the United States "against any and all combinations of foreign powers."[114] The army and navy coordinated their war plans through the Joint Army and Navy Board, which had been reorganized in 1919.[115] Industrial planning was outside the general staff's direct purview, but progressed during the interwar era under the assistant secretary of war. Not until 1939, as the world teetered on the brink of war, did strategic planning begin to focus on more realistic threats to the United States. The results of this new joint army and navy effort—the five Rainbow plans—ranged from a defense of the Monroe Doctrine to an American coalition with Great Britain and France to fight Germany and Italy.[116]

Manpower mobilization, not strategic or industrial mobilization planning, continued as the central focus of the army's interwar planning efforts. Col. James K. Parsons, chief of the G-3 mobilization branch, captured the essence of the War Department's fixation on manpower in a 1928 lecture at the Army War College: "Lack of supply may prevent the mobilization of a particular unit, but it will never prevent a nation's mobilizing for defense. . . . In the last analysis, manpower is the primary factor, and its importance is supreme."[117] Parsons further noted: "The General Mobilization Plan [of 1928] . . . ignores the factors of supply and training, and is based entirely upon the rate which men . . . can be procured and organized."[118] As a result of this mindset, the general staff's interwar manpower mobilization plans remained preeminent and largely unsynchronized with either the strategic color or industrial mobilization plans.[119]

The focus on manpower mobilization had strong doctrinal roots within the War Department. This doctrine glorified the ascendancy of the infantryman on the field of battle and relegated all else to his support: "Whatever auxiliary methods are employed—strategical, tactical, mechanical, or moral, the final method is the physical encounter with bullet and bayonet—the human element is the decisive one."[120] The 1923 edition of the *Field Service Regulations*, in effect until 1939, noted the importance of combined arms warfare, but it stressed that "the mission of the infantry is the general mission of the entire force."[121] And that mission was crystal clear: "The ultimate objective of all military operations is the destruction of the enemy's armed forces by battle. Decisive defeat in battle breaks the enemy's will to war and forces him to sue for peace."[122]

Given this prevailing doctrinal context, the two new military technologies that had shown the greatest potential in World War I—the tank and the airplane—existed solely to support the ground infantry battle. The *Field Service Regulations* defined these roles. The mission of the tank was to "assist in the progression of the infantry by overcoming or neutralizing resistances or breaking down obstacles that check the infantry advance."[123] Similarly, military aviation had the mission of providing observation, attack, pursuit, and bombardment units. In each of these roles, aviation supported the ground mission: observation provided reconnaissance for the ground commander and adjusted artillery fire; attack units assaulted enemy ground units; pursuit cleared the skies of hostile aircraft, thereby protecting ground units; and bombardment attacked ground objectives, especially those "beyond the effective range of artillery."[124] In the minds of many ground officers, the wisest use of offensive aviation was as long-range artillery.

Between 1923 and 1939 a gradual evolution took place in army doctrine. The importance given to combined arms increased. The 1939 *Field Service Regulations* stressed the point that "No one arm wins battles" although the infantry was still "charged with the principal mission in battle."[125] Tanks "as a rule" were "employed to assist the advance of infantry foot troops" although there was growing recognition that they were "a powerful maneuvering force in the hands of a higher commander with which to influence the course of combat" (even though the battalion was generally the largest tank formation).[126] The manual also recognized the increased importance of aviation, but its role was still inextricably linked to "the accomplishment of the mission of the field forces."[127]

In the years between 1939 and 1941 the army attempted to digest the lessons from conflicts in Europe and the Pacific. In May 1941 the War Department issued new *Field Service Regulations*. The new doctrine clearly emphasized combined arms action, with the infantry defined as "an arm of close combat."[128] The role of tanks, found in both GHQ tank units and in the armored divisions after the 1940 creation of the Armored Force, also expanded, with the manual noting that the mobility of the tank should not be restricted by tying it "too closely to foot troops."[129] The section on the armored division stressed the new organization's role in "*offensive operations* against *hostile rear areas*."[130] Finally, there remained a reluctance to admit the powers of strategic combat aviation. The 1941 *Field Service Regulations* still maintained that "The operations of both surface and air forces are directed to the attainment of a common objective. Missions that do not contribute to the attainment of the common objective are avoided."[131] In the American army that "common objective" remained unchanged from the one specified in the 1923 *Field Service Regulations*: "The *ultimate objective* of all military operations is the destruction of the enemy's armed forces in battle."[132]

Doctrinal development, however, remained secondary to the development of manpower mobilization plans. The effectiveness of these plans hinged on the implementation of the provisions of the National Defense Act of 1920. Immediately after passage of the act the army began its reorganization based on a regular army of 280,000 officers and men. The War Department started moving troops to flesh out its plans for regular army divisions in the nine corps areas. When Congress capped the size of the army the War Department decided to adhere to its plan, but filled units at lower levels.

Given the centrality that the size of the regular army played in mobilization planning, the large gap between the 1920 National Defense Act requirement and the numbers authorized by Congress caused considerable concern within the War Department. The army's efforts throughout the interwar era, therefore, remained fixed mainly on increasing active duty manpower so as to better support mobilization plans. When the battle for appropriations became intense, particularly during the depression, the army clung to its position that "everything except personnel, training, and civilian components could be sacrificed."[133]

This "manpower first" policy had a ruinous effect on the army's modernization and equipment programs. Of the $6,169,300,000 appropriated to the army between 1925 and 1940, only $854,556,000 went to fielding improved materiel. Of this modest amount $509,900,000 went directly to army aviation, leaving only $344,656,000, or 5.6 percent, for the "augmentation, modernization and replacement of arms and equipment for the ground elements of the Army of the United States."[134] Within the context of the War Department's fixation on the preeminence of trained manpower for a mobilization-based army, this policy is understandable, particularly when framed by the views espoused by Chief of Staff Douglas MacArthur as late as 1934: "It is easy, of course, to overemphasize the influence of machinery in war. It is man that makes war, not machines, and the human element must always remain the dominant one. Weapons are nothing but tools and each has its distinctive limitations as well as its particular capabilities. Effective results can be obtained only when an army is skillfully organized and trained so as to supplement inherent weaknesses in one type of weapon by peculiar powers in others."[135]

During most of the interwar era the equipment needs of the active army, or of any mobilizing force, had to come from World War I–vintage stockpiles because of the limited level of investment that had taken place. The War Department held that in a national emergency American industry would respond to the army's needs and provide modern equipment by mass producing the "pilot models that had previously been developed through limited funds."[136]

When Gen. Malin Craig succeeded MacArthur as chief of staff in 1935 he began changing the direction of army mobilization planning with the initiation of the Protective Mobilization Plan. This plan centered on a four hundred thousand–man Initial Protective Force, made up of existing regular army and National Guard units, that would defend the country at the beginning of any emergency. Behind this shield the additional six hundred thousand men of the million-man Protective Mobilization Plan would form.[137]

To equip the Initial Protective Force Craig made a decision that effectively stopped the research and development of new weapons. He froze designs so the army could begin procuring standardized equipment for the Initial Protective Force and stockpiling munitions for the remainder of the Protective Mobilization Plan's projected force.[138] In 1939 this resulted in a research and development budget that totaled only $5 million or approximately 0.8 percent of the War Department's budget.[139] Craig's chosen course was surely justifiable, given the worsening international situation and the obsolescence of army equipment. The army had only twelve "modern" tanks in 1934, and only one of these met expectations.[140] Although the army made some progress, the magnitude of the procurement effort prevented completion of Craig's limited plans to supply the Initial Protective Force before the United States entered the war in December 1941.[141]

Unfortunately, Craig's decisions impeded American weapons development programs at a time when military technologies were changing at a rapid pace. A good example of the result of curtailing weapons research and development in order to enable quantity production was the army's decision to procure a 37mm antitank gun of German design. The adequacy of this weapon was questionable when it was adopted as the M3 antitank gun, but the army decided to mass produce it because it was vastly preferable to the machine guns that were then available to defend against tanks.[142] Furthermore, the chief of infantry—the branch chief responsible for antitank developments—favored the light 37-mm gun because he wanted a weapon that "four men could comfortably wheel over the ground."[143] Following the decision to produce the M3, the War Department directed: "No development funds will be expended by the Ordnance Department during the Fiscal Years 1939 or 1940 in the development of antimechanized weapons of larger than 37mm caliber."[144] By 1939 the Germans had begun using antitank weapons "ranging from 50- to 80-mm" and the M3 "was obsolete before it was standardized."[145] It was, however, this pitifully weak 37-mm antitank gun that American troops took into combat in North Africa in late 1942.

The practice of "skeletonizing" the regular army to support mobilization plans resulted in an army that as late as 1939 had few units larger than battalion size. The three "functioning" infantry divisions were at half strength and "scattered among a number of Army posts."[146] The remaining six infantry divisions were only "partially organized" cadre structures—"paper divisions"—and corps, army, and general headquarters special troop units were virtually non-existent.[147]

Skeletonization exacted a heavy toll on readiness and training in two ways. First, the expansion of the army and its restationing required the building of new housing and infrastructure. These programs required a large investment that siphoned funds from an already strained budget.[148] Second, the army spread skeletonized battalions and regiments throughout the corps areas and severely restricted opportunities to conduct maneuvers of units larger than a battalion. Training, readiness, and morale suffered. One frustrated officer wrote in 1926:

> Can you learn to understand a radio set by observing only an antenna? Can you learn to drive an airplane playing with only half a wing? Can you take only the foreleg of a horse and train it to successfully accomplish the stunts of a well trained animal? No! No! Neither can you take eight squads, and, calling it a battalion, teach your men what a fighting battalion is, its parts and their functions; nor can you, by such means, achieve skill in utilizing a fighting battalion; nor can you thoroughly teach such a group of men how the various parts of a fighting battalion carry on their individual tasks and, at the same time, cooperate one with another in the necessary coordinated way.[149]

Skeletonization also restricted the scope of field exercises during the interwar era to "periodic Regular Army–National Guard maneuvers" that were "little more than playacting between notional forces."[150] In 1940 and 1941, as the army mobilized for war, maneuvers finally took on an aspect of reality—and urgency.[151]

In the absence of practical opportunities in the field, officers learned the intricacies of maneuvering and supporting large units through exercises, mainly in army schools.[152] The Command and General Staff School trained officers for duty at the division, corps, and army levels and "dealt exclusively with professional military subjects."[153] The Army War College prepared its students for command and staff at and above the army level and for service on the War Department general staff. Finally, the Army Industrial College opened in 1924 to train officers in wartime procurement and industrial mobilization procedures.[154] Collectively the schools focused on developing officers who could supervise the mobilization, fighting, and supplying of a mass army along the lines of World War I needs. As one scholar of the Army War College noted, the school "failed to produce a Clausewitz, Mahan, Liddell Hart, or Quincy Wright. It contributed only marginally to any body of theory on the phenomenon of war. But that had not been its aim. Its aim had been utilitarian— to produce competent, if not necessarily brilliant leadership that could prepare the Army for war and fight a war successfully if it came."[155]

The same purpose applied generally to all of the army's schools during the interwar era: the production of "able military practitioners" not "military theoreticians."[156] Nevertheless, the schools were a reflection of the institution they served, one dominated by senior officers who "looked with satisfaction on the achievements of World War I, and were cautious and conservative in their outlook."[157] Although the Command and General Staff School at Fort Leavenworth, Kansas, was generally viewed as the "source of Army doctrine and procedure," it was clearly a captive of the army's sanctioned doctrine.[158] Instruction remained riveted on conservative doctrines with little attention to emerging competitive perspectives like mechanization and air power. For example, the curriculum of the 1938–1939 regular course contained 198 hours of instruction on the World War I–vintage four-regiment "square" infantry division, while the study of mechanized units and tanks merited only twenty-nine hours and aviation a mere thirteen hours of the students' time.[159] Small wonder many air officers believed "it was silly to send air officers to the Command and General Staff School for 2 years to learn the minutia of ground officers' duties."[160] In April 1939 the War Department sent Brig. Gen. Lesley J. McNair to Leavenworth to modernize the course of instruction. McNair accomplished little. Before he could significantly change the regular course at Leavenworth the War Department curtailed it, as well as the courses at the War and

Industrial Colleges. The army needed officers in units, not in classrooms, as war approached.[161]

The Command and General Staff School at Fort Leavenworth also reflected the cultural mores of an army imbued with the upper-middle-class traditions of the gentleman soldier.[162] Although the notion of the "indefinable social prestige which the man on horseback, the cavalier, the *hidalgo*, the gentleman" possessed was perhaps most evident within the cavalry branch, the social routine at Fort Leavenworth, like that of many army posts, revolved around horse shows, polo matches, and the hunt.[163] The Command and General Staff School reflected this cultural linkage with the horse—as late as 1939, officers still had to participate in thirty-one hours of equitation.[164] Air corps officers could substitute flying for equitation, but on the days they did not fly they had to join their classmates in learning the "proper adjustment of the saddle and bridle and to riding at all gaits with a comfortable seat."[165] Most students had little problem with the requirement. A survey of the class of 1939 showed that over half of the respondents favored equitation in the curriculum, an indication of the importance of horsemanship in officer culture.[166]

Army culture also had another pervasive influence over the officer corps. Throughout the interwar era the values of an American society caught up in "the business liberalism of the 1920s and the reform liberalism of the 1930s" was bothersome to regular army officers.[167] That the country was seemingly "abandoning its moral anchor and venturing out into a chaotic sea of pragmatism and relativism" was anathema to a conservative officer corps wedded to a belief in the moral superiority of the military life.[168] The end result of this conflict of values was "the isolation forced upon the military by the hostility of a liberal society" and "a renewed emphasis upon military values, and a renewed awareness of the gulf between military values and those values prevalent in American society."[169] One officer wrote in 1936: "If a man cannot find satisfaction in living a purely military life, he should get out of the army. . . . The soldier and the civilian belong to separate classes of society."[170]

Of all the military values one ranked the highest: loyalty. Loyalty was the "cardinal military virtue" stressed during the interwar years, a trait clearly at odds with the prevailing societal value of "individualism."[171] Loyalty placed bounds on initiative, since it required "loyal identification with, and understanding of, the desires of the superior." At the heart of this emphasis on loyalty was "a feeling that as the officer corps came to think alike, to adhere to the same body of doctrine, subjective cohesion would replace objective restraints."[172] In short, officers were expected to conform to the demands of the army's clearly stated policies.

Service periodicals, particularly the *Infantry Journal* and the *Cavalry Journal*, played a role in furthering accepted values and in emphasizing accepted doctrine. Although an occasional article appeared that argued for significant change, editorial policies and the requirement that an author's article receive official sanction from his chain of command generally foreclosed the journals as a venue for freewheeling discussions. The *Infantry Journal* made its rules patently clear in 1922: "Arrangements have been made whereby the Infantry Board will review certain classes of articles that pertain to Infantry equipment, prior to their publication in the *Infantry Journal*. This applies only to those articles that have a tendency to bring into the Infantryman's mind a suspicion that the equipment he is supplied with, is not the very best that can be had for him. It can readily be seen that the army that does not believe its equipment, weapons especially, is equal to, or superior to that of a possible enemy, will suffer to some degree in morale."[173]

This indirect editorial repression, when coupled with the fact that an article that violated the tenet of loyalty would expose an author to criticism, compromised the service journals as a forum for arguing contentious issues.

Innovation in the Interwar Army

Given the prevailing conditions in the War Department between the world wars it would not be surprising to find that little, if any, innovation occurred. This is not the case, although the levels of innovation varied significantly in different areas.

The field artillery developed the concept of rapidly massing the fires of numerous units around the battlefield at the Field Artillery School in the early 1930s. The new procedure emphasized "accuracy, responsiveness, and flexibility" over "sheer volume as measures of effectiveness."[174] The new procedure also required that the battalion, rather than the battery, assume responsibility for fire direction. The ensuing debate over "taking any prerogatives away from the battery commander" prevented adoption of the new concept until 1941. Motorization of the field artillery also faced resistance. Gen. Robert M. Danford, the chief of field artillery from 1938 to 1942, argued before the Army War College in September 1939 that in regards to the light division, elimination of the horse was "an unsound policy." As a consequence, the artillery school continued to teach animal management and equitation as late as 1941, and artillery units had both horse and motor-drawn guns.[175] In the words of one scholar of American field artillery, "with the exception of adoption of the M2 105-mm howitzer and M1 155-mm gun in 1940, the development of improved fuses, and the creation of the fire direction center during the 1930s, the field artillery had not changed much since 1918."[176]

The cavalry was perhaps the most resistant of the branches to change, even though its horses were the most visible anachronisms in a world moving toward machines. Still, growing numbers of cavalry officers saw the need for change in their branch. In 1927 Brig. Gen. George Van Horn Moseley, commander of the First Cavalry Division, wrote to the chief of cavalry, Maj. Gen. H. B. Crosby, that his division had too many "animals" and needed more motor transportation and armored cars. To drive his point home Moseley wrote: "When the cowboy down here is herding cattle in a Ford we must realize that the world has undergone a change."[177]

Diehard proponents of the horse cavalry fought a battle for its retention throughout the interwar era. The foundation of their arguments rested on the premise that the horse had a place in modern war. The cavalry had no greater adherent than Maj. Gen. John K. Herr, its branch chief from 1938 to 1942. Herr believed that the "airplane and the motor cannot displace the cavalry by executing its historic missions."[178] The limit of Herr's acquiescence to technology was the formation of "Horse-Mechanized Corps Reconnaissance Regiments." The Horse-Mechanized Regiment was the cavalry's way of trying to retain horse cavalry in the army. The concept used mechanized elements for distant reconnaissance, while "porté" horse units performed tactical chores and covered difficult terrain. In what the cavalry regarded as an innovative accommodation of machine age warfare, the horse units were provided "strategic" mobility by carting them around the battlefield in large trailers.[179] This admixture of horse and machine is reflective of Herr's underlying approach to technology: "As always, Cavalry's motto must remain: When better roller skates are made, Cavalry horses will wear them."[180] Retention of the horse remained his absolute goal. To this end in January 1942, Herr wrote to Army Chief of Staff Gen. George C. Marshall, urging "in the interests of National Defense . . . an immediate increase in horse cavalry."[181]

Herr's fight to save the horse may seem somewhat quixotic by post–World War II standards. To a generation of officers making the difficult transition from animal to machine, he was in many ways a hero and a standard bearer—a dedicated advocate of a doctrine and martial culture threatened by precipitous reformers. Unfortunately, for innovation in the interwar army Herr, like the other branch chiefs, was very powerful. Their influence was particularly apparent in the army's approach to mechanization.

With the abolition of the Tank Corps following the National Defense Act of 1920, the chief of infantry assumed control of the development of tanks. Most of the officers who had served in the Tank Corps returned to their parent branches when it became obvious that the tank was becoming merely another infantry weapon.[182] Some had briefly tried to argue for a larger role for tanks in the service journals. Maj. George S. Patton Jr. wrote that tanks should be an independent branch of the army, like the air service.[183] Capt. Dwight D. Eisenhower argued a greater role for tanks.[184] Their pleas for innovation were short lived. The chief of infantry censured Eisenhower, who later recalled: "I was told that my ideas were not only wrong but dangerous and that henceforth I would keep them to myself. Particularly, I was not to publish anything incompatible with solid infantry doctrine."[185] Eisenhower returned to the infantry; Patton returned to the cavalry and became one of its principal interwar champions by writing articles that extolled the relevance of the horse in warfare and denigrated machines.[186]

The chief of infantry quickly gained control over tanks. His authority was broad. By the provisions of the 1920 National Defense Act, he was responsible for tank doctrine and for stating user requirements for tank design to the chief of ordnance. Other chiefs, however, also played a role. The army's divisional pontoon bridge had a weight-bearing capacity of fifteen tons and fell within the purview of the chief of engineers. Consequently, tanks had a maximum design weight of fifteen tons. In 1923 the chief of infantry challenged this constraint, since the chief of ordnance could not provide a tank with the capabilities he desired within the weight limit. The chief of ordnance, supported by the chief of engineers, refused to budge and the weight limit stood.[187] A situation developed in which the ordnance department could not manufacture a tank that incorporated infantry requirements within the fifteen-ton limit. The infantry, well within its rights to refuse to standardize equipment that did not meet its requirements, would not accept any of the dozen or so pilot tanks the Ordnance Department designed in the 1920s.[188] Consequently, the infantry remained equipped with World War I machines into the 1930s.[189]

Attempts to challenge the chief of infantry's sole authority over tank doctrine and organization came in 1928 with the constitution of a combined arms Experimental Mechanized Force at Fort Eustis, Virginia. Secretary of War Dwight Davis ordered Chief of Staff Charles P. Summerall to assemble the unit after observing maneuvers of the British Experimental Mechanized Force on Salisbury Plain in 1927.[190] In 1930 the army established a permanent mechanized force after a study by the War Department G-3, over the objections of the chief of infantry, who complained that his prerogatives had been usurped.[191]

The chief of infantry had little cause for concern. General MacArthur disbanded the Mechanized Force in 1931 and directed the decentralization of mechanization efforts to the "traditional arms and services."[192] Maj. Robert W. Grow, a former member of the Mechanized Force, later recalled that the unit disbanded because "shortly after the appointment of General MacArthur, a number of factors presented themselves which caused a change of policy. Among these were a fear of the development of an "elite" corps (the air corps situation was in the limelight), the fact that the National Defense Act would not permit the organization of a separate branch or head of branch, jealousy of the several arms represented in the Force, difficulties in equipment for the above reasons, and finally, a realization that the missions of the Force were, in reality, cavalry missions."[193] In essence the War Department got rid of the Mechanized Force "to compromise conflicts between branches."[194]

Following MacArthur's decision, the development of army mechanization was the responsibility of the chief of infantry and the chief of cavalry. Working with the chief of ordnance they designed doctrine, equipment, and organizations that supported their branches.

The infantry continued designing tanks "to assist the advance of infantry foot troops."[195] The cavalry developed "combat cars"—a euphemism to avoid the 1920 National Defense Act requirement that all tanks remain in the infantry. The "combat cars" were, in effect, "iron horses" designed to perform the traditional cavalry missions of reconnaissance, counterreconnaissance, and security.[196] Neither branch paid much attention to combined arms since such an approach would have exceeded their charters.

The cavalry split between advocates of the horse and a growing number of officers who believed in cavalry missions but who also harbored doubts about the utility of the horse in modern warfare. In 1932 the War Department organized the Seventh Cavalry Brigade (Mechanized).

This unit formed the basis for cavalry experimentation with mechanization until 1940.[197] Cavalry mechanization efforts, however, relied completely upon the support of the chief of cavalry. Until John Herr became chief in 1938, most tried to accommodate both mechanized and horse cavalry, seeing their roles as being complementary. With the German invasion of Poland in 1939, however, pressure increased to expand mechanized cavalry units. The War Department pushed Herr to deactivate horse cavalry units to provide personnel for the new mechanized forces.[198] Herr was incensed and wrote to the G-3: "Any further attempt to encroach on my horse cavalry will meet with bitter opposition. Mechanized cavalry is not the major element of our American cavalry. It bears the same auxiliary relation to the cavalry as does the tank to the infantry.... Under no circumstances will I agree to any further depletion of my horse cavalry. To do so would be a betrayal of the national defense."[199]

Herr was a man of his word and actively campaigned throughout the remainder of his tenure to prevent any decrease in the horse cavalry. In July 1940, following the German blitzkrieg in France, General Marshall created the Armored Force. The Armored Force assumed control of all infantry tank and cavalry combat car units. That such a drastic measure was necessary stemmed from a consensus among the War Department leadership that the parochial chiefs of cavalry and infantry "had procrastinated too long already."[200] As could be expected, both chiefs vehemently protested the creation of the Armored Force.[201] Thus the army did not begin committing to the combined arms concepts of armored warfare, already being used with devastating effect by the Germans in Europe, until mid-1940. Even this beginning would be tentative, however, because Maj. Gen. Adna R. Chaffee, the first commander of the Armored Force, was given virtually complete control over the development of its doctrine, organization, and equipment.[202]

Chaffee was the army's premier mechanized cavalryman, and his views fundamentally shaped the Armored Force and the evolving armored division. The armored division Chaffee created reflected his cavalry bias because "its *primary role is in offensive operations against hostile rear areas.*"[203] The first armored divisions had five components or "echelons": command, reconnaissance, striking, support, and service. The crucial combat element was the striking echelon, a brigade of two light and one medium tank regiments and a field artillery regiment. These iron horses executed the traditional cavalry missions focused on "bold maneuvers executed at high speeds."[204] The role of the infantry in the support echelon was one of merely supporting the striking echelon.[205] In short, "the principle of combined arms was not effectively observed."[206]

The infantry was not, however, forgotten with the formation of the Armored Force. The army retained separate tank battalions, outside the armored divisions, that were "assigned missions, the accomplishment of which will assist the supported troops to reach their objectives."[207] The traditional inclinations of the branches responsible for mechanization of the interwar army—the cavalry and the infantry—were both accommodated within the Armored Force.

The question of how to defend against enemy tanks, however, remained contentious. The infantry maintained that the "best antitank defense lies in the defeat of hostile armored forces by our own armored units."[208] Chaffee agreed.[209] Lieutenant General McNair, chief of staff of the general headquarters, believed differently. He brought his own perspective as a field artillery officer to the equation and defined the problem in a metaphor he understood: "When the armored vehicle faces the antitank gun, the combat is essentially a fire action between a moving gun platform in plain view and a small, carefully concealed, stationary gun platform. The struggle is analogous to that between ships and shore guns, and there is no question that the shore guns are superior—so much so that ships do not accept such a contest."[210]

McNair proposed tank destroyers as the solution to the threat posed by the tank. He was a powerful man; in December 1941 the War Department created a separate tank destroyer organization largely analogous to the Armored Force, which eventually became the Tank Destroyer Command.[211]

The only area in which the army made significant strides during the interwar era was military aviation. Following the creation of the air service by the National Defense Act of 1920, an ongoing insurgency by army air officers wrested control of military aviation from what they viewed as the conservative leadership of a ground-focused War Department.

A growing majority of air officers shared Billy Mitchell's conviction that "As long as our Air Forces remain a part of the Army and Navy, no aerial defense of this country commensurate with the expenditure of effort and money made is possible."[212] In their minds the sinking of the German battleship *Ostfriesland* by aircraft from the First Provisional Air Brigade (personally led by Mitchell) proved the strategic potential of air power.[213] Even the conservative hierarchy Mitchell vilified understood the ramifications of the sinking. On 18 August 1921, the Joint Army and Navy Board, headed by General Pershing, reported to the secretaries of war and navy that airplanes could be the "decisive factor" in coast defense operations and that airplanes could "sink or seriously damage any naval vessel at present constructed." The board also urged the "maximum possible development of aviation in both the Army and Navy."[214]

In the aftermath of the Mitchell bombing tests, the War Department assembled the Lassiter Board to study American aviation. In October 1923 the board reported that the air service "was in a very unfortunate and critical situation" because of personnel shortfalls and the deterioration of its largely World War I–vintage aircraft. The board also recognized that aviation had strategic potential, perhaps even divorced from the ground battle, and recommended: "An Air Force of bombardment and pursuit aviation and airships should be directly under General Headquarters for assignment to special and strategical missions, the accomplishment of which may be either in connection with the operation of ground troops or entirely independent of them. This force should be organized into large units, insuring great mobility and independence of action."

The board also noted that in the absence of military airplane orders, "our aircraft industry is languishing and may disappear."[215] Shortly after the Lassiter Board issued its report, the Morrow Board and the Lampert Committee both convened. These groups also recommended strengthening military aviation, although the more influential Morrow Board was clearly conservative in that it held that "the next war may well start in the air but in all probability will wind up, as the last one did, in the mud."[216]

As the Morrow and Lampert panels prepared their reports, the highly publicized Mitchell court martial began. That Mitchell would be convicted was scarcely in doubt, even among his closest supporters.[217] Nevertheless it was probably through his "martyrdom" rather than his "vision" that Mitchell made his central contribution to the cause of American air power: he fundamentally transformed the limits of what constituted sanctioned behavior for army aviators. Forty years after the trial, retired Lieut. Gen. Ira Eaker, a captain at the time of the court martial who helped prepare Mitchell's defense, recalled that he "formed a great admiration for his method, learned a lot from him about how to influence the Congress, how to influence the public, how to draw attention to individuals and ideas and concepts . . . we were told by General Patrick, the Chief of the Army Air Corps, that we must be very careful or we might jeopardize our entire military careers. We realized this as well as he did, but we, in council, after talking it over and deliberating carefully, thoroughly, decided we'd rather stand with Mitchell for a principle and for the future of airpower than to save our necks and skins."[218]

In this way air officers transferred their loyalty from the army to the higher goal of an independent air force. One officer later asserted: "To favor a separate Air Force—that was a religion at that time. . . . Anyone who didn't accept that wouldn't go far in the Air Corps."[219]

In 1926 Congress passed two bills, the Air Commerce Act and the Air Corps Act, that became benchmarks for American aviation. The Air Commerce Act created a direct linkage between the civilian aviation industry and military aviation, because the "Army and Navy would sustain the manufacturers as well as their own air branches with contracts for new aircraft."[220] The Air Corps Act authorized the "Air Corps" to increase its officer strength from 900 to 1,514, and its enlisted force from 9,760 to 16,000, and required the maintenance of 1,800 serviceable airplanes. Congress specified that the army was to meet the increases in personnel and aircraft through the execution of a "Five-Year Air Corps Program." The War Department was upset by this legislation since the increase in the Air Corps had to come from within existing personnel authorizations.[221]

Army aviation also became a closed society. Maj. Gen. Mason M. Patrick, air corps chief, insisted that shortages of field grade officers should be corrected by internal promotions not by the transfer of willing majors and lieutenant colonels into the branch. The Air Corps Act stipulations that ninety percent of each grade had to be qualified as pilots and that all aviation units would be commanded by flying officers provided Patrick with the leverage he needed to keep the air corps under the control of its current officership. Even if a middle-grade ground officer became an emphatic convert to the cause of aviation, he could not break into the air corps fraternity unless he became a qualified pilot. Among air officers it was common knowledge that "it was very, very difficult to teach a person in the grade of major to fly an airplane."[222]

These 1926 acts also created a symbiotic relationship between civilian aircraft manufacturers and military aviation since the "only research money was in the military services, in their own testing and engineering programs, and implicitly in the experimental contracts they were authorized to make with manufacturers for the development and delivery of new aircraft."[223] Developments in either would benefit both. Additionally, the air corps did not have to rely on the Ordnance Department for its equipment.

Progress in airplane technology in the 1920s was phenomenal. By the 1930s the cloth and wood biplanes of World War I were artifacts. In their place, American industry introduced the "all-metal, stressed-skin, low-wing, twin-engine monoplane with variable-pitch propellers, flaps, and retractable landing gear."[224] As aircraft capabilities improved, air officers began formulating a doctrine that would harness their potential and justify an independent air force.

Strategic bombing came to dominate American air power doctrine between the wars. It had antecedents in the views of a number of air power advocates, most notably Giulio Douhet of Italy and Hugh Trenchard of Great Britain. The real work of crafting the American air power doctrine, however, was done at the Air Corps Tactical School. There, beginning in the mid-1920s, some of the best minds in the air corps worked to develop a doctrine that would capitalize on the what they believed were the inherent strengths of bombardment aviation.

In 1931 the Air Corps Tactical School stated explicitly the central assumption that governed doctrinal development in the army air arm: *"Bombardment aviation, under the circumstances anticipated in a major war, is the basic arm of the Air Force."*[225] Although tactical aviation in support of ground troops did not disappear—the army had attack aircraft and units throughout the interwar era—the emphasis clearly shifted to strategic bombing. Indeed, attack aviation languished "from a benign sort of neglect,"[226] because the ground "Army asked little of it,"[227] while "within the Air Corps a certain amount of official lip service was given to the attack mission in order to escape the wrath of the General Staff, but on the whole very little constructive effort was put into the program."[228]

The most radical notion developed by the Air Corps Tactical School, however, was the nature of the targets that bombers would attack. Unlike the ground army, which focused on the destruction of opposing military forces, American air power advocates made the enemy's industrial capacity to wage war the decisive target. Although long-range bombers were officially justified as defensive weapons (that is, as a component of the Army charged with "defending the coasts, both in the homeland and in overseas possessions"), air officers firmly believed that the bomber was an offensive weapon.[229] Their consistent focus was on developing the technologies and doctrines that supported this view. Given the physical isolation of the United States from the other major powers, army air officers campaigned for bombers of great range. Thus, even though the United States embraced "a National Policy of good will and a Military policy of protection, not aggression," the doctrine being developed by the air corps was clearly offensive.[230] Indeed, by 1935 the *Bombardment* text used at the Air Corps Tactical School argued for bombers of great range whose "ultimate radius of action . . . is that which will enable us to strike the nerve centers of any potential enemies from our own territory."[231] In short, the best defense was a good offense.

By 1934 school lectures reflected a doctrine centered on attacking an enemy's "industrial web" made up of interdependent raw materials, transportation, and power components. The theory stressed that one need not destroy the complete industrial capacity of an opponent, only the "critical nodes" because "modern industrial nations are susceptible to defeat by interruption of this web, which is built to permit the dependence of one section upon many or all other sections." This resulted from the conclusion that "to continue a war without machinery is impossible" and that machinery could not be produced after an "interruption" of "the industrial fabric which is absolutely essential to modern war." Instructors confidently lectured that because the industrial web, generally protected deep within an enemy's territory, was only susceptible to strategic bombing, air power could be the decisive, war-winning force.[232] Indeed, one instructor declared: "Since armies and navies cannot attack the roots of a nation's power, it is maintained that the air force should be the principal arm in future warfare."[233]

During the 1930s, technological developments made the achievement of this strategic bombing construct seem ever more plausible. Air officers argued that new bombers such as the B-17, bristling with machine guns and flying in large formations at high altitudes, could defend themselves. In this way the threat from enemy pursuit aircraft and anti-aircraft artillery was negated, as well as any requirement for escort fighters for the bombers.[234] By 1939 these views had crystallized to the point that the commander of the general headquarters air force, Maj. Gen. Frank M. Andrews, could state with confidence: "Once a powerful Air Force leaves its base, though it may suffer losses, it cannot be stopped by any man made weapons."[235] Finally, the revolutionary Norden bomb sight gave bombers the capability to deliver bombs with precision, if used in daylight.[236]

The growing conviction that the bomber was preeminent and all but unstoppable made other classes of aviation less important. Detractors of what became an air force dogma were marginalized. One of the most vocal of these was Maj. Claire L. Chennault, a pursuit aviation instructor at the Air Corps Tactical School from 1931 to 1936.[237] Chennault maintained that pursuit, not bombardment, was the most important class of military aviation. His arguments posed a direct challenge to the contentions of the bomber advocates because he questioned the organic assumption that "pursuit can never be effective for the denial of hostile bombardment."[238] Chennault contended that air defense warning systems, using a vastly improved radio technology to link far-flung listening posts and pursuit aircraft, could deny bombers the element of surprise. They would be detected and intercepted by pursuit aircraft. Furthermore, advances in armament enabled the intercepting force to attack a bomber formation with great effectiveness.[239] Hence Chennault concluded that a crucial component of the bombardment theory—that bombardment could not be stopped by pursuit—was flawed.

In 1937 Claire Chennault retired and with him went the greatest internal challenge to bomber advocates. Gen. Laurence Kuter, a former bombardment instructor, later recalled the victory of the bomber advocates over Chennault: "We just overpowered Claire; we just whipped him."[240] Kuter further noted that the bomber advocates edged out Chennault (and all others) in a number of critical areas: "attention by the chief's office, for appropriations, for personnel assignment. . . . We got money for B-17s; he didn't get anything."[241]

Bomber advocates also downplayed the role of supporting ground troops. Between 1926 and 1936 the doctrine prescribed for attack aviation shifted from "It precedes and accompanies the troops in their advance, increasing the fire action when necessary at any section of the line" to "Air attacks are not made against objectives within the effective range of friendly artillery, or against deployed troops, except in cases of great emergency."[242] In 1939, "attack" as a category disappeared, and was replaced by "light bombardment."[243] Light bombardment was even more separated from the ground battle: "To use this force on the battlefield to supplement and increase the firepower of ground arms is decidedly an incorrect employment of this class of aviation, since it would neglect the more distant and vital objectives."[244] Consequently, "When World War II began in Europe, there was still no consolidated, clear-cut, concrete body of doctrine, nor for that matter even a field manual dealing with air-ground cooperation and direct support of ground troops."[245]

In the summer of 1941 President Roosevelt directed the army and navy to develop "the over-all production requirements required to defeat our potential enemies."[246] The assumption that Germany would be defeated first, followed by Japan, guided the planning.[247] Before the services could provide to the president the information he had requested they first had to decide on a strategy for the employment of the nation's armed forces. As part of this effort, the Air War Plans Division developed a plan for a bombing offensive against Germany called AWPD-1. AWPD-1 boldly stated that, given adequate resources, an American bombing campaign could "virtually defeat the sources of military strength of the German state" by bombing 154 targets vital to the industrial fabric of Germany in the categories of electric power, transportation, synthetic petroleum production, airplane assembly plants, aluminum production, and magnesium production.[248]

AWPD-1 was compelling for a number of reasons. First, the plan offered an opportunity to end the war without a costly ground attack because it specified: "If the air offensive is successful, a land offensive may not be necessary."[249] Second, the bombing campaign could be started in April 1942, well before any major ground operations could be launched.[250] Finally, the plan was attractive for pragmatic reasons: "There was something very attractive in the claim that air power alone might achieve victory by destroying the will of the enemy to resist. There was certainly much to be gained if it worked. If it did not, the Army and Navy would be called upon to do what they had been planning on doing anyway."[251]

Secretary of War Henry L. Stimson approved AWPD-1 on 25 September 1941. It seemed army air power advocates had finally received authority to conduct an air campaign that could prove once and for all that air power had a decisive, independent role. Their paradigm was absolute: unescorted, high altitude, daylight, precision bombing formations, fighting their way to key industrial targets without unacceptable losses, would be the deciding factor in the outcome of the war.

The internal arrangements within the interwar army, when coupled with an inherently conservative culture and the institutional insurgency among air officers yearning for autonomy, created barriers to service integration and innovation. Intraservice cooperation was stifled by the parochialism of each of the branches and the absence of any requirement to coordinate across branch lines. The War Department general staff did not fill this void. As one would expect, the chiefs of arms concentrated on what was good for their branches. Advocacy turned into parochialism, and the army remained a collection of parts rather than an integrated whole. As one astute officer noted in 1929: "*Our Army is lacking a suitable agency for general research, experimentation, and development.* We have branch boards (Infantry Board, Tank Board, Air Corps Board, Field Artillery Board, and so on), each of which can make studies, within limits. But these minor agencies are severely limited as to what they may do, and they have, individually, scant resources with which to operate. . . . The missing element should be supplied."[252] Unfortunately, the "missing element" was not supplied before the United States entered World War II.

The autonomy of the arms and services had another influence: the creation of branch filters that shaped perceptions of external experiences. Lessons from China, Ethiopia, the Spanish Civil War, Poland, and France all had different meanings, depending on who did the analysis. The "system" for collecting and disseminating technical intelligence relied mainly on officers assigned as observers and attachés in foreign countries as well as published sources for information. Military observers forwarded reports to the War Department G-2, which then passed the reports to the relevant arm or service. There was no "systematic routine for following up information."[253]

Within this decentralized and ad hoc intelligence apparatus the branch chiefs interpreted the lessons of modern warfare from their own perspective. The chief of cavalry stressed that the German horse cavalry had "proven valuable in seizing and occupying positions the mechanized forces had overrun."[254] General Chaffee, then commanding the Seventh Cavalry Brigade, believed his proposed "mechanized cavalry division"—which eventually formed the basis for the first American armored division—was superior to the German panzer division because it was "organized along traditional American concepts."[255] The chief of infantry concluded that the success of German panzer divisions in France proved the need for more infantry tank units to support the "assault missions of our foot infantry."[256] Finally, the army air forces clung to their conviction of the correctness of unescorted daylight precision bombing—even after the German failure in the Battle of Britain and after the British shifted to nighttime area bombing because of the horrendous bomber losses to fighters. Lieut. Gen. Henry H. "Hap" Arnold believed that with the "greater defensive fire power of our bombers, and a carefully developed technique of formation flying with mutually supporting fire, that our bombers may be able to penetrate in daylight beyond the radius of fighters."[257] Others were less charitable. One air officer blamed the British change in strategy on inadequate training and "the unpalatable fact that the bombardment combat crews of the RAF [Royal Air Force] are no longer trying."[258] These examples, although limited, show the pervasiveness of "branch culture" in the interwar army's attempts to analyze foreign wars.

On 28 February 1942 President Roosevelt signed Executive Order 9082, which directed a wholesale reorganization of the War Department.[259] The reorganization was "intended to streamline the General Staff and subordinate elements of the Army in order to facilitate speedy and most effective control of mobilization and operations."[260] Gone was the unwieldy, decentralized structure created by the National Defense Act of 1920 that resulted in some sixty agencies having the authority to report to the chief of staff directly.[261] The new War Department centralized mobilization and training functions in three large agencies: the Army Ground Forces, the Army Air Forces, and the Services of Supply. The war plans division became the chief of staff's command post, while the general staff focused on "broad policy planning and co-ordination."[262]

Thus, in the darkest days of the American involvement in World War II the organization that had directed the army in peacetime was scrapped because it was incapable of leading it in war—just as in the World War I reorganization under General March. The chiefs of the ground combat arms vanished, and the bureaus and services came under the control of the Army Service Forces. Their legacies, however, remained. The attention of the Army Ground Forces and Army Service Forces was riveted on mobilizing, training, and supplying a rapidly expanding army of millions. Existing weapons designs were rushed into mass production. Similarly, prewar doctrines formed the basis for wartime procedures and organizations and they reflected the branch parochialism that provided their foundations. Therefore, army ground doctrine was more a collection of branch doctrines rather than the integrated combined arms approach inherent in the German blitzkrieg. The doctrine of the Army Air Forces, however, reflected the triumph of the concept of strategic bombing while the very creation of the Army Air Forces largely sanctioned an independent army air arm.

The acid test of combat revealed the organic technological and doc-trinal deficiencies in the American army's way of making war. American tanks—designed as they were for mobility, reliability, and deployability—lacked the armored protection and firepower necessary to contend on equal footing with German panzers. The tank destroyer failed to remedy this disparity, and postwar studies recommended "the replacement of the tank destroyer with a tank" capable of destroying other tanks.[263] American combat units developed their own combined arms concepts, since they had to "compensate for . . . inferior equipment by the efficient use of artillery, air support, and maneuver."[264] This combined arms approach resembled the German blitzkrieg concept, which incorporated close air support but differed radically between theaters since, in the absence of direction from the War Department, "new and different tactics . . . developed for the support of ground troops in each active theatre separately."[265]

The central technological assumption that undergirded Army Air Forces doctrine—that the firepower of an unescorted heavy bomber formation would preclude "unacceptable losses" during missions—failed in the fall of 1943 over the German cities of Schweinfurt and Re-gensburg.[266] Bomber crews endured exorbitant losses. General Arnold reported to General Marshall in December 1943 that "On the basis of 25 missions to be performed during a tour of duty . . . only 36 out of every 100 crew members starting on a tour of duty would complete the prescribed tour."[267] The reason for these losses was the same as had been predicted by Chennault in 1933: the claimed invincibility of the bomber was specious, because it would not prove to be "the first exception to the ancient principle that 'for every new weapon there is an effective counter weapon.' "[268] The Luftwaffe responded to the bomber threat by devising an efficient radar and ground control system that enabled the detection of attacks and the massing of fighters to intercept them.[269] The Luftwaffe negated the defensive firepower of the American bombers by equipping attacking aircraft with rockets and heavy caliber cannons that could attack bomber formations from outside the range of the .50 caliber machine guns that supplied their defensive firepower.[270] The German aircraft executing this tactic were cumbersome and would have been highly vulnerable to fighter aircraft—but there were no American escort fighters to challenge them. The Luftwaffe thus inflicted devastating losses on the Eighth Air Force; and, consequently, "by the fall of 1943, growing enemy fighter power precluded bomber operations to targets deep in central or southern Germany until long-range fighters were available to provide full escort."[271]

There are several insights from the American army's interwar experience that warrant summarizing. Clearly, the post–World War I army was an institution that had to make the difficult cultural shift from a frontier constabulary to a modern army. The highly favorable experience of the AEF in World War I seemingly validated army tactical doctrine, but also highlighted in the minds of the army's leadership the need to have the capability to mobilize and supply a mass army. The National Defense Act of 1920 provided the structure and regular army strength to accomplish these requirements in the event of an emergency—if Congress appropriated the necessary funds to realize the provisions of the act.

Domestic and international events during the interwar era created a climate within which the Congress chose not to fund the army to its desires. Given the centrality of manpower to its plans, the army consistently chose to spend its money on personnel and related expenses. Doctrine, based on a World War I construct, supported this approach. Investment in technology went wanting, since modern weapons remained secondary to manpower in a conservative military culture still largely ambivalent about machines. Instruction in army schools emphasized existing doctrine and focused on preparing graduates to mobilize and lead a mass army. Within the army's branches each parochial chief fought hard for his own share of a small budget. The tank, submerged as it was in the infantry and cavalry, never had a constituency to push for its advancement or to develop a doctrine that specified anything beyond the support of existing branch concepts.

The air corps was the one exception to the interwar fixation on manpower. Air officers and their ground contemporaries generally viewed machines from a different perspectives. The former embraced technology as the crucial factor in warfare. Machines attacking the enemy's means of producing machines epitomized their way of war. In the quest to realize their vision the air officers developed a doctrine at the Air Corps Tactical School that hinged on the ability of the emerging bomber technology to meet their expectations. In their quest for autonomy air officers also became largely isolated from ground officers and assiduously avoided any attempts to subordinate air power to a ground campaign. Consequently, close air support received limited attention within the air arm.

The army was also largely isolated in American society because its ethos stressed loyalty to the organization. Denied a voice in any debate over national policy, the army increasingly turned inward. There was, however, little tolerance within the army for dissent. The system repressed those who agitated for change, and early advocates of a larger role for tanks quickly abandoned their cause. Again, the air arm was different. Air officers transferred their loyalty from the army to the concept of an independent air force. The means to effect this ideal was the development of air power as a decisive, war-winning instrument—not solely tied to the ground war. Bomber advocates dominated the air arm and suppressed air officers who did not share their views.

When the War Department reorganized in 1942 it tacitly recognized this existing institutional duality by creating largely autonomous ground forces and air forces. Given the realities of the interwar American army it is difficult to imagine any other arrangement as a possibility.

In the final analysis the American army that entered World War II was a reflection of the biases and institutional arrangements that existed in the War Department throughout the interwar era. Branch parochialism, a largely powerless War Department general staff, tension between air and ground officers, a conservative culture, and disparate views about technology all conspired to inhibit innovation and intraservice cooperation. Even though the War Department's focus on manpower issues enabled it to create and deploy a mass army in World War II, this same manpower focus constrained weapons research and development throughout the interwar period.

How valid is the traditional interpretation of the army's unpreparedness for World War II that, in the main, Congressional penury and public malaise caused the army's deficiencies? The answer to this question can be derived only through speculation about what the army would have done had it been more generously funded. Given the pervasiveness of the internal dynamics that were operating within the army throughout the interwar period, more resources would probably have resulted in more of the same. The ground army, focused on manpower mobilization, would almost surely have used any additional resources to fill the 280,000-man structure authorized by the National Defense Act of 1920—and probably would have pressed for even more. The air arm, bent on achieving autonomy, just as certainly would have invested any increased funds toward strategies that would facilitate its long-cherished goal. In short, the ground army would have bought more manpower and the air army would have bought more bombers. Thus the unpreparedness of the American army for World War II, although clearly exacerbated by the realities of tight budgets and an isolationist-minded Congress and public, was as much or more a result of internal factors within the army itself than any forced upon it by the external political-social milieu.

Notes

1. C. V. Wedgwood, *William the Silent* (London: Jonathan Cape, 1967), 35, quoted in Guenter Lewy, *America in Vietnam* (Oxford: Oxford University Press, 1978; Oxford University Press paperback, 1980), 420.

2. Mark S. Watson, *Chief of Staff: Prewar Plans and Preparations* (Washington: OCMH, 1950; reprint, 1985), 17.

3. John S. Wood, "Memories and Reflections," quoted in Hanson W. Baldwin, *Tiger Jack* (Fort Collins CO: Old Army Press, 1979), 75. Wood commanded the Fourth Armored Division from June 1942 to December 1944. The citation is from his unpublished memoirs, used by Baldwin in writing *Tiger Jack*.

4. Watson, 17.

5. Martin Blumenson, "Kasserine Pass, 30 January–22 February 1943," in Charles E. Heller and William A. Stofft, eds., *America's First Battles, 1776–1965* (Lawrence: University Press of Kansas, 1986), 226.

6. Johnson Hagood, *The Services of Supply* (Boston: Houghton Mifflin, 1927), 22ff, quoted in Watson, 63.

7. Hagood, 22.

8. James E. Hewes Jr., *From Root to McNamara: Army Organization and Administration, 1900–1966* (Washington: OCMH, 1975), 6.

9. Russell F. Weigley, *History of the United States Army*, 2nd ed. (Bloomington: Indiana University Press, 1984), 327–33.

10. Timothy K. Nenninger, *The Leavenworth Schools and the Old Army: Education, Professionalism, and the Officer Corps of the United States Army, 1881–1918* (Westport CT: Greenwood Press, 1978), 56–59.

11. Nenninger, 57.

12. Weigley, 320.

13. C. Joseph Bernardo and Eugene H. Bacon, *American Military Policy: Its Development Since 1775* (Harrisburg PA: Military Service Publishing Company, 1955), 313–17; Weigley, 347–50.

14. Weigley, 35–58; and Peter Young and Michael Calvert, *A Dictionary of Battles, 1816–1976* (New York: Mayflower Books, 1977), 321–22.

15. Edward M. Coffman, *The War to End All Wars: The American Military Experience in World War I* (New York: Oxford University Press, 1968; reprint, Madison: University of Wisconsin Press, 1986), 8.

16. "Preliminary Report of the Commander-in-Chief," in *United States Army in the World War, 1917–1919, vol. 12, Reports of the Commander-in-Chief, AEF, Staff Sections and Services* (Washington: Department of the Army, 1948; reprint, 1991), 2–3.

17. "Reports of the Army Schools," in *United States Army in the World War*, 14:334.

18. "Final Report of G-3," in *United States Army in the World War*, 14:60; and Coffman, *War to End All Wars*, 156–58.

19. "Final Report of G-3," in *United States Army in the World War*, 14:60.

20. Hewes, 19; and Otto L. Nelson Jr., *National Security and the General Staff* (Washington: Infantry Journal Press, 1946), 217–18.

21. Hewes, 41.

22. Corelli Barnett, *The Swordbearers: Supreme Command in the First World War* (New York: William Morrow and Company, 1964), 356.

23. Edward M. Coffman, *The Hilt of the Sword: The Career of Peyton C. March* (Madison: University of Wisconsin Press, 1966), 171.

24. "Final Report of G-3," in *United States Army in the World War*, 14:60.

25. "Report of Superior Board on Organization and Tactics," 1 July 1919, Office of the Chief of Cavalry, correspondence, 1921–42, box 13, Records of the Chiefs of Arms, Record Group (RG) 177, National Archives (NA), Washington DC, 1–4. The membership of the board included Maj. Gen. J. T. Dickman (senior member), Maj. Gen. J. L. Hines, Maj. Gen. William Lassiter, Brig. Gen. Hugh A. Drum, Brig. Gen. W. B. Burtt, Col. George R. Spaulding, and Col. Parker Hitt. See also Boyd L. Dastrup, *King of Battle: A Branch History of the U.S. Army's Field Artillery* (Fort Monroe VA: Office of the Command Historian, United States Army Training and Doctrine Command, 1992), 180–85; and "Final Report of the Chief of Artillery," in *United States Army in the World War*, 15:195–98. Aside from the Superior Board, the most notable of the boards that convened in the immediate aftermath of the war were the Hero, Lassiter, and Westervelt (or Caliber) Boards that studied field artillery, and a special committee formed by Secretary of War Newton D. Baker in 1920 to determine the proper organization of the division.

26. "Report of Superior Board," 18–62, 132–84.

27. "Report of Superior Board," 20–21.

28. "Report of Superior Board," 21.

29. "Report of Superior Board," 20.

30. U.S. War Department, *Field Service Regulations* (Washington, 1914), 67.

31. "Report of Superior Board," 20.

32. These data obtained from <http://www.army.mil/cmh-pg/war.htm> accessed 30 March 1999.

33. "Report of Superior Board," 18.

34. "Report of Superior Board," 77–78.

35. "Report of the Chief of Staff," in *War Department Annual Reports, 1919,* 473.

36. *War Department Annual Reports, 1919,* 474.

37. Peyton C. March, *The Nation at War* (Garden City NY: Doubleday, Doran, and Company, 1932), 331–33; and "Report of the Secretary of War," in *War Department Annual Reports, 1919,* 60–61.

38. Weigley, 396.

39. Weigley, 396–97; Emory Upton, *The Military Policy of the United States* (Washington DC: Government Printing Office, 1907), xiv.

40. "General M'Andrew's Figures," *New York Times,* 24 September 1919, 16. This editorial comment supported a recommendation made by Maj. Gen. James W. McAndrew, AEF chief of staff, during the army reorganization hearings that in peacetime a 300,000-man regular force was sufficient.

41. Weigley, 599; U.S. War Department, *Official Army Register for 1916* (Washington, 1916), 670; and *Army Register, 1921,* 1402. The regular army had 5,033 officers and 93,511 enlisted men in 1914, while the postwar numbers eventually settled at approximately 14,000 officers and 120,000 to 126,000 enlisted (until increases began in 1936). On 1 December 1916 the War Department had legislative support for thirty-seven general officers. By 1921 the authorization had risen to ninety-four (sixty-eight general officers of the line and twenty-six in the various arms, services, and departments). Thus officer and general officer authorizations almost tripled, while the enlisted component increased only by roughly one-third.

42. Weigley, *History of the United States Army,* 394–400.

43. "Oppose an Army of 576,000," *New York Times,* 4 September 1919, 4.

44. "Report of Chief of Staff," in *War Department Annual Reports, 1919,* 60–61; and "March Defends Army Plan," *New York Times,* 18 August 1919, 18.

45. Watson, 33. Watson further notes that a review of newspapers during the interwar period shows no "noticeable expression" of War Department disagreement with this congressional mandate to exhaust existing weapons and equipment surpluses before buying new materiel.

46. Congress, Senate, Committee on Military Affairs, *Reorganization of the Army: Hearings before the Subcommittee of the Committee on Military Affairs,* 2 vols., 66th Cong., 1st sess., 1919, 2:1578.

47. "Report of the Secretary of War," in *War Department Annual Reports, 1920,* (Washington, 1921), 1:11–14; and John M. Palmer, *America in Arms: The Experience of the United States with Military Organization* (New Haven: Yale University Press, 1941), 178.

48. *Report of the Chief of Staff United States Army to the Secretary of War* (Washington, 1921), 12.

49. Hewes, 53.

50. Nelson, 289.

51. Hewes, 51.

52. Weigley, 404–5.

53. Weigley, 405; Coffman, *War to End All Wars*, 183–86; and Hewes, 52.

54. U.S. War Department, *Acts and Resolutions Relating to the War Department Passed during the Sixty-sixth Congress, Second Session, 1 December 1919, to 14 June 1920* (Washington, 1920), 424–30; and Nelson, 108, 292.

55. Hewes, 50.

56. Hewes, 50–51.

57. *Acts and Resolutions Relating to the War Department*, 436.

58. "Report of Superior Board," 29.

59. Nelson, 292–93, 311. The seventeen branches, bureaus, and services were the chief of infantry; chief of cavalry; chief of field artillery; chief of coast artillery; chief of air corps (air service until 1926); chief of engineers; chief signal officer; inspector general; judge advocate general; quartermaster general; chief of finance; surgeon general; chief of ordnance; chief, Chemical Warfare Service; chief, National Guard Bureau; chief of chaplains; and chief, Bureau of Insular Affairs.

60. Hewes, 51.

61. Hewes, 53.

62. Bernardo and Bacon, 386.

63. Nelson, 213–17, 293.

64. Memorandum, Maj. Gen. W. A. Holbrook, chief of cavalry, to the director, war plans division, "Duties and Responsibilities of the Chiefs of Combatant Arms," 8 September 1920, file 323.362/316, Office of the Chief of Cavalry, Correspondence, 1921–42, box 7a, Records of the Chiefs of Arms, RG 177, NA; and U.S. War Department, *Army Regulations No. 70–5: Chiefs of Combatant Branches* (Washington, 1927), 1–3.

65. R. Earl McClendon, "A Checklist of Significant Documents Relating to the Position of the United States Army Air Arm in the System of National Defense," TMS, p. 1, 239.04–17 (February 1949), in USAF Collection, United Sates Air Force Historical Research Agency, Maxwell Air Force Base, Alabama (USAFHRA), 21; and "Aeronautics in America," *New York Times*, 14 August 1919, 8.

66. Coffman, *Hilt of the Sword*, 205; "Baker Opposes Single Air Bureau," *New York Times*, 13 August 1919, 15; McClendon, 22; and Maurer, *Aviation in the U.S. Army, 1919–1939* (Washington DC, 1987), 41.

67. Maurer, 41. Although the 1919 bills by New and Curry were the first aeronautics legislative measures seriously considered by Congress, there were earlier efforts to create an independent air organization. The first attempt to legislate a separate Department of Aviation (H.R. 13838) was submitted in March 1916 by Representative Charles Lieb of Indiana. The Lieb bill set a precedent; virtually every session of Congress would have before it a similar bill until the 1947 establishment of the U.S. Air Force. See McClendon, 7, and "Digest

of Legislative Proposals for a Department of Aviation and/or Department of National Defenses," tab A:1–4, p. 1–2, in "Legislation on: A Separate Air Force; a Department of Aviation; a Department of National Defense, 1916–1943," February 1944, 168.04–14 (1916–43), USAFHRA.

68. Maurer, 41.

69. Senate, *Reorganization of the Army*, 1:182–83, 279, 287; 2:1258–98, 1686.

70. "Report of Superior Board," 81–82.

71. Senate, *Reorganization of the Army*, 1:300, 2:1258–1302.

72. *Acts and Resolutions Relating to the War Department*, 424, 426, 435; Maurer, 44; and McClendon, 26.

73. Harry P. Ball, *Of Responsible Command: A History of the U.S. Army War College*, rev. ed. (Carlisle Barracks PA: Alumni Association of the United States Army War College, 1994), 167.

74. Robert H. Ferrell, *American Diplomacy: The Twentieth Century* (New York: W. W. Norton, 1988), 155.

75. Thomas A. Bailey, *A Diplomatic History of the American People*, 8th ed. (New York: Appleton-Century-Crofts, 1969), 627.

76. Department of State, *Papers Relating to the Foreign Relations of the United States, 1919*, vol. 2 (Washington, 1934), 866, 873.

77. Robert H. Ferrell, *Woodrow Wilson and World War I, 1917–1921* (New York: Harper and Row), 166.

78. Charles A. Beard and Mary R. Beard, *A Basic History of the United States* (New York: Doubleday, Doran and Company, 1944), 436.

79. John Maynard Keynes, *The Economic Consequences of the Peace* (New York: Harper and Row, 1971; reprint, New York: Penguin Books, 1988). The reprinted edition contains a useful introductory essay by Robert Lekachman that assesses the influence of the book in the United States and contains a quote by Senator William E. Borah, a leading "irreconcilable," who recommended the work to his colleagues before the vote on the Versailles Treaty.

80. Bailey, 624–25.

81. Ferrell, *Woodrow Wilson and World War I*, 235; and Ferrell, *American Diplomacy*, 176.

82. Robert H. Ferrell, *Peace in Their Time: The Origins of the Kellogg-Briand Pact* (New Haven: Yale University Press, 1952), 219, 263–65.

83. *Report of the Chief of Staff, 1921*, 19–20.

84. "New Army Policy Fixed by Harding," *New York Times*, 25 July 1921, 4; and "Disarmament Feelers Are Well Received," *New York Times*, 11 June 1921, 3.

85. Weigley, 599.

86. "Pershing Favors 5-Power Disarming," *New York Times*, 3 February 1921, 5.

87. "Says Army Officers Must Not Criticize," *New York Times*, 25 June 1922, 21.

88. *New York Times*, 25 June 1922, 21.

89. "Coolidge Unmoved by Bureaus' 'Alarm' Over Budget Cuts," *New York Times*, 26 August 1925, 1.

90. "Text of President's Address to the Legion in Omaha," *New York Times*, 7 October 1925, 2.

91. *New York Times*, 7 October 1925, 2. Mitchell had reverted to the grade of colonel when he was not reappointed assistant chief of the army air service, a position that carried with it the temporary grade of brigadier general for the officer holding the post.

92. "Mitchell Charges Force Davis to Act," *New York Times*, 6 September 1925, 6; and Maurer, 128–29.

93. "Davis to Enforce Strict Discipline on Army Factions," *New York Times*, 21 December 1925, 1.

94. "Assails Army Economy," *New York Times*, 12 October 1927, 23.

95. "Coolidge Halted Summerall Trip," *New York Times*, 14 October 1927, 52.

96. "Summerall Awaits Call," *New York Times*, 19 October 1927, 27.

97. "A Warning as to Suggestions," *New York Times*, 30 October 1927, sec. 3, 2.

98. Letter, Adjutant General to All Chiefs of Branches and Bureaus, AG 333 E.P. (7-30-29), 1 August 1929, file 333, Office of the Chief of the Chief of Cavalry, correspondence, 1921–42, box 12, RG 177, NA.

99. Richard B. Morris, ed., *Encyclopedia of American History* (New York: Harper and Brothers, 1953), 337, 511–12.

100. Omar N. Bradley and Clay Blair, *A General's Life* (New York: Simon and Schuster, 1983), 68.

101. John W. Killigrew, *The Impact of the Great Depression on the Army* (New York: Garland Publishing, 1979), app. 1.

102. Robert H. Ferrell, *American Diplomacy in the Great Depression: Hoover-Stimson Foreign Policy, 1929–1933* (New Haven: Yale University Press, 1957), 138–39.

103. H. C. Engelbrecht and F. C. Hanighen, *Merchants of Death: A Study of the International Armament Industry* (New York: Dodd, Mead and Company, 1934), 9.

104. Robert Dallek, *Franklin D. Roosevelt and American Foreign Policy, 1932–1945* (New York: Oxford University Press, 1979; Oxford University Press paperback, 1981), 85, 95, 102–3; Weigley, 402–3; and Dwight D. Eisenhower, *At Ease: Stories I Tell to Friends* (Garden City NY: Doubleday and Company, 1967), 215–18.

105. Bailey, 706.

106. U.S. War Department, *Biennial Report of the Chief of Staff of the United*

States Army, 1 July 1939, to 30 June 1941, to the Secretary of War (Washington, 1941), 2.

107. Robert A. Divine, *Roosevelt and World War II* (Baltimore: Johns Hopkins Press, 1969; reprint, Baltimore: Penguin Books, 1971), 27–29.

108. Mark S. Watson, *Chief of Staff: Prewar Plans and Preparations* (Washington: OCMH, 1950; reprint, Washington, 1985), 367–410; Morris, 366; and Elliot Roosevelt, *As He Saw It* (New York: Duell, Sloan and Pearce, 1946), 19–46.

109. R. Elberton Smith, *The Army and Economic Mobilization* (Washington: OCMH, 1959; reprint, 1991), 4.

110. Weigley, 599.

111. Maurice Matloff and Edwin M. Snell, *Strategic Planning for Coalition Warfare, 1941–1942* (Washington: OCMH, 1953; reprint, 1990), 1.

112. Ray S. Cline, *Washington Command Post: The Operations Division* (Washington: OCMH, 1951; reprint 1970), 35.

113. Cline, 35.

114. Cline, 36.

115. Weigley, 405.

116. Watson, 103–4.

117. Lecture by Col. James K. Parsons (Ch. G-3 Mob Br) to the Army War College, 13 Sep 1928, "War Department General Mobilization Plan," quoted in Marvin A. Kriedberg and Merton G. Henry, *History of Military Mobilization in the United States Army, 1775–1945* (Washington: OCMH, 1955; reprint, 1989), 417.

118. Parsons, 417.

119. Parsons, 417.

120. U.S. War Department, *Training Regulations No. 10–5: Doctrines, Principles, and Methods* (Washington, 1921), 2.

121. U.S. War Department, *Field Service Regulations, United States Army, 1923* (Washington, 1924), 11.

122. *Field Service Regulations, 1923*, 77.

123. *Field Service Regulations, 1923*, 13.

124. *Field Service Regulations, 1923*, 22.

125. U.S. War Department, FM *100–5, Tentative Field Service Regulations: Operations* (Washington, 1939), 5.

126. *Field Service Regulations, 1939*, 7.

127. *Field Service Regulations, 1939*, 21.

128. U.S. War Department, FM *100–5, War Department Field Service Regulations: Operations* (Washington, 1941), 5.

129. *Field Service Regulations, 1941*, 278.

130. *Field Service Regulations, 1941*, 263.

131. *Field Service Regulations, 1941*, 13.

132. *Field Service Regulations, 1941*, 22. Emphasis in the original.

133. Killigrew, v-8.

134. Excerpts from letter by Harry W. Woodring, secretary of war, to House Military Appropriations Subcommittee, and to House and Senate Committees on Military Affairs, 28 May 1940; quoted in Killigrew, app. 2.

135. U.S. War Department, *Report of the Chief of Staff U.S. Army, 1934 (Extract from Annual Report of the Secretary of War, 1934)* (Washington, 1934), 11.

136. *Report of Chief of Staff, 1934,* 6–7.

137. Watson, 29–30.

138. U.S. War Department, *Annual Report, 1936* (Washington, 1936), 40.

139. Watson, 31–32.

140. *Report of Chief of Staff, 1934,* 9.

141. *Biennial Report 1941,* 10.

142. Weigley, 416; and Watson, 42–43.

143. Letter of Col. Steven L. Conner, quoted in Green, Thomson, and Roots, 184–85; see also Christopher R. Gabel, *The U.S. Army* GHQ *Maneuvers of 1941* (Washington: CMH, 1991), 31.

144. Letter of the Adjutant General to the Chief of Ordnance, 11 August 1938, subject: Responsibility for Development of Antitank Guns and of Tactical Doctrine for Their Use, quoted in Green, Thomson, and Roots, 184.

145. Green, Thomson, and Roots, 183–84.

146. *Biennial Report, 1941,* 1–2.

147. *Biennial Report, 1941,* 1–2; and Gabel, *Army* GHQ *Maneuvers,* 8.

148. See Killigrew, app. 2. From 1925 to 1940 the army spent 86.1% of its budget on "recurring charges and improvement of plant." For good examples of the urgency of the housing debate see Congress, House, Committee on Military Affairs, *Housing Bill: Hearings before the Committee on Military Affairs,* 69th Cong., 1st sess., 20 March 1926; and Congress, Senate, Committee on Military Affairs, *Construction at Army Posts: Hearing before the Committee on Military Affairs,* 69th Cong., 1st sess., 16 April 1926. The War Department eventually received approval from Congress to sell surplus property to fund housing construction (*Annual Report, 1925,* 19), thus somewhat defraying the costs. An excellent survey of the generous quarters the army built for its officers during the interwar period is in the useful study by Bethanie C. Grashof, *A Study of United States Army Family Housing Standardized Plans,* 6 vols. (Washington DC: Department of the Army, 1986).

149. Ralph E. Jones, "The Recent Factors," *Infantry Journal* 28 (February 1926): 148.

150. Gabel, *Army* GHQ *Maneuvers,* 5.

151. Weigley, 424; Gabel, *Army* GHQ *Maneuvers,* 5.

152. John W. Masland and Laurence I. Radway, *Soldiers and Scholars: Military Education and National Policy* (Princeton NJ: Princeton University Press, 1957), 88–89.

153. Masland and Radway, 88.

154. Masland and Radway, 90.

155. Ball, 253.

156. Ball, 253.

157. Blumenson, in Heller and Stofft, 231.

158. Masland and Radway, 88.

159. Letter, Brig. Gen. L. J. McNair to the Adjutant General, 31 August 1939, subject: Annual Report, School Year 1938–1939, in U.S. Army Command and General Staff College library collection.

160. Oral history interview of Maj. Gen. Donald Wilson by Mr. Hugh Ahmann, 10–11 December 1975, K239.5012–878, USAFHRA, 74. See also oral history interview of Gen. Laurence S. Kuter by Hugh N. Ahmann and Tom Sturm, 30 September–3 October 1974, K239.0512–810, USAFHRA, 130. Kuter was even more blunt, noting that "It [the Command and General Staff School course] was a wasted year. . . . It was, again, good if you wanted to know how to patrol the trenches, how Gettysburg should have been fought." See also Timothy K. Nenninger, "Leavenworth and Its Critics: The U.S. Army Command and General Staff School, 1920–1940," *Journal of Military History* 58 (April 1994): 224. Nenninger notes that the representation of air officers in the Leavenworth courses increased over the interwar period. He believes the reason for the higher attendance was "linked to the Air Corps' organizational expectations and agenda. Officers who were not graduates of the CGSS could not be named to the general staff eligible list, and thus could not serve on the War Department general staff. If the air corps wanted representation on the general staff—one means of enhancing its organizational status as a branch within the army or to influence War Department policy to increase branch autonomy—it had to qualify officers by sending them to Leavenworth."

161. Larry I. Bland and Sharon R. Ritenour, eds., *The Papers of George Catlett Marshall*, vol. 1, in *The Soldierly Spirit: December 1880–June 1939* (Baltimore: Johns Hopkins University Press, 1981), 702–3.

162. See Morris Janowitz, *The Professional Soldier: A Social and Political Portrait* (New York: Free Press, 1971), 90–93. Janowitz presents evidence that the majority of the officer leadership of the interwar era had their origins in the upper and upper-middle social classes of American society (over 70 percent between 1910 and 1935).

163. Citation from John K. Herr and Edward S. Wallace, *The Story of the U.S. Cavalry, 1775–1942* (Boston: Little, Brown and Company, 1953), 254; and Orville Z. Tyler Jr., *The History of Fort Leavenworth, 1937–1951* (Fort Leavenworth KS: U.S. Army Command and General Staff College, 1951), 1–2.

164. Letter, Brig. Gen. L. J. McNair to the Adjutant General, 31 August 1939, subject: Annual Report, School Year 1938–1939, in U.S. Army Command and General Staff College library collection.

165. *Instruction Circular No. 1, 1939–1940* (Fort Leavenworth KS: U.S. Army Command and General Staff School, 1939), 10.

166. McNair, Annual Report, 1938–1939. See also Ira C. Eaker, "The Air Corps Tactical School: As Seen by an Air Corps Officer," *Air Corps News Letter* 19 (15 April 1936): 10. Eaker wrote that in the 1936 course at the Air Corps Tactical School students were required to participate in one hour of equitation instruction every other day, although there was "considerable agitation on the part of the present class to make riding optional."

167. Samuel P. Huntington, *The Soldier and the State: The Theory and Politics of Civil-Military Relations* (Cambridge: Belknap Press of Harvard University Press, 1957), 311.

168. Huntington, 310.

169. Huntington, 309.

170. *Infantry Journal* 43 (1936): 237–38, quoted in Huntington, 310.

171. Huntington, 304.

172. Huntington, 304.

173. "Notes from the Chief of Infantry," *Infantry Journal* 21 (August 1922): 196. See also Stetson Conn, *Historical Work in the United States Army, 1862–1954* (Washington: CMH, 1980), 62–63, 73; and Ball, 215, 229, 241. The only interwar attempt by the army to publish a historical analysis of World War I was the 1929 monograph *The Genesis of the First Army*. This document highlighted the triumph of the AEF in maintaining its autonomy from the Allies and, unfortunately, appeared at the same time General Pershing was in France for the funeral of Marshal Foch. Pershing was incensed and demanded the suppression of the book and a later War Department directive required that "in future no manuscript of any kind on the World War will be published until it has been submitted to General Pershing and until it has received the personal approval of the Chief of Staff." (Conn, 63). *Genesis* was finally republished, over the objections of the adjutant general, in 1938. Not until 1939 did the Historical Section of the Army War College receive a directive to compile a study of the army of World War I. This effort was finally published in 1948 as *United States Army in the World War, 1917–1919*. Virtually every branch and service had its own journal, while the Command and General Staff School published the *Military Review*. The one notable exception was the air corps, which published its own in-house *Air Corps News Letter*.

174. Gabel, *Army GHQ Maneuvers*, 11.

175. Dastrup, 192–201.

176. Dastrup, 201.

177. Letter, Brig. Gen. Geo. Van Horn Moseley to Maj. Gen. H. B. Crosby, 9 December 1927, file 322.02, Office of the Chief of Cavalry, correspondence, 1921–42, box 7a, RG 177, NA.

178. "Cavalry Affairs Before Congress," *Cavalry Journal* 48 (March–April 1939): 130–35.

179. Herr, 248–49; *Field Service Regulations, 1941*, 8; and FM 2–5, *Cavalry Field Manual: Horse Cavalry* (Washington, 1940), 112–13.

180. First Indorsement from Maj. Gen. J. K. Herr, Chief of Cavalry, to the Commanding General, Washington Provisional Brigade, 9 February 1940, file 322.02 (cavalry), Office of the Chief of Cavalry, correspondence, 1921–42, records of the Chiefs of Arms, RG 177, box 7b, NA.

181. Memorandum from Maj. Gen. J. K. Herr, Chief of Cavalry, for the Chief of Staff, 26 January 1942, file 322.02 (cavalry), Office of the Chief of Cavalry, correspondence, 1921–42, records of the Chiefs of Arms, RG 177, box 7b, NA.

182. Dale E. Wilson, *Treat 'Em Rough: The Birth of American Armor, 1917–1920* (Novato CA: Presidio Press, 1989), 227–31.

183. George S. Patton Jr., "Tanks in Future Wars," *Infantry Journal* 16 (May 1920): 958–62.

184. D. D. Eisenhower, "A Tank Discussion," *Infantry Journal* 17 (November 1920): 453–58.

185. Eisenhower, *At Ease*, 173.

186. See, for example, George S. Patton Jr., "What the World War Did for Cavalry," *Cavalry Journal* 31 (April 1922): 165–72; and George S. Patton Jr., "Motorization and Mechanization in the Cavalry," *Cavalry Journal* 39 (July 1930): 331–48.

187. Letter, John H. Hughes to the Adjutant General CI-470.8/2164-B, 14 September 1923; 1st Ind, Ordnance Office to the Adjutant General, O.O.451.25/1870, 19 September 1923; 2nd Ind., Chief of Engineers to the Adjutant General, 470.8-E-4, 25 September 1923; 3rd Ind., Adjutant General to the Chief of Infantry, AG 473.1 (9–14-23), 18 October 1923, file 470.8, Office of the Chief of Infantry, correspondence, 1921–42, box 90, RG 177, NA; and Constance M. Green, Harry C. Thomson, and Peter C. Roots, *The Ordnance Department: Planning Munitions for War* (Washington: OCMH, 1955; reprint, 1990), 190–91.

188. Timothy K. Nenninger, "The Development of American Armor, 1917–1940," (master's thesis, University of Wisconsin, 1968), 79–81. The infantry requirements, mainly that the medium tank have enough armor to stop a .50 caliber armor-piercing bullet, made it impossible for ordnance designers to build a 15-ton tank unless engine weight was reduced. Unfortunately a lighter engine would cause the tank to be underpowered and it would then fail to meet performance criteria.

189. Ralph E. Jones, George H. Rarey, and Robert J. Icks, *The Fighting Tanks Since 1916* (Washington: National Service Publishing, 1933), 153–68.

190. Nenninger, "Development of American Armor," 85–86.

191. Memorandum, Chief of Infantry for the Assistant Chief of Staff, G-3,

537.3 (3–20-28), 26 March 1928, RG 94, NA, cited in Nenninger, "Development of American Armor," 95–96.

192. Incl. 1, letter, Gen. Douglas MacArthur to letter, Adjutant General to Commanding Generals of all Corps Areas and Departments, Commandants of all General and Special Service Schools, Superintendent, United States Military Academy, Chiefs of all Arms, Services and Bureaus, and the War Department General Staff, 1 May 1931 AG 537.3 I.R. (12–18-34), file 322.012, Office of the Chief of Cavalry, correspondence, 1921–42, box 7a, RG 177, NA; and *Annual Report, 1931*, 42–43.

193. Memorandum, Maj. R. W. Grow for Colonel Kent, 21 December 1936, file 322.02, Office of the Chief of Cavalry, correspondence, 1921–42, RG 177, NA.

194. Memorandum, Brig. Gen. George P. Tyner for the Chief of Staff, G-3/21500, 25 October 1937, file 470.8, Office of the Chief of Infantry, correspondence, 1921–42, RG 177, NA.

195. *Field Service Regulations, 1939*, 7.

196. *Field Service Regulations, 1939*, 8.

197. Gabel, *Army GHQ Maneuvers*, 22–23.

198. Memorandum, Brig. Gen. F. M. Andrews for the Chief of Cavalry, G-3/42070, 23 February 1940, file 322.02, Office of the Chief of Cavalry, correspondence, 1921–42, box 7b, RG 177, NA.

199. Memorandum, Maj. Gen. J. K. Herr for the Assistant Chief of Staff, G-3, 322.02, 28 February 1940, file 322.02, Office of the Chief of Cavalry, correspondence, 1921–42, box 7b, RG 177, NA. Emphasis in the original.

200. Gabel, *Army GHQ Maneuvers*, 23; and *History of the Armored Force, Command and Center*, Historical Section, Army Ground Forces, study No. 27 (Washington, 1946), 6–7; and Memorandum, Brig. Gen. F. M. Andrews for the Chief of Cavalry, G-3/41665, 1 June 1940, file 322.02, Office of the Chief of Cavalry, correspondence, 1921–42, box 8, RG 177, NA.

201. Memorandum, Maj. Gen. George A. Lynch for the Assistant Chief of Staff, G-3, 2 June 1940; and Memorandum, Maj. Gen. J. K. Herr for the Assistant Chief of Staff, G-3, 3 June 1940, file 322.02, Office of the Chief of Cavalry, correspondence, 1921–42, box 8, RG 177, NA.

202. Memorandum, Brig. Gen. F. M. Andrews for the Adjutant General, G-3/41665, 5 July 1940, and Memorandum, Brig. Gen. F. M. Andrews for the Chief of Cavalry, 5 July 1940, file 322.02, Office of the Chief of Cavalry, correspondence, 1921–42, box 8, RG 177, NA.

203. *Field Service Regulations, 1941*, 263.

204. *Field Service Regulations, 1941*, 269.

205. *Field Service Regulations, 1941*, 264.

206. Gabel, *Army GHQ Maneuvers*, 25.

207. *Field Service Regualtions, 1941*, 278.

208. Letter, Maj. Gen. George A. Lynch to the Assistant Chief of Staff, G-3, AG

320.2 (7–3-40) M-C, 3 July 1940, headquarters, Commanding General, General Decimal file, 1940–44 (McNair files), box 8, RG 337, NA.

209. Gabel, *Army* GHQ *Maneuvers*, 33.

210. 2rfd Ind., Brig. Gen. L. J. McNair to the Adjutant General, AG 320.2 (7–3-40) M-C, 29 July 1940, headquarters, Commanding General, general decimal file, 1940–44 (McNair files), box 8, RG 337, NA.

211. Christopher R. Gabel, *Seek, Strike, and Destroy: U.S. Army Tank Destroyer Doctrine in World War II* (Fort Leavenworth KS: U.S. Army Command and General Staff College, 1985), 1, 44.

212. Memorandum, Brig. Gen. Wm. Mitchell for Chief of Air Service, 29 August 1921, 248.222–69 (April–August 1921), USAFHRA.

213. Maurer, 113–20.

214. U.S. Navy Department, *Report of the Joint Board on Results of Aviation and Ordnance Tests Held During June and July, 1921 and Conclusions Reached* (Washington, 1921), 5–7.

215. "War Department Committee Report on the Organization of the Air Service [Lassiter Board]," 27 March 1923, 167.404–6 (24 April 1923), USAFHRA, 6.

216. *Report of the President's Aircraft Board* (Washington: Government Printing Office, 1925), quoted in Maurer, 73.

217. See oral history interview of Lieut. Gen. Ira C. Eaker by Arthur Marmor, January 1966, K239.0512–626, USAFHRA, 28–29; Oral history interview of Gen. Carl A. Spaatz by Mr. Alfred Goldberg, May 19, 1965, K239.0512–755, USAFHRA, 9; and Arnold, *Global Mission*, 120. Eaker, Spaatz, and Arnold all recognized Mitchell's "guilt" within the context of acceptable officer behavior.

218. Eaker, oral history (K239.0512–626), 28.

219. Eugene Beebe, *The Reminiscences of Eugene Beebe* (1959–1960), oral history collection of Columbia University; quoted in James P. Tate, "The Army and Its Air Corps: A Study of the Evolution of Army Policy Towards Aviation, 1919–1941" (Ph.D. diss., Indiana University, 1976), 33.

220. Alex Roland, "The Impact of War Upon Aeronautical Progress: The Experience of NACA," in Alfred F. Hurley and Robert C. Ehrhart, eds., *Air Power and Warfare: The Proceedings of the 8th Military History Symposium, United States Air Force Academy, 18–20 October 1978* (Washington: Office of Air Force History, 1979), 371. Roland notes that "Finally in 1926 Congress passed the Air Commerce Act along with the Army and Navy aircraft procurement programs, all of this following close upon the Air Mail Act of 1925. The essence of these laws was that local and state governments would provide facilities for civilian aviation, the federal government would regulate civil aviation through the Bureau of Air Commerce and nurture it with air-mail contracts, and the Army and Navy would sustain the manufacturers as well as their own air branches with contracts for new aircraft."

221. Congress, Senate, Committee on Military Affairs, *The Army Air Service:*

of 'Mechanized Cavalry,' 29 September 1939," TMS, p. 31, Mechanized Cavalry Board Maneuvers, 1929–39, box 1, RG 177, NA.

256. Memorandum, Maj. Gen. George A. Lynch for the Assistant Chief of Staff, G-3, 2 June 1940, file 322.02, Office of the Chief of Cavalry, correspondence, 1921–42, box 8, RG 177, NA.

257. Letter, Lieut. Gen. H. H. Arnold to Air Chief Marsh. Sir Charles F. A. Portal, 9 March 1942, file "Correspondence—Commanders in the Field," Arnold Papers, box 38, LC.

258. Memorandum, L. S. K. [Laurence S. Kuter] for the Chief of Staff, 13 January 1942, 168.7012 (1942–43 SL-3), USAFHRA.

259. Cline, 92–93.

260. Memo, Major General McNarney for Maj. Gen. A. D. Surles, 27 February 1942, subject: Outline of Reorgn of WD, quoted in Cline, 95.

261. Hewes, 63.

262. Hewes, 68–69.

263. U.S. Army, Forces in the European Theater, General Board, Armored Section, *Organization, Equipment and Tactical Employment of Separate Tank Battalions*, study number 50 (n.p., n.d. [1946]), app. 2, 2.

264. Letter, Maj. Gen. Maurice Rose for Gen. Dwight D. Eisenhower, 21 March 1945, in DDE Pre-Presidential Papers, "Rose, Maurice," Eisenhower library, 1.

265. Letter, Lt. Col. B. B. Troskoski to Maj. John P. Crowder, 3AF 337 (15 May 1944), 248.122 (1944), USAFHRA. See also United States Forces, European Theater, General Board, Air Section, *The Tactical Air Force in the European Theater of Operations*, study number 54 (n.p., n.d. [1946]), foreword. This report noted that "Because of the hesitancy on the part of the War Department to publish a Field Manual or Training Circular. . . . The splendid cooperation between the Tactical Air Commands and the Armies was developed during operations."

266. Headquarters, Eighth Air Force, Operational Analysis Section, "An Evaluation of Measures Taken to Protect Heavy Bombers from Loss and Damage," November 1944, 6, USAMHI.

267. Memorandum, Gen. H. H. Arnold for the Chief of Staff, 27 December 1943, file "BC to GB 7-'44 to," Arnold Papers, box 48, LC.

268. Chennault, "Role of Defensive Pursuit," 12.

269. Command Information Intelligence Series, no. 43–121, "German Day-Fighter System," 31 August 1943, 142.034–3 (31 August 1943), USAFHRA.

270. Command Informational Intelligence Series, no. 43–124, 17 September 1943, "Interview with Brig. Gen. H. S. Hansell, 9 August 1943," 142.05 (1942–43), USAFHRA.

271. "An Evaluation of Measures Taken to Protect Heavy Bombers from Loss and Damage," 6. Lieut. Gen. James H. Doolittle, Commander of the Eighth Air Force, approved this report, noting "the conclusions are considered sound."

6. MILITARY INNOVATION AND THE WHIG PERSPECTIVE OF HISTORY

Dennis E. Showalter

Change in military systems remains one of the last strongholds of the Whig perspective of history. In this intellectual matrix, innovation—be it technical, operational, or structural—is regarded as unambiguous. Its parameters and its implications are clear to anyone with eyes un-blinded by whatever scales are fashionable to denounce: class prejudice and professional ignorance are the most familiar whipping boys. The consequences are presented in a kind of standings chart. At the top are the armed forces which either win their wars or are accepted as looking good while losing; the Union army of the American Civil War and Nazi Germany's Wehrmacht are examples. In the middle of the pack come the systems that eventually got most of it right: the United States after 1941, the Soviet Union of World War II, and, by recent definition, the British Expeditionary Force (BEF) of 1918. Bringing up the rear are those who did not get or could not hear the word. France from 1918 to 1940 and Italy at any time are familiar examples. Geoffrey Wawro is making a single-handed effort to have Francis Joseph's Habsburg Empire added to the short list of losers who deserved their fates.[1]

The period between the world wars offers a clear illustration of the limits of this approach. The Great War of 1914–18 arguably had a greater impact on military change than any modern conflict before or since. Its impact is best understood in the metaphor of a prism refracting light across a spectrum. Prior to 1914 the world's armed forces were fairly symmetrical. Armies in particular were based on the common assumption of general citizen service in case of general war. Even powers such as Britain and the United States, which retained the volunteer system for first-line recruitment, recognized it as a stepping stone to national mobilization in case of a full-scale war. In the aftermath of the Haldane reforms of 1906, for example, Britain's militia was intended to keep the regulars at full establishment in the context of an expected 80 percent wastage rate in the first year of war. The territorial force was understood as a reinforcement for the half-dozen expeditionary divisions created out of what had been de facto a mixed bag of training and garrison formations.[2]

As for the "citizen" concept, the world's major military powers expected ultimately to draw on a cross-section of their general populations; they also expected that cross-section to serve willingly, with no more than administrative compulsions. In that context even the Romanov and Habsburg Empires, with their strong multiethnic elements, sought to develop into what Friedrich Meinecke has called "state nations" with loyalty to a general political system as opposed to a particular cultural identity.[3]

The symmetries extend further. Great-power armies were regarded as existing essentially to fight their counterparts, constabulary and colonial missions were secondary. The BEF was conceived in principle as a general deterrent capable of being deployed anywhere in the world. But once it reached its destination it was expected to face an enemy like itself.[4] French mobilization plans increasingly projected stripping African garrisons to reinforce the metropole; a few enthusiasts like Charles Mangin advocated creating a "Black army" to counter German numerical superiority.[5]

Technology, doctrine, and organization offered even fewer grounds for distinguishing among great-power armies. Their weapons were alike, even down to the caliber. They shared a common commitment to the tactical and operational offensive. They copied each others' force ratios and organizations blindly, then rationalized the imitations.[6] The virtually universal binary organization of corps and divisions, for example, did not originate for tactical reasons. It was a product of the relationship of line to Landwehr in the Prussian army of the Biedermeyer era, imitated and continued despite its obvious operational shortcomings.

The Great War reinforced these symmetrical relationships. Its issues were common to all major combatants except the United States, whose experience was clearly an anomalous consequence of its short exposure. In the context of national policy the other great powers uniformly strained the loyalty of their citizens to its limits and beyond. In Russia, Austria, and Germany, the people came to loathe their own governments even more than they feared their enemies. Operational problems such as developing and implementing coherent theater strategies were similarly congruent, posing the same challenges in Galicia, Palestine, and Mesopotamia that they did in Flanders.[7]

The battlefield gridlock created by the imbalance between firepower on one hand and mobility and protection on the other remained a norm until 1918. Even then neither German infiltration tactics nor the early versions of the all-arms battle developed by the British were clear portents for the future.[8] Nor did any of the combatants achieve clear, objective technological superiority. Germany, for example, lacked tanks because the high command decided against emphasizing their development and production not because either task was beyond the wartime Reich's capacities.

This military symmetry, so long a norm, vanished in the aftermath of the Versailles Treaty. That did not mean that the experience of 1914–18 was ignored or distorted by some parties while others enjoyed clearer insight. It reflected, rather, new definitions of security issues generated by total war, growing specialization of conflict types, and a broader spectrum of military necessities and military options available in the great-power system.

The new Red Army confronted the most general paradigm shift. Its geopolitical environment was the legacy of a thousand years of Russian history. Overlaying and overlapping it was the ideological principle of international class warfare against an unappeasable hostile capitalism. Then came the mission of deterring internal challenges to a regime whose legitimacy had largely been achieved at gunpoint. Finally, the army was regarded as having a key role in developing the "new Soviet man." The response was the development of a "warfare state" unprecedented in modern history. Jacob Kipp presents the interwar evolution of the USSR into a comprehensive security system that functioned in a Hobbesian matrix of all against all. The Soviet model of future war was of a total war waged in ideological as well as operational dimensions. Such a conflict would involve overcoming internal enemies—"wreckers" and "deviationists"—as well as destroying hostile armies. It called for extending revolution as well as winning battles. Victory was ultimately defined as transforming hostile societies while furthering the USSR's progress toward communism.[9]

Soviet visions were thus far more ambitious than National Socialism's blinkered focus on merely destroying the "other." Military innovations such as "deep battle" were merely the cutting edge of a comprehensive project. Beginning in the 1920s the Red Army developed a hitherto-unmatched synergy between mass and mechanization. Instead of regarding them as antithetical, as German general Hans von Seeckt and British theorist B. H Liddell Hart did, Stalin's generals achieved modernity on a large scale in the context of an economic development disproportionately focused on military production.[10]

Their success reflected as well a commitment to the concept of "proletarian development." In the communist world-view anyone could learn to do anything. A key to the revolution's eventual triumph involved simplifying processes to the point where, in Lenin's trope, a village schoolmistress could take a leave of absence and run the country. The principles of simplicity and expendability that shaped weapons design policies throughout the Soviet Union's history were in no small measure a response to this ideological postulate.

The interwar Red Army was not, however, able to succeed in making military service a transforming experience for a rank and file that as late as 1945 fought for the motherland rather than for communism. The army was increasingly removed as well from direct confrontation with internal enemies as peasant soldiers proved less than ideal enforcers of collectivization.[11] Nevertheless it was the first in modern history to accept its identity as being fundamentally a political institution. A major theme of Soviet history between 1921 and 1939 is the ultimately successful effort to integrate the armed forces as part of the triad of army, party, and police that sustained the Soviet Union until its dissolution. In that context even the purges that decimated the army's cadres and enhanced its vulnerability to German invasion were an acceptable price to pay.

Great Britain is a more subtle example of paradigmatic military change. After 1918, as before 1914, political and strategic decisions were made in the context of a dialectic between continental and imperial responsibilities. On one hand Britain never seriously considered a return to a policy of "splendid isolation" that even in its salad days had been more myth than reality. The familiar mantra of "no major war for ten years" was a guide for restraining expenditures rather than planning.[12] The army in particular accepted the principle that its core mission involved preparation for conventional warfare in a great-power context on the continent of Europe. That preparation involved accepting what today would be called a high tech matrix. Critics of the interwar British army have made a case for what amounts to deliberate demodernization, a conscious return to "real soldiering" as a reaction not only to the horrors of the trenches but to the institutional traumas generated by national mobilization. In this model the army turned its back on "temporary gentlemen" in the officers' mess; on civilians playing soldier; and on greasy, smelly artifacts like tanks in favor of huntin', shootin', fishin', and the occasional spot of native-bashing in remote imperial corners.[13]

Reality was less convenient. Harold Winton's essay shows the existence of a reasonably high level of consensus on the nature and requirements of the modern style of warfare. The debate between advocates of mechanization and supporters of armored warfare involved distinctions rather than dichotomies. Seen from the perspectives of J. F. C. Fuller, B. H. Liddell Hart, and even Leslie Hore-Belisha, "mechanizers" were temporizers seeking at best to pour new wine into old bottles. Seventy years' perspective suggests, however, that interwar concepts of armored warfare analogizing the future land battle to war at sea, with fleets of specialized armored vehicles maneuvering at will, proved inapplicable even in the North African desert—the closest possible approximation to a land ocean. It was mechanization, the comprehensive introduction of internal combustion engines followed by the addition of tracks, protection, and armament, that made possible the combined-arms combat teams that set the parameters of operational effectiveness during World War II.

As much to the point, even the army's old guard rejected the firepower-attrition model of the Great War—and had indeed rejected it during that conflict, developing by 1918 a semi-mechanized BEF able to sustain semi-mobile operations.[14] The crucial interwar questions in this context involved not the implementation of change but the details of change. This problem was significantly exacerbated during the 1930s, as Winton demonstrates, by the dilemma of responding to an increasingly threatening international climate while governing an electorate apparently committed to avoiding any repetition of the 1914–18 experience.

More significant in shaping approaches to change, however, was an imperial commitment both increasingly more significant and significantly more complex than its prewar version.[15] It was clear to individuals from across the political spectrum that the Great War had demonstrated that Britain's survival as a great power, perhaps indeed Britain's survival at all, depended on Britain's overseas connections. The mandate system provided unfamiliar challenges, Palestine and Iraq being the most obvious examples. Even on its traditional imperial grounds the British army faced more demanding responsibilities. Events from the Third Afghan

War to the Mohmand and Waziristan campaigns of the 1930s demonstrated that the northwest frontier was no longer what it had been. Tribal armament and tribal politics alike were growing more sophisticated. Nor was internal security in the age of Gandhi any longer a matter of "aiding the civil power" by waving placards instructing an unruly crowd to disperse, then shooting a few "ringleaders." The Irish Republican Army waged the first modern guerrilla war from 1919 to 1922. At the other end of the interwar era, a dual insurgency in Palestine absorbed two divisions of troops and a corresponding level of intellectual energy.

Before the Great War the institutions and training methods appropriate for modern conventional warfare were reasonably congruent with the requirements of imperial wars and imperial policing. The Boer War highlighted not so much the British army's shortcomings as a counterinsurgency force as its failure to prepare effectively for combat against an enemy able to utilize modern rifles effectively. At battalion and brigade levels, skills acquired at Aldershot were generally applicable in the Khyber Pass. The devil was in the details not in the matrix. During the interwar years that commonality disappeared. It was increasingly clear that the demands of mechanization diverged from the requirements of empire. Automatic weapons enhanced firepower and trucks improved logistics, but at the bottom line it was riflemen and mules that were needed to police frontiers and control interiors. Armored cars might impress a crowd once, perhaps twice. Thereafter they became large targets for gasoline bombs. On the other hand even experience gained against live ammunition in Waziristan or Palestine was regarded as having little direct relevance to the demands of operations based on the internal combustion engine.[16]

An increasing body of British professional literature advocated specialized training in the modern versions of small wars and constabulary work. This solution was, however, consistently rejected by a War Office and a senior officer corps determined to avoid the risk of creating two armies, one for Europe and one for the empire.[17] The decision was sound in principle, particularly given the truncated military budgets of the period. Practice, however, was another matter. Far from being indifferent to change, the army of interwar Britain was dominated by it—but at micro levels. Officers and formations rotating through the spectrum of stations and missions characteristic of interwar Britain responded by seeking common denominators, developing principles and procedures that met the requirements of both grande guerre and imperial policing.

The result was a general purpose army, one that lacked virtuosity and did nothing especially well. It was a force of "good plain cooks," the kind who sustain life without enhancing it. It was also a classic case study in the limits of adaptability.

For France the Great War was an object lesson in the ultimate danger of wishing: the wish might be fulfilled! After 1918 France inherited Germany's position as not the hegemon but the primary power of Europe. At the same time, neither the state nor the society were willing—or, indeed, able—to alter the matrix of France's security system. Eugenia Kiesling establishes a point too often obscured in general histories. The French army did not deliberately set out to lose the next war! It understood and accepted its place in a parliamentary republic that was committed to the principle of a conscript army and valued loyalty above brilliance in its generals. The army also understood France's new position as a status quo power—and the corollary that any drastic change in the country's military system was likely to upset a postwar international balance whose fragility was becoming increasingly apparent.

The French army therefore chose to refine processes rather than alter parameters. The empire became increasingly a source of troops permanently deployed in France as compensation for political and demographic factors that produced shorter terms of service for lower numbers of Frenchmen. Mechanization was implemented within existing force and branch structures. Its doctrines were largely extensions of principles developed between 1916 and 1918. Tanks were integrated into combined arms formations in the context of "managed battle" conducted at a foot soldier's pace. The light mechanized divisions organized in the 1930s did not differ much in structure from the panzer divisions emerging in Germany. Their mission, however, was to screen rather than to penetrate and exploit. France led the world in motorizing its artillery, but its artillery tactics were based on predetermined fire plans. And underlying any perceived lacunae in the active forces was the policy-level commitment to total mobilization during wartime. In that context the serving soldiers needed to do no more than hold the ring until the "real" France, the nation in arms, should take the field.[18]

It is important to remember that the French army did not have serious reasons to question its institutional understanding of modern war. As Kiesling demonstrates, its study of German (and Soviet) practices tended to reinforce confidence in French methods. In the long run those methods were by no means inapplicable. The French indeed were arguably closer to the achievable norms of modern war than were the Germans, who were so often credited as being masters of the battlefield. By 1943 at the latest, the halcyon days of blitzkrieg were at an end, never to return against a reasonably competent enemy. Antitank defenses had reduced the tactical flexibility of armor. At the operational level managed battle dominated; neither Montgomery, Zhukov, nor Bradley epitomized shoot-from-the-hip opportunism. In strategic contexts World War II was decided by national mobilization—and by second lines of armed forces that in 1942–43 took over from those that covered the mobilizations.[19] It is one of military history's overlooked ironies that rather than being behind the curve the French army of 1940 may have actually been ahead of its time.

The three forces discussed above had in common a complex network of ongoing commitments that shaped their definition of and their responses to change. The interwar American and German armies, by contrast, were for all practical purposes irrelevant to national security in their existing forms. The absence of mundane responsibilities did not, however, necessarily facilitate comprehensive change. David Johnson makes a case that the U.S. army accepted the necessity of national mobilization for any future general war. It insisted as well on the necessity for implementing that process in matrices established by the peacetime professionals. But branch parochialism, air-ground tensions, and diverging views about the best ways to apply modern military technology kept the interwar army a collection of fiefdoms whose perspectives even on limited issues of doctrine and equipment were too often shaped by tunnel vision and wishful thinking. Put to the test, four-engine precision daylight bombers did not win the war by themselves. American tanks proved inferior to their German counterparts in firepower and survivability. As late as 1953, a former chief of cavalry argued in a widely circulated book in favor of the potential value of mounted troops in the Korean peninsula![20]

In demonstrating the U.S. army's lack of institutional focus Johnson concentrates on its internal structure and dynamics. Relevant as well is the external absence of a "clear and present mission" around which interwar planning could focus. To paraphrase a familiar and obscene limerick, just what was the army supposed to do, where, with what, and to whom? The post–Civil War constabulary mission had long since disappeared, and in any case the army had never configured itself for that purpose.[21] The American empire generated neither small wars nor internal security problems. Mexico and Canada posed no threats worth considering, despite Canadian contingency plans to attack the U.S. should war break out! As for the fear of invasion by a great power, dramatized so clearly in the early years of the century by Homer Lea and Hudson Maxim, the events at Gallipoli and the movement to France of the American Expeditionary Force combined to demonstrate the practical impossibilities of forcing and supporting such an operation in a transatlantic context. As for aircraft, nothing on wings could reach the United States with a meaningful payload even on one-way missions—a condition that endured until the 1950s.

Even had the U.S. Army possessed a true general staff or had the War Department been more interested in operations than administration, processes of change would nevertheless have been limited and parochial-ized by the residual free security America still enjoyed during the inter-war period.[22] Military modernization meant accepting the large-scale projection of American power—a concept as politically impossible as it was strategically meaningless. The limited, mutually competitive pattern Johnson describes represented an unconsciously realistic response to the Army's circumstances. That pattern, moreover, nurtured the intellectual flexibility that gave the army the remarkably steep learning curve it demonstrated throughout World War II.[23] It fostered as well a significant ability to maximize the strengths of weapons systems and doctrines. The B-17 and the Sherman tank may have had limitations relative to their combat environments. Yet institutions using them accepted these limitations as the consequence of their specific decisions—as opposed to some externally imposed master plan—and made the best of them rather than the worst. For the U.S. army of World War II, change was a pragmatic concept not an abstract principle.[24]

The German army in contrast knew precisely what it wanted: a program of changes that would enable it to re-fight the Great War and this time win. The reform of doctrine, organization, equipment, training, and education begun by the Reichswehr and implemented by the Wehrmacht were focused on revising the Treaty of Versailles by reestablishing Germany as a credible military power. This aim was congruent with the avowed policies of both the Weimar Republic and the Third Reich, which created minimal friction with other government departments.[25] Nor did the Reichswehr have the display and deterrence missions that shaped French military behavior. However impressive the annual German maneuvers may have been, no one seriously believed the

Weimar Republic could either defend itself or influence its neighbors with the armed forces it had at its public disposal.[26]

The relative weakness of vested internal interests also fostered flexibility. Branch rivalry, for example, had limited consequences in a Reichswehr whose size and force structure reduced such pretensions to the level of children in a sandbox. As James Corum demonstrates, the Germans developed a spirit of critical analysis that structured a comprehensive approach to change. One might suggest as well, however, that the German army changed successfully because, of all the armies considered in this text, it changed the least of all. Factors outside its narrowly focused perspective of winning the next war by winning its first battles tended to be ignored or overlooked. Domestic economic mobilization and exploitation of conquered resources were alike implemented in a Hobbesian context of interservice and army-party rivalries that squandered irreplaceable assets: human and material. Hitler's increasing degree of control over the military command apparatus correspondingly excluded the armed forces from any significant role in developing policy or strategy. Joint forces planning never moved beyond the ad hoc low-level processes of the Norway campaign, whose success depended heavily on Norwegian weakness and British fecklessness. A concentration on the near future left Germany's soldiers neither the time nor the inclination to consider any changes except those they predicted. As had been the case in 1914, the army found itself forced to revert to increasingly random improvisations when its original bag of tricks emptied in the autumn of 1941 somewhere between Smolensk and Moscow.[27] As Germany's enemies learned how to make war, the German army fell farther and farther behind the curve of change, "demodernizing," living on its past performances, sustaining itself by will power and brute force.

In moving from particular case studies to general conclusions, four points stand out.

First, change in military affairs is contextual. There are no hard and fast rules, be it in mobilization plans, doctrinal concepts, or weapons systems. To take the latter as an example, the German army did not develop a general recipe for the optimal use of armored fighting vehicles. They did develop a synergy among machines, tactics, and command style that proved devastating against obliging enemies in the context of high force-to-space ratios.[28] But principles and techniques conceptualized elsewhere—not least in France—first checked the blitz then forced its modification. Contemporary advocates of maneuver warfare insist on the German roots of the Desert Storm ground plan to a point John Mearshimer describes as "Wehrmacht penis envy." In the process they fail to consider whether the correspondingly derided French might in fact have developed a viable alternate general paradigm of modern war.[29] Nor in a similar context did it make sense for the U.S. army of the interwar period to think in terms of tanks able to meet German panthers on equal terms—or, indeed, to develop any but the most general contingency plans for a future war whose theaters, enemies, and circumstances remained ephemeral for most of the period.

These contextual analyses lead to the general conclusion that far from being rigid or retrograde the armies of the interwar period were significantly flexible in reacting to new conditions. The British responded successfully to an increasingly sophisticated role as imperial constabulary while at the same time managing to remain a major participant in the field of armored warfare—and perform both roles on a shoestring budget. The adaptability of German and Soviet systems in the context of their respective political pressure cookers scarcely requires comment. Even the French, so often excoriated for their blinkered approach between 1918 and 1940, managed to get a good deal right about the nature of modern war.[30]

The second general observation focuses on the network of external constraints in which armies operate. Armies reflect, far more than do navies or air forces, the core dynamics—and the core anxieties—of their societies and their governments. The latter services are set apart by their symbiotic relationship with complex technologies. By comparison, the tools of land war are relatively simple, involving variations on a smooth rock to throw, a heavy rock to crush skulls, and a sharp rock to slit throats. Navies and air forces also operate in environments unnatural for human beings. Eventually aircraft must land and ships must dock—and then their crews can be called to account. Armies are also directly present where people live; they are capable of prompt, sustainable action. These factors combine to make them political institutions as well as policy instruments. The French Republic was able to tolerate a royalist navy, but even the theoretical concept of a professional, technocratic army was too much for the system to stomach.[31]

Political and social systems of the day structured military change in other ways as well. The Wehrmacht and the French army, for example, both faced significantly different human dynamics. In the first case, National Socialism's ideological emphasis on service and community acted as a bridge between a small professional force that had developed artisanal methods of training and task-oriented officer-man relationships and a cohort of young men willing to accept military service as a rite of passage denied them by the Versailles Treaty.[32] In the second the army was committed to an industrial model of making soldiers. French conscripts were entering a system that had been in place for three-quarters of a century, one that had lost most of its luster. Even the barracks were dilapidated. The Third Republic was characterized by levels of entropy that militated against a strong sense of community while in uniform. The army had no mandate to act as the school of a nation that could no longer agree on a curriculum.[33] This dichotomy, it must be stressed, did not make either German victory or French collapse in 1940 inevitable. It did mean, however, that the two military cultures were asymmetrical in ways that made it all but impossible to develop similar responses to the common situation posed by their confrontation.[34]

A third issue determining the nature of change is the nature of internal interest groups. What Harold Winton calls "service cultures" are, like all subcultures, inherently limited in their flexibility. They are also significantly different even in similar systems. Compare, for example, the relative strength of branch loyalty in the British and U.S. armies. The latter combined an undefined mission, a small officer corps, and a weak regimental system. The U.S. Army was also part of a society that affirmed individual competition and was intolerant of prescriptively sanctioned routine. In that context a strong branch identification was arguably the best practical source of institutional change—not least because officers across the spectrum of opinion on an issue (such as the proper role of tanks) tended to support one of their own against an "outsider."[35]

The British army's patria chica, in contrast, was the regiment. Branch loyalties in the infantry and cavalry were expressed in regimental terms. Even in the Royal Artillery, ostensibly a corps characterized by cross-posting, small unit identity died hard. The interwar years indeed witnessed an arguably stronger emphasis on the regiment than had been the case immediately before 1914—part of a conscious effort to provide to the officer corps some emotional compensation for what was increasingly a privately subsidized career in a period of shrinking real income among Britain's middle and upper classes.[36] The result of all this was a tendency for British advocates of change to seek a balance between innovation and isolation—their own isolation. Whether voluntary or not, exile from the fellowship of one's regiment imposed personal and professional stresses unlikely to be casually incurred. Change in the British army was a process of tradeoffs and triangulation at micro levels in comparison to the more spectacular branch clashes of the Americans—and correspondingly difficult to translate into general concepts.

A fourth factor affecting the dynamics of change was the difficulty of testing innovations. The increasing divergence between the demands of small wars outside Europe and the projected requirements of *grande guerre* involving industrial powers rendered traditional practice sites all but irrelevant. In a context of asymmetrical systems, neither theoretical literature nor practical exercises could be mined for comparisons to the degree possible before 1914. The German willingness to test abstract concepts with hypothetical forces has been widely praised—but some of the same authorities excoriate British and American makeshifts of the 1930s, with their dummy weapons substituting for the real thing and flags substituting for dummies. The French army's refusal to simulate material it did not possess invites interpretation as lack of imagination. But on the other side of the coin, a solid case can be made for the aphorism "train as you expect to fight." Of the armies discussed here, only that of the Soviet Union possessed the resources, and not least the space, to test its concepts of deep battle in something like a systematic fashion. Ironically, the Red Army's first real tests were under circumstances where the terrain, the enemy, and the political circumstances combined to impose a significantly different form of warfare than any they had anticipated. Nomonhan and Finland featured head-down slugging matches with little scope for operational maneuver groups, deep penetration, or other refinements developed with such care in Soviet war colleges.[37]

In sum, military innovation in peacetime is a complex process whose interfacing variables defy easy categorization. They might indeed be said to defy categorization at all. Students of innovation in modern armed forces tend to assume a Marxist-industrial model in which systems are identifiable, stable, and controllable—the "Whig" approach mentioned at the beginning of this essay. The years between the world wars suggest as well the relevance of a "third wave," a "chaotic" model in which specific innovations, technical or institutional, are less significant than the creation of a positive synergy among material and doctrine, "service cultures," and the wider social and political systems to which those cultures belong. The creation of such synergy, however, is not an end in itself. It is, rather, a sophisticated tool in the hands of reformers whose ultimate responsibility is to enhance the security of the state and the society they serve by changing military institutions to meet the problematical demands of an uncertain future.

Notes

1. Cf. inter alia Wawro's *The Austro-Prussian War: Austria's War With Prussia and Italy in 1866* (Cambridge: Cambridge University Press, 1996) and "Inside the Whale: The Tangled Finances of the Austrian Army, 1848–1866," *War In History* 3 (1996): 42–65.

2. E. M. Spiers, *Haldane: An Army Reformer* (Edinburgh: Edinburgh University Press, 1980). For the conscription issue specifically see M. I. Allison, "The National Service Issue, 1899–1914," Ph.D. dissertation, University of London, 1977.

3. Cf. Johann Christoph Allmayer-Beck, "*Die bewaffnete Macht in Staat und Gesellschaft,*" in A. Wandruszka and P. Urbanitsch, eds., *Die bewaffnete Macht*, vol. 5, of *Die Habsburgermonarchie 1848–1918* (Vienna: Verlag der Oesterreichischen Akademie der Wissenschaft, 1987), 65–141, and Walter T. Wilfong, "Rebuilding the Russian Army, 1905–1914: The Question of a Comprehensive Plan for National Defense" (Ph.D. dissertation, Indiana University, 1977).

4. John Gooch, "Mr. Haldane's Army: Military Organization and Policy in England," in *The Prospect of War: Studies in British Defence Policy, 1847–1942* (London: Cass, 1981), 92–115.

5. Cf. Charles Mangin, *La Force Noire* (Paris: Hachette, 1910) and the limited realities presented in M. Michel, "*Un Mythe: La 'Force Noire' avant 1914,*" *Relations Internationales* 1 (1974): 83–90.

6. The best recent analysis is David Herrmann, *The Arming of Europe and the Making of the First World War* (Princeton: Princeton University Press, 1996).

7. This point is highlighted in the context of an operation long regarded as an exception to the generalization in Matthew Hughes, "Allenby and the Palestine Campaign, 1917–1918," *The Journal of Strategic Studies* 19 (1996): 59–88.

8. Jonathan Bailey, "The First World War and the Birth of the Modern Style of Warfare," Strategic and Combat Studies occasional paper, 1996, is a stimulating overview of the subject.

9. Earl Ziemke, "Strategy for Class War: The Soviet Union 1917–1941" in W. Murray, M. Knox, and A. Bernstein, eds., *The Making of Strategy: Rulers, States, and War* (Cambridge: Cambridge University Press, 1994), 498–533, is the best English-language complement to Kipp's essay. Cf. also Mark von Hagen, *Soldiers in the Proletarian Dictatorship: The Red Army and the Soviet State, 1917–1930* (Ithaca NY: Cornell University Press, 1990), and Sally Stoecker, "Forging Stalin's Army: The Sources and Politics of Military Innovation in Russia" (Ph.D. dissertation, Johns Hopkins University, 1995).

10. Holland Hunter and Janusz S. Szyrmer, *Faulty Foundations: Soviet Economic Policies, 1928–1940* (Princeton: Princeton University Press, 1992), 136 ff., surveys this relationship.

11. Roger R. Reese, *Stalin's Reluctant Soldiers: A Social History of the Red Army, 1925–1941* (Lawrence: University Press of Kansas, 1996), 87ff.

12. John R. Ferris, *Men, Money, and Diplomacy: The Evolution of British Strategic Policy, 1919–1926* (Ithaca: Cornell University Press, 1989).

13. Among the most familiar presentations of this line of argument is Shelford Bidwell and Dominick Graham, *Fire-Power. British Army Weapons and Theories of War, 1904–1945* (Boston: Allen & Unwin, 1985), 152 ff.

14. Cf. inter alia T. E. H. Travers, *How the War Was Won: Command and Technology on the Western Front, 1917–1918* (London: Routledge, 1992), and Bill Rawlings, *Surviving Trench Warfare: Technology and the Canadian Corps, 1914–1918* (Toronto: University of Toronto Press, 1992).

15. On this issue generally, see K. Nielson and G. Kennedy, eds., *Far Flung Lines: Studies in Imperial Defence in Honour of Donald Mackenzie Schurman* (London: Cass, 1996), a comprehensive challenge to the continental perspective on British strategy developed by Michael Howard and Paul Kennedy.

16. T. R. Moreman, " 'Small Wars' and 'Imperial Policing': The British Army and the Theory and Practice of Colonial Warfare in the British Empire, 1919–1939," *Journal of Strategic Studies* 19 (1996), 105–31, is the most up-to-date survey of this issue. Cf. as well David Omissi, *Air Power and Colonial Control: The Royal Air Force 1919–1939* (Manchester: Manchester University Press, 1990).

17. T. R. Moreman, *The Army in India and The Development of Frontier Warfare, 1849–1947* (New York: St. Martin's, 1998).

18. The most detailed overview is the official account by Col. André Paoli, *L'Armée française de 1919 à 1939*, 4 vols. (Paris: Service Historique de l'armée, 1969–1971). Best in English are Robert Doughty, *The Seeds of Disaster* (Hamden CT: Archon Books, 1985), and Eugenia Kiesling, *Arming against Hitler: France and the Limits of Military Planning* (Lawrence: University Press of Kansas, 1996).

19. On this subject generally see Richard Overy, *Why the Allies Won* (New York: Norton, 1995), and Gerhard Weinberg, *A World at Arms* (Cambridge: Cambridge University Press, 1994).

20. John K. Herr and Edward S. Wallace, *The Story of the U.S. Cavalry* (Boston: Little, Brown, 1953), 258ff.

21. Cf. inter alia Robert Utley, *Frontier Regulars: The United States Army and the Indian, 1866–1891* (New York: Macmillan, 1974); Perry Jamieson, *Crossing the Deadly Ground: U.S. Army Tactics, 1865–1899* (Tuscaloosa: University of Alabama Press, 1994); and Graham Cosmas, *An Army for Empire: The United States Army in the Spanish-American War* (Columbia: University of Missouri Press, 1971).

22. See most recently Brian Linn, *Guardians of Empire: The U.S. Army and the Pacific, 1902–1940* (Chapel Hill: University of North Carolina Press, 1996);

and William Odom, *After the Trenches: The Transformation of U.S. Army Doctrine, 1918–1939* (College Station: Texas A & M University Press, 1999).

23. The clearest brief demonstration of this is Allan R. Millett, "The United States Armed Forces in the Second World War," in A. Millett and W. Murray, eds., *Military Effectiveness* (Boston: Allen & Unwin, 1988), 3:45–89. Cf. as well Geoffrey Perret, *There's a War to be Won: The United States Army in World War II* (New York: Random House, 1991).

24. David E. Johnson, *Fast Tanks and Heavy Bombers: Innovation in the U.S. Army 1917–1945* (Ithaca NY: Cornell University Press, 1998).

25. Cf. the survey by Dennis E. Showalter, "Past and Future: The Military Crisis of the Weimar Republic," *War & Society* 14 (1996): 49–72. Peter Krueger, *Die Aussenpolitik der Republik von Weimar* (Darmstadt: Wissenschaftliche Buchgesellschaft, 1985), and Gerhard Weinberg, *The Foreign Policy of Hitler's Germany*, vols. 1–2 (Chicago: University of Chicago Press, 1970–1980), are detailed treatments strong on the military-political interface.

26. Michael Geyer, *Aufruestung oder Sicherheit? Die Reichswehr in der Krise der Machtpolitik, 1924–1936* (Wiesbaden: Steiner, 1980) remains the best treatment of this issue.

27. This by-now-conventional wisdom is a major theme of the contributions to Horst Boog, et al., *Das Deutsche Reich und der Zweite Weltkrieg*, vol. 4, *Der Angriff auf die Sowjetunion* (Stuttgart: Deutsche Verlag, 1983). Cf. also Bernhard Kroener, "Der 'erfrorene Blitzkrieg': Strategische Planungen der deutschen Fuehrung gegen die Sowjetunions und die Ursachen ihres Scheiterns," in *Der Zweite Weltkrieg: Grundzuege, Analysen, Forschungsbilanz* (Munich: Piper, 1989), 133–48.

28. See most recently Karl-Heinz Frieser, *Blitzkrieg-Legende: Der Westfeldzug 1940* (Munich: Ordenburg, 1995).

29. A salient example is R. Hooker, ed., *Maneuver Warfare: An Anthology* (Novato CA: Presidio, 1993). Its contents include Bruce Gudmundsson's "Maneuver Warfare: The German Tradition"; David A. Grossman's "Maneuver Warfare in the Light Infantry: The Rommel Model"; and John F. Antal's "The *Wehrmacht* Approach to Maneuver Warfare: Command and Control." In contrast Robert A. Doughty's "From the Offensive *à Outrance* to the Methodical Battle" is a case study of how to get things wrong for the right reasons.

30. On this issue see Dennis Showalter, " 'A Stopped Clock Is Right Twice A Day': What the French Got Right about the Nature of Modern War," in M. Vaisse, ed., *The Fall of France as Seen by Foreign Historians* (forthcoming).

31. Ronald Chalmers Hood III, *Royal Republicans: The French Naval Dynasties between the World Wars* (Baton Rouge LA: Louisiana State University Press, 1985).

32. Stephen Fritz, *Frontsoldaten: The German Soldier in World War II* (Lexington KY: University of Kentucky Press, 1995) and Omer Bartov, *Hitler's Army*

(New York: Oxford University Press, 1991) both accept this postulate from significantly different perspectives.

33. Kiesling, *Arming against Hitler*, is the best recent analysis of the army in French society during this period. See as well Eugen Weber, *The Hollow Years: France in the 1930s* (New York: Norton, 1994).

34. On this last point see (in English) Jeffrey Gunsburg, *Divided and Conquered: The French High Command and the Defeat of the West, 1940* (Westport CT: Greenwood, 1979), and Martin Alexander's more controversial *The Republic in Danger: General Maurice Gamelin and the Politics of French Defence, 1933–1940* (Cambridge: Cambridge University Press, 1992).

35. This pattern is demonstrated comprehensively in Johnson, *Fast Tanks and Heavy Bombers*, passim.

36. For the "character and ethos" of the interwar army see Brian Bond, *British Military Policy between the Two World Wars* (Oxford: Oxford University Press, 1980), 45ff.

37. Cf. Alvin Coox, *Nomonhan: Japan against Russia 1939*, 2 vols. (Stanford: Stanford University Press, 1985), and Carl van Dyke, *The Soviet Invasion of Finland* (London: Cass, 1997).

CONTRIBUTORS

James S. Corum is Professor of Comparative Military Studies, School of Advanced Airpower Studies, Air University. He received his Ph.D. in history from Queens University and is the author of *The Roots of Blitzkrieg: Hans von Seeckt and German Military Reform* and *The Luftwaffe: Creating the Operational Air War, 1918–1940* as well as numerous articles on military and airpower history.

David E. Johnson, a retired army officer and military historian, received his Ph.D. in military history from Duke University. He is the author of *Fast Tanks and Heavy Bombers: Innovation in the U.S. Army, 1917–1945*.

Eugenia C. Kiesling is an associate professor of military history at the United States Military Academy. She received her Ph.D. in history from Stanford University and is the author of *Arming against Hitler: France and the Limits of Military Planning* and " 'If It Ain't Broke, Don't Fix It': French Military Doctrine between the World Wars," *War in History* (1996), and is the editor and translator of Adm. Raoul Castex's *Strategic Theories*.

Jacob W. Kipp is a senior analyst with the U.S. Army's Foreign Military Studies Office at Fort Leavenworth, Kansas, and holds the position of adjunct professor of Russian and East European Studies at the University of Kansas. He received his Ph.D. in Russian history from Pennsylvania State University. He edited the English translation of V. K. Triandafillov's *The Nature of the Operations of Contemporary Armies* and has published numerous articles on Russian and Soviet military, naval, and aviation history.

David R. Mets is Professor of Technology and Innovation, School of Advanced Airpower Studies, Air University. He holds a Ph.D. in history from the University of Denver and is the author of *Master of Airpower: General Carl A. Spaatz*, NATO: *An Alliance for Peace*, and *Land-Based Air Power in Third World Countries* as well as numerous articles and reviews on airpower technology, arms control, and military thought.

Dennis E. Showalter is a professor of history at the Colorado College. He earned his Ph.D. in history from the University of Minnesota. He is coeditor of *War in History* and the author of *Tannenberg: Clash of Empires*, *The Wars of Frederick the Great*, and *Railroads and Rifles: Technology and the Unification of Germany* as well as numerous articles and reviews in the field of military history. He served as president of the Society for Military History from 1997 to 1999.

Harold R. Winton is Professor of Military History and Theory, School of Advanced Airpower Studies, Air University. He holds a Ph.D. in modern European history from Stanford University and is the author of *To Change an Army: General Sir John Burnett-Stuart and British Armored Doctrine, 1927–1938* as well as numerous articles and reviews on the subjects of doctrine, military reform, and military biography.

INDEX

Academy of the General Staff (Soviet),
  120
Adam, Ronald, 97
airborne tactics, 51, 56
Air Commerce Act, 194
Air Corps Act, 194
Air Corps Tactical School (U.S.),
  195–97, 202
air doctrine: American, 181–82,
  192–98, 200–202; German, 53–54
air-ground operations: American, 195,
  197, 219 n.265; German, 51–53
air service (U.S.), 174, 192
Air War Plans Division (U.S.), 198
American army. *See* United States
  Army
American Expeditionary Force,
  165–66, 202
American strategy. *See* strategy:
  American
André, Louis, 2
Andrews, Frank M., 196
antitank guns: American development
  of, 183–84; American views of, 18;
  German, 184
Armiya I revolyutsiya (Army and
  revolution), 111
armored cars, 14, 30 n.61
armored divisions: American, 199;
  British, 96, 98; French, 18–23;

German, 50–51
armored doctrine: American, 181,
  189–92; British, 89; French, 21–23,
  32 n.81; German, 23, 50–51
Armored Force (U.S.), 181, 191–92
armored warfare, 74, 78–80, 89–90,
  159 n.92. *See also* mechanization;
  motorization
Army Air Corps (U.S.), 193–98
Army Air Forces (U.S.), 200–202
Army General Staff College, (U.S.),
  165
Army Ground Forces (U.S.), 200
Army Industrial College (U.S.), 185
Army Laws of 1927–1928 (French),
  7–9
Army Regulation 487 (German army).
  See *Leadership and Battle with
  Combined Arms*
Army Service Forces (U.S.), 200
Army War College (U.S.), 185
Arnold, Henry H. "Hap," 199–200
artillery doctrine, 187–88
assault guns, 58–59
AWPD-1, 198

B-17, 196–97
Baker, Newton, 168, 173
Baldwin, Stanley, 77, 88, 92–93
battaille conduite. See methodical battle
Battle of Britain, 199